A Antonia,

Con los más cálidos de
amor, y con mucho af
amabilidad hacia Mí.
tiempo de Angustia.

Tu nuevo amigo

Sara Jane
Ano: Viernes 11ª Febrero 2022.

To
Antonia,
With Warmest good Wishes and love,
and much appreciation for your
kindness in my time of distress.
XX

No Ordinary Life

Sara-Jane Cromwell

Copyright © Sara-Jane Cromwell, 2021
First Published in Ireland, in 2021, in co-operation with
Choice Publishing, Drogheda, County Louth, Republic of Ireland.
www.choicepublishing.ie

ISBN: 978-1-913275-35-8
ISBN: 978-1-913275-36-5 (eBook)

A CIP catalogue record for this book is available from the National Library.

Dedication

This book is dedicated to my beloved late father and Pastor, Liam Joyce; who adopted me as his daughter and made sure I knew I was the daughter he always wanted, and of whom he was immensely proud, It was my father Liam who made sure I could begin my amazing journey and become the woman he knew I was born to be, and it was *he* who revealed for the first time that I am a pathfinder and that it is through my work that I would help change Ireland and many lives here and abroad. This has indeed proven to be prescient on his part, and I dedicate all of it and this book to his loving memory.

Contents

Part Three - Letting Go

Part Four - Endings & Beginnings

Acknowledgments

A joyful and pleasant thing it is to be thankful.
[Psalm 147:1]

It is a truism to say that publishing a book is not possible without the help of others and it is certainly true in this instance. There are a few people I wish to thank for helping bring this book into being. I would like to thank Deirdre Devine and her team at Choice Publishing, who have done so much work in bringing this book together. Thanks, is also due to those who read the book and made suggestions and pointed out the typing errors etc., i.e., Paul Reinhardt, Antoine, Gamble, Jacqui O'Riordan and Hilary Dring. I am immensely grateful to Mary P. O'Connor for the beautiful cover design. We went through many attempts before getting to the cover we have now. I am forever thankful for all your work.

Much of what I've achieved over the past several years is due in no small way to my colleagues at UCC, in particular Dr Rola Abu Zeid O'Neill, who first invited me to speak to her students in 2017 and my colleagues at the Staff LGBT Network who invited me to participate in various activities over the last several years. Their support collectively and individually has made an immense contribution in helping me to keep going to the point where I now have my own UCC course on Gender Identity in Ireland. This simply would not have been possible without them.

This book records numerous achievements not previously published: however, they could not be published at all were it not for one person. I am referring to the wonderful Teresa Ryan at the Family Resource Centre in Carrigtwohill. Teresa's colleagues are also worthy of praise and gratitude. It is due to Teresa's intervention and support over the past two years that has enabled me to survive to tell this amazing story. It was Teresa more than any other person who gave me constant and regular support over the entire period and linking me up with her colleagues that has unquestionably helped me to reach this point. So, for those who are grateful I am still alive and able to continue with my work (and I know there are), please remember this remarkable lady and her wonderful colleagues at the Carrigtwohill Family Resource Centre; equally those amazing people at Pieta House, Cork, without whom I quite possibly would not be here.

Introduction
Changing Times and Changing Lives

There must be a beginning to any great matter, but the continuing unto the end until it be thoroughly finished yields the true glory.
[Sir Francis Drake]

I was born Sara-Jane Duffy, FEMALE, on the 26th June 1960. It took a mere fifty-five years to make this official by having it stated on my Birth Certificate. But you will never hear me cribbing about it, because I am far too grateful for the fact that we live in a time when such errors can be corrected. So, in a real sense, this book is a celebration of this and the many other wonderful achievements that have been made possible since my first autobiography *"Becoming Myself"* was published in 2008. This book is an update, but it is so much more. It brings my entire gender journey to a most wonderful completion and marks the beginning of a new life and new stories, being, and yet to be written. It also answers the numerous questions I received about what happened to my family's situation which was still pending in 2008. There were also questions about my family's reaction to the book, and whether I completed my gender reassignment. This book will answer these questions and others besides.

Such has been the changes and developments since 'Becoming Myself' was published that I have chosen to use my birth surname rather than the pseudonym used previously. The reason is twofold; firstly, is the number of my siblings who went public following the 2008 publication and fully identified themselves to the media. The second reason was the family name being published across the media reporting of our father's appearance before the courts and my sister's victim impact statements. However, I have chosen, in most cases, to continue using pseudonyms for their first names. This is because I have no wish to have a go at them personally, but simply to recount events as they transpired.

Whilst the book was universally well received, it was however missing some of the material I really wanted to have included in the first version, especially the positive contributions others have made to my life over the years (few though they were). I am thinking especially of people like Peter Parkinson and the folks at Caring for Life in Leeds, and my late father and Pastor, Liam Joyce of Evangelical Church Fellowship, Dublin. Also, the published version omitted the influence my namesake had on my decision to change my name by Deed Poll. These are important, as are the accounts of my suicide attempts. I am delighted that I can correct them here.

What the first book could not have included in 2008 was the economic crash that took place within months of its publication, and the devastation the crash caused to so many. This was just one of the many events that occurred since then and is worthy of inclusion here, especially as they have contributed in one way or another to my extraordinary journey and the legacy that has already been created, and which I hope to create in the future.

Whilst parts of this book are difficult to read, readers will be well rewarded as they continue. I have made it one of my goals not to use hyperbolic language when describing the various events recorded here. Indeed, it has been quite gratifying to hear people say this and how they were very taken with the matter-of-fact way in which the story is told, while some described it as sitting across from me in my living room and it being part of a normal conversation. Others expressed their amazement that I did not present myself as a victim, nor sought people's pity; choosing instead to see things for what they were and deal with them on that basis, with a grim determination not to be completely overcome by them. There is something quite exhilarating about *not* being a victim, or the realisation that even if we were victims at some stage, we do not have to remain so. Because the truth is, being a victim can become a *state of mind* which continues long after any horrible traumatic event has occurred, and it is this *state of mind* which continues to do the greatest harm. Life and experience have taught me that this need not be the case, and I fervently hope that my story will be a demonstration of this; thereby giving hope to those who read this book, that they too can overcome and go on to achieve extraordinary things in their own lives.

So, it is fair to say that this book serves three very worthy goals: firstly, to update in a more rounded way what was already an amazing story. By rounded I mean that there is far more in this story than the emphasis on my gender journey; there were the challenges of being left-handed, being tall, being well spoken (I kid you not), leaving school so early and having to educate myself, and for me the enormous lifelong challenge of trying to prove that I wasn't *mentally retarded*. Of all these, the last one was by far my greatest challenge, probably greater than the physical, psychological and emotional abuse experienced over many years. And of course, at the centre of all these was living in the wrong body.

My second goal is to inspire people to believe in what is possible despite the many obstacles, challenges and setbacks that might otherwise prevent them from achieving their life's purpose (assuming they know what it is). And thirdly, to motivate people to never give up on their dreams and goals, but to continue instead and fulfil their own particular journey and potential, whatever that journey and potential might be. If this book can do this, then it will have been completely worthwhile.

Sara-Jane Cromwell
Cobh, Co. Cork
15th January 2021

PART ONE
Early Days

Chapter One

I'm Here, But Who Wants Me?

'I do not love him because he is good, but because he is my little child'
[Rabindranath Tagore]

'There is something I have to tell you about why I've been the way I have been towards you all this time. I always hated you, since you were a baby. I've never been able to explain it to myself, but I have resented you and there are times when I still do.'

My mother told me this when I was forty-three years of age. Finally, I felt vindicated by the knowledge that I had not been imagining it all these long years; feeling that she really never loved me and that she really didn't want me around. The reason why is harder to explain, although I know that at the time of my birth, my mother's life was far from easy.

Even before I was born, events in my mother's life were conspiring against her ever wanting or accepting me as one of her own. Like so many other women, she, too, had her dreams and ambitions. And like so many other women at the time, she had her dreams and ambitions crushed and destroyed. I know that she had a dream of becoming an interior designer, for which she was ideally suited. And no doubt she had dreams of a fulfilling marriage and of raising a healthy, happy family, but this dream was also shattered. These crushed hopes undoubtedly led to great and lasting feelings of disappointment, resentment and bitterness. All of this was crystallised during a series of tragedies which occurred around the time I was born, and I am sure they contributed to my mother's resentment of me.

My life started in the Coombe Hospital on 26 June 1960. At least my male life started on that date. When I came into the world, I was given the name Thomas. I was two weeks overdue; a late starter. This late start seems to have been a dominant theme in my life. Apparently, I only came into the world following a scare from a German shepherd. My mother opened the back door only to be greeted by a rather enthusiastic dog that jumped at her and scared the living daylights out of her, literally! She went into labour and I was the result.

I'm the third of twelve brothers and sisters and am now officially (at last) the eldest girl! This means there are now six boys and six girls in the family. It was often said that we were a football team plus one. There were two boys before the first girl arrived. Apparently, being third in line is not the best place to be, especially if you're the third boy, but it was the same if you were a girl, at least in my case.

I was barely two months old before my mother fell pregnant again which doesn't bear thinking about. She simply hadn't the resources to look after three of us, never mind four, but that never mattered in Catholic Ireland of the 1960s. All that mattered was that women accede to the sexual demands of their husbands. They were machines for producing Catholic babies and they did so efficiently and without question.

Women were expected to satisfy their husband's conjugal rights, without any regard to their own or to the dire consequences of constantly producing children, for which they could not adequately provide. And if these women failed to satisfy their husband's needs (lusts), well, then they were raped. I did not visually witness such rapes as a child, but I certainly heard them, just feet away from where I slept, and was terrified. On more than one occasion I heard my frightened mother plead with my father not to come near her as it was too soon after having yet another baby. Then I heard the smacks and the shouting at her to 'shut the fuck up!' Then there was crying, then whimpering, then silence and then the creaking of the bed and then total silence, and then I eventually went to sleep crying for her. I cry for her now.

Before my parents moved into their new house in Ballyfermot, around the time when I was born, they had lived in married quarters in McKee or Collins Barracks, as my father was in the Army Motor Squadron. He later joined the military police. And it was here that they were to experience some of the most traumatic events of their lives.

My father was staying in McKee Barracks the night before he was due to fly out on a tour of duty to the Congo with the United Nations. On that fateful day my mother learned that a man who had raped her some years earlier had moved just three doors down from her. Not surprisingly, she had a breakdown, putting her hands through the glass window of our front door. My father was called home to take care of her and she was taken to St Loman's Hospital. As a consequence, my father's best friend was sent to the Congo in his place.

This friend would be killed, along with nine others, during a massacre at Niemba in September 1960, barely three months after I was born. It is almost impossible to imagine, the impact this must have had on both their lives. They also knew some of the other soldiers killed, which only served to multiply their sense of loss and sorrow.

It is hard to think that they did not blame themselves in some way for their friend's death and that they were not wracked with guilt for a long time after the event. I know for certain that my mother attributes these events and others for causing my father to 'go off the rails'; what we now know as post-traumatic stress disorder. Of course, such a diagnosis did not exist then and those suffering with the condition received absolutely no help whatsoever. She assured us that our father was not always the violent man we knew him to be while growing up; that in fact he had been a very different man before these tragic events occurred.

I can say with a high degree of certainty that the difficult relationship that developed between me and my mother has its roots in this particular period of time. Although I find her animosity towards me, which bordered sometimes on hatred, difficult to understand. I remember a woman who made it abundantly clear that she did not want me and did not love me and is best summed up in her own words and through gritted teeth: *'I had twelve mistakes and you were my biggest mistake of them all!'* In all her bitterness and disappointments, she was all too human and imperfect, just like the rest of us.

My father remains something of an enigma to me and, like my mother, I feel that I hardly know him at all. I never had the kind of relationship with him that would allow me to get to know him better. What I do know about his earlier life comes from my mother and one of my brothers. He came from County Louth and had three other brothers that I know of. From what I've learned, he also had a terrible life: he was sexually abused while growing up and had more than his fair share of brutal beatings.

He spent long periods abroad on UN duty and when he was home, he was in the Curragh or on weekend camps with the army. When he wasn't away with the army, he was working on nixers for the owner of the local pharmacy. If he wasn't working outside the home, then he was working at home, painting, wallpapering and building the kitchenette, which I helped him to build. At one stage, he left the army for a few years and went to work in a local weaving factory, where I went to work some years later. I used to bring him his lunch while he was at work and remember being overawed by the size of the machines and the noise they made. And the fluff! He eventually went back to the army and joined the military police. I always associated his uniform with aggression and violence and of being told what to do without the right to speak up. Unlike many men of his time, he was not much of a drinker and rarely, if ever, smoked, though later on he smoked a pipe. This gave him an air of calm which I rarely ever experienced.

There can be no doubting that he was hard working, and, in fact, he was truly gifted with his hands, in much the same way as my mother was gifted in her ability in interior design. It is fair to say that in another time and under different circumstances they both would have been hugely successful in business. But it was not to be. As with my mother, my father was a product of his own time and experiences and he certainly brought them into his marriage and his role as a father.

Every time I hear the Furey's song 'The Oul Man', I am reminded of what I never had with my father and what I never will have with him. There are so many songs that are full of resonances of my younger years and they fill me with emotion as I recall the various experiences to which those songs relate. No doubt that's true of us all. Something that distressed was how I looked like him. I wanted to have no reminders of him whenever I look in the mirror, nor have people tell me I looked the image of my father.

For me, everything I have come to know about my father, every personal experience I had with him, taught me how not to be a man. In fact, people have asked me upon hearing this, if this was the reason I felt I was a girl? My answer is emphatically <u>no</u>, especially as my behaviours were far too instinctive and natural and predated any conscious decision on my part <u>not</u> to be like him, or my brothers for that matter. The one thing I will say about him was that, unlike my mother, he was equal in the severity of the beatings he gave us. In other words, he was impartial in his brutality.

One exception, and something that used to bother me was the time he spent with the other girls and not with me. He would have them sit on his knee and play with them. It never occurred to me that there was something else entirely going on and that far from having any reason to be envious of them, I would have every reason to feel horrified.

My earliest memories of family life go back to when I was about three or four, before I started school. I remember going to the zoo and crying because I wanted to sit in the front of the coach. I got my way and was very happy. Another memory is of being taken to the army barracks for parties. We would be allowed to climb into the armoured cars and other military vehicles. These were pleasant memories, as were our trips to the seaside.

I also remember how my mother liked to be out of the house as much as possible, preferably without us in tow. There can be no doubting that bringing up so many children with, so little income had to cause great stress to my parents. They used to go off together on my father's Honda 50 motorbike. One of their favourite places was the Embankment in Tallaght, where they went to see Brendan Grace, Barleycorn, the Bards etc. But it was also true that she liked to take her children out and about. We were also taken to the beaches at Gormanstown, Rush and Portmarnock, where our father tried to teach us to swim. Sometimes a row would ensue between them because my father either didn't want to take us or because he complained of not having enough money for petrol, which was often his cover for not wanting to take us. This wasn't a problem by the time the younger ones came along as we older ones were bringing home significant income, which eliminated my mother's money worries; something she never acknowledged.

So, there were good times when I was a child. But there were also the darker more distressing times. One of my most disturbing memories is of being locked into the bedroom for long periods of time. This was a common occurrence. It is hard to describe my feelings aged four when I had been left behind by my mother, but I do remember feeling unwanted and abandoned and that I was nothing but a nuisance, something I was to feel many, many times since. I wrote my first ever poem on this very subject.

Big! With chalky brown walls;
'Go in and be quiet.' The key turns
In the lock and I'm alone.
What did I do to be left alone?
Please open the door, I'm only four.

Was it once or more? I can't always recall,
But I remember the tears and the fears.
What wrong did I do to be left alone like this?
Please open the door, I'm only four!

Being on my own was like an eternity.
I felt they had abandoned me, that they
Didn't want me. No-one talks to me, not a sound.
Just me, here, alone.
Please, open the door, I'm only four.

And now I see the prophetic vision of it all.
My life has been like that empty room, with
No-one there and no-one here. No-one wanting
To talk or play. No, I was getting in the way.
Please open the door, I'm only four
And I can't bear the loneliness anymore.

That room was empty, devoid of human care.
There was no-one there to love me.
And still I'm alone, with no family and no place
To call my home. The key is still turned in the door
And I'm alone.
Please, please open the door, I just can't take the
Loneliness, pain and rejection anymore!

I don't know the reason why my mum left me in the room so often. Probably it was to go shopping or maybe she couldn't cope with the house and raising four children, three boys and a girl, and maybe she just needed her space. Whatever it was, it made me feel totally alone and unwanted; feelings that were to dominate my life.

From the earliest age I can remember the stress that filled our house; a house that for me at least, never felt like a home. It was a house I was glad to leave when I was nineteen years of age. This wasn't helped by so many people living in such a small space. We lived in a two-up and two-down. We did have an indoor bathroom and toilet, but although the houses were considered quite modern for their time and a big improvement on what had gone before, it was completely inadequate to accommodate fourteen people.

Of course, there was no privacy to be had for anyone, including my five sisters, who had to share the same bedroom with their brothers. That can't have been easy for them. We slept in a double bed and bunk beds. Up to five of us slept in the double bed; three at the top end and two at the bottom. There were another five sleeping in the bunks, with brothers and sisters having to sleep together. We would sleep under blankets and army overcoats. There was a constant battle to hold onto the bit of blanket or bit of coat. It was a constant tug-of-war trying to stay warm, especially in the winter months. There was no central heating in those days and the only fire was the one in the kitchen. There was an open fireplace in our bedroom, but it was never used. Imagine waking during the night and in the morning with your brother's smelly, long-nailed feet in your mouth and sticking up your nose or cutting into your skin. Added to this were the broken springs that kept pricking us. It was so uncomfortable and very difficult to get a good night's sleep. At Christmas and Easter, though, we were bound to have clean crisp sheets and blankets. My mother would threaten us not to tear them by telling us that we were not 'to so much as breathe' on them. Of course, we would try to make a joke out of this by holding our breath.

This was the situation until we got the new bed-settee in the parlour and the eldest brother was moved down. Later, another was moved down, and this gave some more space to those of us left upstairs. After the eldest brother got married and left the house, the second eldest then moved down and I followed soon after. The parlour was great, because we could leave the light on for longer and read. We also had the record player and radio unit in the parlour, which meant that we could listen to our favourite radio station, Radio Luxembourg and the European Top 40.

During the earlier years the stress in our house came mainly from the rows and fighting between my parents, or, should I say, my father beating my mother and her screaming and begging him not to hit her.

This legacy of aggression was to be passed on to some of my brothers; while I was to become very passive and open to physical violence from males and females alike. Some of the worst rows came around Christmas, when my mother would go all-out to get us the best of presents and the best of clothes. Christmas was the one time of the year when we were sure to have new clothes, in fact new everything. But it would be spoiled by my father's shouting at my mother and her screaming with fear and pleading with him not to hit her, but to no avail. When we heard the screaming and shouting we would start crying and then my mother would have to come and comfort us and try to reassure us that there was nothing wrong. But we always knew. I came to hate my father for what he was doing to her.

But it really didn't take a lot to make either of them angry and resort to violence towards us. It could be something like soiling our clothes while out playing, or losing money while going to the shops. Even something as innocuous as coming home late from school or, crossing in front of the television as my father was doing the Pools on a Saturday evening. On quite a few occasions, they beat and berated me for wetting the bed. The bedwetting was, I think, because I lived in a constant state of emotional distress, partly because of my family, partly because of school and also because I had all the emotions and instincts of a girl, but without the right to express them.

I remember trying to resist reading girl's comics and magazines, even pretending that I hated them, but all the while I always felt like reading them. I was in a constant state of uncertainty about who I was and who I was meant to be. There was such a need to belong, but hating what I had to do to fit in.

My sensitive personality was also becoming more pronounced as I grew, along with my empathic spirit. I had a growing sense of being split in two, but without ever knowing why. The tensions became a constant in my life and left me feeling extremely unsure of myself in how I was to behave. I found myself preferring the company of girls far more than boys, yet still trying to fit in and be accepted as normal, which of course meant playing with boys.

My parents took issue with my being so sensitive and gentle as did my siblings and they were not averse to calling me a cissy, because of my very girlish ways of dealing with things, and the way in which I would cry when hurt, or when I saw my brothers and sisters were hurt. Whenever I came home from school upset because of something that had happened, my parents would call me 'a fucking whinger', or they would tell me to stop crying or they would give me 'something to cry about'. Like the others, they chose to view my girl-like behaviour as attention-seeking on my part.

My mother knew that my father was extremely bad-tempered and violent; that he would give us severe beatings for even the most minor misdemeanours. If we did something wrong — at least in her eyes — my mother would threaten us with our father's violence. I remember the time I'd lost money while going to the shops and having to come home and tell my mother. Or the time I had money stolen from me and I tried to convince my mother that it really was stolen, knowing full well she wasn't going to believe me. I would receive the inevitable threat: 'Wait till your father gets home; he's going to fuckin kill you!'

It is so hard remembering these all-too-frequent experiences and the absolute terror they instilled within me without becoming upset. I can still remember the times I would urinate in my short trousers while walking home from school, knowing that I was going to get a beating. The nearer I got to home, the worse the urinating became. When I'd get home, I would be sent straight to bed without any food, and I would have to stay there until my father got home. My stomach would churn relentlessly in anticipation of what was going to happen. But no amount of anticipation could really prepare you for the roar: 'Sara-Jane, get the fuck down here now. And don't have me to tell you twice!'

No matter how much I anticipated it and tried to prepare myself for it, I was still completely frozen with terror. I knew that the only thing worse than delaying the inevitable was what would happen if I didn't go down straight away. While he was sitting there as a petulant god, I would be standing there and peeing on the floor in sheer terror at what awaited me. Sometimes, the only clothes I wore were my vest and underpants.

'Come here, you bastard. I said come here! I'll teach you to lose money. You're nothing but a fucking troublemaker. You bastard. I'll fucking kill you the next time you lose money … the next time to tear your clothes … then next time you come home late from school again!' He would get up from his chair, taking the belt from his trousers and start belting me sometimes on the bottom, the back and as I struggled to escape, on the head or face. Or he would hit me with his huge fists pounding against my little head. His huge fists pounding my little face and me peeing again on the floor. 'I'll give you something to piss about!'

These beatings were always accompanied by him shouting abuse at me while he pounded me. Telling me how worthless I was while he lashed his belt across my bottom, across my back and across my face as he lost control and started to kick me around the floor with his army boots. At other times he would use lengths of wood and beat me wherever he could inflict the most pain; all the while shouting and screaming at me while I tried to get away, which of course just made him worse, and even more vicious.

While he was beating me to a pulp, she would be screaming: 'Don't do it, Frank. He's not worth it, the bastard! Frank, the bastard isn't worth it. Frank, please, he's not fuckin worth it.' These words and the vehemence with which they were spoken affected me for decades afterwards.

At no time in the following decades of my life did I ever associate the word *trauma* with my abuse but in reality, that is exactly what it was. And I am suffering that trauma at the present time, except that now I know what it is and the horrific effects it has had and continues to have on so many areas of my life. I just recently discovered this to be the case after I bought a book from the book vouchers, I received from UCC (more about UCC later). I went to buy some books in Waterstones and the first one I saw was *The Body Keeps the Score* by Bessel Van der Kolk. It is a truly astonishing book, especially as it describes every one of the issues affecting me to this day, from what I now know to be my childhood abuse traumas, and why my life has turned out to be so incredibly difficult and why it is that I can finally stop blaming myself for what I once regarded as my many inadequacies failings and mistakes. In short, I never knew that I was brain damaged by what had happened to me and that the trauma has been affecting my physical health and welling since my childhood.

However, I wasn't alone in being beaten. One of the worst and most savage beatings I ever witnessed was that of my brother, Peter. He was given a flask to take to school, but unfortunately for him he dropped it. Of course, it broke, and he had to come home and tell my mother. She in turn told my father, who was repairing the television at the time. 'How did you manage to break the fucking flask?' he roared.

'It slipped out of my hand, Dad.'

'Come here, you stupid little bastard,' he shouted back.

Peter tended to laugh whenever he was nervous or distressed and the more distressed he became, the more he laughed. My parents always interpreted this as him not caring, but nothing could be further from the truth. My father went into a complete rage and started beating Peter with his fists. The more he did this, the more distressed Peter became. The more distressed he became, the more he laughed. The more Peter laughed, the more viciously my father beat him. The more he laughed, the more my father screamed, 'Cry, you bastard. Cry, you bastard! He punched him, broke a stick across his back then proceeded to kick him with a viciousness I had rarely seen, even against me.

The reason I think that I remember this beating above all is that Peter was always my star. I loved him like none of the others. We were just eleven months apart in age, I am the older of the two. I loved his company and his cheerfulness. I loved being out with him amongst our friends and felt so proud to be by his side. Because of my own sense of inferiority towards him and my other brothers and sisters, it was vital that he accept me and allow me to get close. We did play together a lot in the younger years: our beds were used very frequently during our playtimes. Peter and I would play a game called the Funny Men on the bed. We would pretend we were working up ladders painting walls. Suddenly, we would push each other off each other's imaginary ladder to fall into a bath of paint. At other times we used the double bed as a pick-up van and the bunk beds as a double-decker bus. We would drive our Dinkies around the bedroom floor, imagining the legs of the beds as corners of high-rise buildings. However, as Peter became more aware of how I was perceived by others, as a cissy, as different, he started to avoid me at every opportunity and even joined in the name-calling and put-downs. We had come a long way from the days of playing the Funny Men and football and going on our long adventures together with our friends. Peter would be lost to me out of his need to be loved and to be popular at home and amongst our friends.

My relationship with my brother Fred was fraught with sibling rivalry. We fought at every turn and it took very little to provoke either one of us to fight the other. He was eighteen months older than me and was understandably closer to our oldest brother James than to me. It seemed that no matter what I did, he had to find a way of beating me. I hated it and tried my best to avoid it and him, not an easy thing to achieve in such a small house and where we had to share the same bed.

Fred suffered terribly with asthma and frequently missed school because of it. He had very nasty attacks and on several occasions, we thought he was going to die. As much as I didn't like him at times, I certainly didn't want that. And despite my feelings towards him, I wanted to protect him.

We spent the best part of nineteen years in our bedroom. It was this bedroom that kept our secrets, that witnessed all our emotional highs and lows, wherein we held our little confabs about the injustices that were so much a part of our lives; well, at least some of us. This was the room in which we expressed our joys and sorrows. The place in which we found comfort, but which also served as our prison cell. It was the holding area for those who were to be victims of the most vicious beatings and the place we would go to, to soothe our wounds, both physical and emotional. It was here that I kept my record player, cassette recorder, records, cassettes and my wonderful books; the few that I had. The record player was on my side of the bed, so I was able to listen to my music through my headphones. We grew up on all kinds of music including Jim Reeves, Perry Como, Nat King Cole, Slim Whitman, Dean Martin, and Connie Francis, Glen Campbell and Patsy Cline, to name just a few. As we got older we developed our own tastes. Music was to be one of my greatest comforters and my greatest inspiration for coping with all my difficulties.

Such was my desperation for my mother's love and acceptance that I was prepared to go to any lengths to please her. So much so that I would wait until everyone was asleep in their beds before getting up and going down stairs to clean up and get the kitchen and sitting room gleaming. I would wash all the ware, clean the cooker, do the dusting, wash and polish the floors and set the table for the whole family. I would then go to bed, hoping everything would be a pleasant surprise for my mother and that she would treat me better. It was a complete waste of time: but it took years to accept this. All my family commented on was my setting the table for left-handers! It drove them all crazy. Can you imagine it a table set for fourteen lefthanders!

After some time, Peter realised that I had been getting out of bed after everyone else was asleep and he came downstairs to see what I was doing. He kept me company some of the time and so we started to play football between the table and chairs which we'd placed at either end of the sitting room to act as goal posts and used a tennis ball as our football. It was very enjoyable and made us tired enough to go back to bed after all the work was done. It was a bit like the story of the 'Elves and the Shoemaker', except of course that this little elf was doing the domestics rather than making shoes for the poor cobbler. Looking back to those times, it is so obvious how completely natural it was for me to act instinctively as a girl and to play homemaker, because that is in effect what I was doing. The truth is though that I genuinely loved doing it.

One exception to the stress of our household was those Christmases that were free of rows between our parents, which could be truly wonderful. My mum would pull out all the stops at Christmas to make sure it was the best it could be. Christmas was the one time of the year — along with Easter — that we never wanted for anything. We loved to put up the Christmas tree and decorations and to see all the other preparations being made, including the puddings. I had a strong liking for raw pudding mix and used to go to where they were hidden in the kitchen and stick my fingers in and scoop out nice big amounts and eat them till I made myself sick, not realising that we would have none left for Christmas if I kept eating it. We loved putting up our Christmas stockings on the bedposts and looking forward to the surprise fillings when we awoke on Christmas morning. They would be filled with Lemons sweets and we would get stuck into them, even before we came down for our toys. We would sneak downstairs about six or seven in the morning, trying not to wake our parent's. The atmosphere of coming into the sitting room and seeing all the presents under the tree was just the best thing ever and so very exciting.

Our aunts and uncles came to our house every year to say Happy Christmas and to get their Christmas drink. That was also very exciting. There was such a wonderful and for the most part, peaceful, atmosphere for these few days, before we would revert to what was to be our version of normality. We loved most of the Christmas programmes on the telly, especially Wanderly Wagon, Ludín and His Magic Flute, Chitty-Chitty Bang-Bang, Top of the Pops, Mike Yarwood, the Morecombe and Wise Show and so on. On Christmas morning we would all be marched off to mass at Our Lady of the Assumption. We were like the Von Trapp children, all wearing identical clothes and shoes. The girls always looked so pretty in their dresses and lovely ribbons. I always loved looking at girls in their curls and ribbons and wondered why I couldn't wear them. This was a very frustrating experience but I daren't say a word about it.

I was quite a performer and storyteller as a youngster. During the mid-60s, I would stand on the road and tell tall stories to whoever would listen, of how I saved my father's life while he was in the Congo with the United Nations. He was being crushed to death by a huge python snake and I would come to his rescue by getting a knife and fighting the snake until he released my dad. I was paid a few pennies for telling this story. I also sang 'Walk Tall' by Val Doonican and, 'Walking the Streets in the Rain' by Butch Moore. In fact, I got the nickname, 'Butch Moore'. These songs became my party piece whenever we had some special occasion. I loved to sing at special occasions but was often upstaged by Peter who would get in my way and put me off singing, normally with some kind of derogatory remark that had everyone laughing, except me.

There is no doubt that times were hard financially when we were growing up. I can distinctly recall a period during the 70s when my father was taking home about £16 a week, which had to feed at least ten of us at the time. He had to work extra hours in order to supplement his income and to try to provide us with a decent living. It wasn't always possible, and this necessitated the older children giving up school to go out to work for a living.

Our situation was made worse by my mother's constant borrowing to make ends meet. It was a case of constantly robbing Peter to pay Paul. It had to be deeply frustrating for him to see her spending money the way she did and yet she needed to do what she thought was right, based on the way she was brought up. It was a no-win situation for either of them.

My mum kept a beautiful house, with my help, of course. Everything was immaculate. She had a definite talent for interior design, as amply demonstrated over the years with the various designs she came up with for the house. The house décor was always kept up to date. I recall the very vivid floral colours and patterns on the walls and floors, which were typical of the 60s and 70s. We had linoleum in every room which made them very cold during cold months of the year. We couldn't afford carpets back then. Keeping up with the trends meant getting knee-high in debt and this affected how we were dressed and fed. We never starved, but some of the meals were decidedly short on substance. My mother's need to keep up with the trends created problems for my father as he was the one who had to do the painting and decorating, and later build the new kitchenette. The debts angered my father greatly; as did the constant changes and they had ceaseless rows because of it.

The fact is, we were poor throughout my earliest years and into my early teens, and this was reflected in our meals and clothing and the fact that we rarely, if ever, got new books for school. We got a lot of our meals from the Stew House on Glass Lane. It was also reflected in the fact that all of the older boys never got to finish school. They were all taken out of second-level, except me: I left primary school when I was just eleven years old. The truth is that school was never really a priority for my mother. She preferred us do the housework and go out to work as soon as we were old enough.

Some of us were expected to do housework when we came in from school, sometimes before we could eat. And we would be sent to bed around 6 or 7 p.m. depending on our mother's mood. There was very little time for doing our homework after our chores and even when we did, we would be too tired. This meant getting into trouble with the teachers. Sometimes my mother would not give me a note for the teacher even though it wasn't my fault that the homework didn't get done. Sometimes I would be slapped or clattered and then get lines to write:

I must do my homework every day.
I must do my homework every day.
I must do my homework every day.

When we went to the Stew House we would have to stand in a queue and we would be taunted by people passing by on their way to and from school. We would put in our three or four pots and out would come the aromatic smell of fresh, hot food. We would get large pots of stew and potatoes for just two shillings a pot. We also got corned beef and chicken-and-ham roll. The food tasted fabulous and it certainly beat the usual bread and jam, bowls of soup or bread and margarine which we sometimes had as our main meals. The nearest we ever got to butter and ham was when we would have visitors. Sometimes, we would try and hang around until they left, to see if they had left any sandwiches behind. That was a rare treat.

A lot of our clothes came from the Iveagh Market on Francis Street, in the Liberties. They came to us via the O'Keeffe's from Ballyfermot Drive. Up the road they would come with their oversized Dick-Whittington-style sack, except it was a loud orange bed sheet with all the clothes inside. Of course, there was the usual mortification at the sight of the sack being taken into our house, but we weren't too mortified if it meant getting a new pair of much-needed shoes, albeit second or even third-hand. Sometimes, I was so desperate to get a pair that I would pretend they fit, even though they were crushing my feet. I couldn't take any more of sticking pieces of linoleum tile into my shoes because of the gaping holes in my soles, or because the soles had come away and were constantly flapping up and down. It was especially noisy when walking up the school corridors. People would say *Here's flapping-soles Duffy!* And '*scruffy Duffy.*' But wearing tight shoes was to prepare me for fitting into another form of tight shoes many years later, I suppose!

We had very little money, so my mother would borrow money from Mr Beagle. He would come to the house on Fridays with a box of groceries. Sometimes, there would be long slim bars of Cadbury's chocolate and we would wait to see if we would receive a piece. Sometimes we did and sometimes we didn't. At other times she would borrow money from Mrs Tallan, a neighbour, or from men who would call to the house every Friday. It was at a young age that we were taught to lie; at least when it suited her to have us go to the door and tell the callers that she wasn't at home. I could never understand why it was okay for us to lie when our parents told us to, but that we were never to lie ourselves. When I questioned this double standard, I would be beaten and told that I was a 'cheeky little bastard'.

We did our weekly shop in the Elephant supermarket on Le Fanu Road. There we would buy thirteen sliced pans, along with all the other bits and pieces. We would live on this food for a few days, but there would often not be enough to last the week. So, we had to get by on bread and jam. And that included sandwiches for work, which often amounted to nothing more than bread and margarine. Not much for a young girl expected to work twelve hours a day. And if we expressed our frustration or the fact that we were still hungry our mother would make us feel guilty by calling us a 'shower of ungrateful bastards'. This was often accompanied by smacks across the head and face.

As children we thought nothing of changing our clothes for toys, as toys were hard to come by after Christmas. Every few weeks the Travellers would come around in their Ford vans or the horse and wagon. They had all kinds of toys, including cowboy hats, balloons, guns and holsters, planes to throw, wind-up helicopters, whistles and sometimes footballs and beach balls. It was so exciting when they came but, of course, our mother refused to allow us to exchange our clothes for toys; no surprise there, especially as our clothes were all hand-me-down and down and down again, but, on the rare occasions we were allowed to exchange clothes for toys, there was so much pleasure to be had. Even then, I was disappointed that I couldn't trade clothes for girls' toys and had to settle for boys', but it was better than nothing.

The Ballyfermot I remember was new and bright, with rows of six houses, small front gardens and slightly larger gardens at the back. Wrought-iron railings separated each house and in the early years, no-one really bothered with putting up walls or fences. They weren't considered necessary then. The walls were pebble dashed, and everything looked the same. That changed over the years and, it has to be said, not for the better.

Every second week, Farmer John would come round with his large drums on his wagon to see if we had any waste food for his pigs. He had a small farm beside the canal. It was very exciting when he would allow us to climb up onto the wagon and travel along with him. Sometimes, he would let me sit up front and at others he would allow us to stay on all the way up to the farm. The Johnston, Mooney and O'Brien van was another visitor to our streets. It would stop across from our home and when the bread man pulled up the shutter, the aroma of fresh bread and cakes filled the air. Again, it was rare, but every now and again my mother would buy shortbread fingers, chocolate éclairs and cream slices or batch bread. Those were the days when bread actually tasted like bread, so fresh it was still warm when buttered.

I was made to do a lot of the household chores from as young as seven or eight years of age. My working life also started at a very early age, as did my career as an entrepreneur. When I was around nine or ten I would go up to Young's Bar on Le Fanu Road and mind the cars for the customers. When they left the pub and approached their cars, I went over to them and said, 'Excuse me mister, I was minding yer car for ye.' I normally received a few pennies, or a sixpence; sometimes as much as a shilling!

At other times I would go out on Saturday and Sunday mornings to work with the milkman. He would pay me sixpence but sometimes as much as one or two shillings. I would nearly always spend the money before going home because I knew my mother would take it from me and I would never see it again. When I would ask her were my money was, she would tell me to stop annoying her, or she would clatter me across the face and tell me to, 'Shut up or I'll break your fucking neck', and if it wasn't threats, then it was reminders of how ungrateful I was for all that she had done for me.

Despite all that had happened at this tender age, I was already living with purpose and developing a resilience that was to stand me in good stead in the years to come. And my god did I need them. I was also developing an innate desire to help others and make a difference. Even from a young age I was learning from my experiences. I was also learning to find reasons to smile despite how difficult things might be. I was learning that people, including parents will lie through their teeth and get their children to do the same on their behalf. I was learning that I was expected to behave differently from how I knew myself to be. And more importantly than these was learning that even at a young age I could learn to think for myself and have my own voice. And I did.

Chapter Two

School and My First Jobs

Tis education forms the common mind,
Just as the twig is bent, the tree's inclined.
[Alexander Pope]

It is hard to describe to the present generation what it was like to be left-handed in the sixties and seventies. People today can hardly believe that a left-handed child could be subject to continual cruelty abuse and humiliation, but that is precisely what it was like for youngsters back then. Being called an antichrist was not merely a spur of the moment thing, it was a strongly held belief and it was accompanied by other forms of verbal abuse and numerous forms of punishment, including having our hands slapped until they were so red and painful as to render holding a pencil, or any other item in our left hand impossible. Indeed, being left-handed and refusing to use my right-hand resulted in my being regarded as mentally retarded, which brought its own problems.

School started for me when I was just five years old. I went to the Dominican Convent boys' school on Ballyfermot Road. It was such a strange place and very imposing to a young child. There were scary statues and long corridors with polished floors. The walls were painted a mixture of the usual institutional cream or yellow on top with blue or green on the bottom. The classrooms seemed very big and contained large press units where all the books and chalks were kept and there were long blackboards and sloping desks with wooden bench seats attached.

The strangest thing of all for me were the nuns with their long habits and serious unfriendly looking faces. The other thing that was strange to me was sitting with so many boys. Where were the girls? I felt completely cut off from everyone and everything familiar. I had a strong sense of not fitting in with my classmates and they weren't slow in recognising this. Nothing made sense to me. Because of the isolation, I found it very difficult to learn and at no time in my school life did I feel natural as a boy, despite all my best efforts to fit in.

My mother was told by one of my teachers that there was something wrong with me: I should not be writing with my left hand and I should be discouraged from doing so, and that I was extremely sensitive for a boy. It was also the case that in those days, being left-handed was a sign that you were backward in some way. In school I would be shouted at if I was caught using my left hand, or as mentioned earlier, I would have my hand slapped until it was too sore to hold a pencil. At other times I was made to stand in the corner with my face to the wall and listen to the teachers and classmates calling me a dunce.

When I went home and told my mother that the teachers had slapped me, she would tell me I must have done something to make them hit me, so she would hit me too and tell me I was 'nothing but a fucking troublemaker'. I was still just a child and I found this kind of treatment overwhelming. I learned from the earliest age that I was to have no refuge from the very people who were supposed to be my guardians, my protectors, my nurturers. This was also the case when I was beaten on my way to and from school, or if I was wrongly accused by a neighbour

Mealtimes, too, were a complete nightmare. If I was caught using my left hand, my mother would shout at me to use my right hand. I tried, but it was just so awkward, and I had no coordination or strength to use it, so, I would quickly put the fork or spoon back into my left hand, only to have my mother or my father come over and beat me over the head and shout at me, calling me a 'cheeky little bastard!' or, an 'awkward little fucker'. While at other times my mother would grit her teeth and say, 'you're nothing but a fucking antichrist! I'll break your hand if you don't stop using it.' This was extremely hard to cope with and I started to withdraw further into myself. It got so bad and mealtimes were becoming so stressful I was unable to eat properly. Instead of chewing my food I would swallow it in order to get my meals over with as quickly as possible to avoid getting into trouble for using my left hand. But my mother would shout at me: 'Chew your food and don't swallow it.' Or it would be my brothers and sisters squealing and telling her: 'Mam, Sara-Jane is using her left hand', or, 'Mam, Sara-Jane is swallowing her food.' This went on for years.

My difficulties with my mother worsened after she was told by some teacher that I was 'mentally retarded'. I had to be taken to the doctors in Thomas Street and to St John of God Hospital in order to check me out and get me to do different tests to assess my mental abilities. I was able to do them okay and I was given a bag of sweets by the doctors. But at home and in school I was treated as anything but normal. It got out that I was supposed to be retarded and this led to years of bullying. I was frequently referred to as the 'retard', the 'spa' or the 'head case'; all serving to remind me that I was abnormal. To add to my woes at this time, I was taken out of my class and placed in a special class. The teacher was a kind, elderly lady and she would give me sweets if I would go to her classroom, but, conscious of the fact that I would be bullied on my return, I did everything I could to resist and remain in my old class, but it was to no avail. I cannot remember her name, but I do remember her gentleness and kindly nature; a very rare experience during these years. She never shouted at me or called me names and that felt really strange at the time. I won a set of rosary beads while in her class; the first thing I'd ever won. I had to attend elocution classes where I learned to say: 'This, That, These and Those, That's the way the TH goes.'

Being told I was retarded then has had a horrendous effect upon my life ever since. It was used by so many people to put me down and to make me feel completely inadequate as a child, that my life was useless and worthless and simply not worth the bother. It worked exceptionally well and served to hold me back for most of my life. So much so that this along with so many other things made life very difficult to cope with, by the time I was sixteen, I was already taking medication for coping with stress and depression and contemplating suicide. This feeling was to return many times over the next thirty years.

As a result of these feelings and the damage they caused, I spent most of my life trying to prove to myself and to everyone else that I am just as 'normal' as them. I thought that by working really hard, by spending my money on my family and so on that I would convince people that I was worth loving. But it never seemed to work, so I just worked harder and harder in a completely futile pursuit of approval. It was like climbing Mount Everest on my bare hands and knees. Every setback was perceived as yet another confirmation of how useless and unwanted I was.

At school we had to ask in Irish for permission to go to the toilet. We were often refused permission to go, which resulted in some of us wetting our pants. On one such occasion, when I was six, I asked for permission: 'An bhfuil cead agam dul amach, más é do thoil é?' I was refused, but I told the teacher that I really needed to go and that, if I didn't, I was likely to go in my pants. She told me to sit down and stay quiet. I couldn't hold back any longer and excreted into my pants. This was humiliating, but it was made worse by the fact that it was diarrhoea and was running down the legs of my short pants. I stood up and told the teacher, who, without saying anything, left the classroom. While she was out my classmates were laughing at me and calling me names.

The teacher returned to the classroom and called me out. 'Sara-Jane, you are to go home with these girls.' She pointed to the two older girls she had brought back with her into the classroom. They looked like teenage girls. They had a high pram and told me to sit into it, which I did. They pushed me along Ballyfermot Road and up the street where I lived, all the while laughing at what had happened to me. When I got home my Nana and Aunt Nancy were in the kitchen with my mother and they all thought my predicament was something to laugh about. Rather than be taken upstairs to the bathroom, I was told to strip and get onto the draining board. My mother proceeded to wash me in front of them. I was mortified and humiliated.

Telling this story in the first version of my book had an unexpected result. The aunt I mentioned as being present read this account and informed her children and other family members that it was true and that she was present when it happened. Apparently she told them that she felt ashamed at seeing how humiliated I was made to feel and for having not at least said something about it. I heard some other wonderful things to corroborate other events recounted here, but they are for later.

It was around 1967 or '68 when I first went to the De la Salle boys' school. Our special class was the last to move across and we were broken up into other classes. I arrived with some others into Master Mullally's class. I was sent straight to the back of the class and left there. Any pupil who was thought to be slow was left behind. This led to me withdrawing more and more into myself on the one hand while desperately trying to fit in on the other, but I just didn't know how. I hated being in school, especially as this is where I experienced so much of the bullying. There was nowhere I could turn for refuge when trouble came.

Matters became so much worse when word spread that I was supposed to be retarded. People thought I was an easy target, and they were not wrong. When my classmates wanted to have a laugh, they would tell me I was 'nothing but a fucking spa!' Or, 'Duffy, you're a bleedin weirdo.'

Mr Mullally has stayed in my memory because he wore odd shoes and socks. The worst thing I could say about him was that he seemed almost completely indifferent to me and to the rest of the class. This was better than those teachers and brothers who had no compunction about treating us harshly and humiliating us in front of our classmates. Here too, I was frequently slapped by teachers and brothers until it was so painful that I could not hold a pen or pencil, never mind that this would preventing me from writing. On other occasions they would belt me across the back of the head or clatter me in the face, or pull me up by my ears and shout insults at me:

'You're completely stupid, Duffy, what are you?'

'I'm completely stupid, Master.'

'Say that louder, Duffy, we can't hear you.'

'I'm completely stupid, Master.'

'And why are you stupid, Duffy?'

'I don't know, Master.'

'Because you can't even use your right hand, isn't that it, Duffy?'

'Yes, Master.'

'Can't hear you, Duffy.'

'Yes, Master.'

'Now, get back to your seat.'

'Yes, Master.'

At this age, I was frequently kept back from school to clean the house. I also cooked for the whole family, dressed my younger brothers and sisters, changed their nappies, bathed them, took them out in their prams etc. And so, I would be slapped for missing school, because I'd been kept at home, and would be made to stand in front of the class until I came up with a believable excuse. The longer it took me to come up with something, the more I was slapped. Then there were the times when I would not be allowed to go to school until my work was finished. When I finally did turn up I would be slapped, clattered or given lines to do:

I must not be late for school.
I must not be late for school.
I must not be late for school.

Passing the girls' school was particularly difficult as it made me feel that I should have been on the other side of the wall and be attending the same classes as all the other girls. It was a deeply lonely experience. It was also around this time that I felt the growing need to dress and feel like a girl, but there were no clothes other than my mothers. So, when I was kept home from school and she was out of the house, I would go to her room and put on her clothes and try to look like a girl. She had lovely crimplene, crêpe and chiffon dresses. I would try to put on her make-up, but not very well, mostly because my hands would be trembling with a mixture of fear and excitement. What was most fantastic about this was the feelings of wholeness and of being right within myself. Every part of my body, except one, felt completely girlie. These were precious times for me, so much so that I would volunteer to stay at home from school, knowing that my mother would go out for a few hours and this would leave me free to get dressed. Of course, there was always the risk of getting caught, but it was worth it to be able to spend time being myself and feeling some way normal.

The experience was full of delight and terror at the same time. I was exhilarated and wonderfully content being a girl for that short time, but I was also terrified at being found out. I was caught once by one of my brothers, but he never let on that he saw me. It was years later before I discovered why he never said anything, and his reasons were to reinforce for me the fact that I wasn't dressing for kicks, but for an altogether more profound reason. The truth is, I felt like a freak inside while I was living, or should I say trying to live as a boy, but when I was dressed in my mother's clothes, I felt truly normal.

There were a few occasions when I was nearly discovered by my mother. I remember running and hiding in the wardrobe with my heart racing, waiting for her to come up the stairs and to open the wardrobe only to find me standing there in her clothes. However, not even this fear was enough to deter me from taking every opportunity to dress and be a girl; to be my true self. But, like it or not, I also had to live my life as the girl with no name. That is what I was until my friend Kathy gave me my new name in 2003. These rare opportunities were to end after I started working, and once I became a teenager, it was to be at least another ten years before the opportunity to be a girl, well, to at least <u>feel</u> like a girl, was to present itself.

There were many occasions when my mother's favouritism and, in particular, her dislike of me, were felt very strongly. There is one I remember above all others. I had been begging to go the film being shown at school, *The Vikings*, with Kirk Douglas and Tony Curtis. Both my brother Fred and I were promised faithfully by my mother that we could both go and see the film after school. I had to do a load of chores in order to be allowed go. On the day of the film I was hardly able to concentrate due to the excitement. I couldn't wait to go home for lunch and get the money to pay for my ticket and maybe a few sweets. I came home for lunch, which I ate very quickly as I wanted to get back to school as quickly as possible, such was my excitement. We went to my mother to get the money for the tickets, but she told us that only one of us could go to see the film and that someone was Fred. I was truly devastated by this, it was just so bloody unfair. It was not the first time it had been done to me, and not the first time I was left feeling devastated and angry at the blatant favouritism. I returned to school determined that I was going to see the film, so I decided to take matters into my own hands. I went to see the head brother, Brother Sebastian, and told him that my mother told me to ask him if there were any spare tickets for the film, because she could not afford to send me to the pictures. It was, of course, a lie on my part, just as it had been on my mother's. She had the money, but just wanted me to be at home doing the housework as usual.

Brother Sebastian gave me the ticket and I got to see the movie. It was spectacular and I enjoyed every minute of it, and it didn't matter that I had no money to spend on sweets; I got to see the film and that's all that mattered. I did this knowing full well there would be a major showdown when I arrived home, but, just this once, I was too determined to be afraid. It was amazing how much courage I found to stand up to my mother.

'Where were you until this hour?' my mother asked when I got home.

'I was at the film,' I said, trembling; knowing that I was in serious trouble and that I would be sent to bed without anything to eat and the prospect of a severe beating, along with the usual shouting and verbal abuse. I was determined though that she was not going to win out this time, especially after what she had done to me in not keeping her promise. It was showdown time!

'And where did you get the money for the pictures?' She asked this with a tone that was clearly designed to terrify me into confessing. But I was adamant that I was not going to cave in. This was one beating she was not going to give me, nor for that matter was my father, not if I had anything to do with it.

'I won the ticket in a raffle,' I said.

'You're lying! Get down on your knees here and tell me the truth.'
I had to kneel on the hard floor in front of her and my smirking brothers. It was awful, but I was still determined. I never had a single victory or let-off with my parents up to this incident, but this time it was going to be different. I started to cry, but said nothing for a few moments.

'You will stay there until you tell the truth', she said. So, I thought for a few moments then said: 'I found the ticket in the school yard and brought it to Brother Sebastian. He told me to go around to all the classes and see if anyone lost it. Then he said if no-one claimed it then I could keep it, so no-one claimed it and I was allowed to keep it and go to the film.'

She remained unconvinced, but I remained steadfast and immovable. True to her word, she kept me kneeling there for what seemed like an age, but the longer I knelt there the more courageous and determined I became. Suddenly she said: 'I'm going to send your brother Fred in to see Brother Sebastian tomorrow and if he says you're lying, I'll fucking kill you, you little bastard!'

My brothers looked on with an air of superiority and were convinced that I was most likely going to get the hiding of my life the next day. But neither they nor I could have predicted what was to occur. I was in class the following day, finding it impossible to concentrate on my lessons, not that unusual for me, but particularly hard when all I could think about was the inevitable beating that awaited me when I returned home; not to mention being sent straight to bed for the umpteenth time without dinner.

A pupil knocked on our classroom door: 'Master Mullally, Sara-Jane Duffy is to go down to Brother Sebastian's office immediately.' This is the moment I had dreaded. I was convinced that I was going to be exposed and pay the consequences. This filled me with the most awful terror and my stomach, not for the first, or the last time, was in terrible pain. I went down to Brother Sebastian's office and knocked at the door.

'Come in.'

I went in very sheepishly. 'Brother Sebastian, I'm Sara-Jane Duffy and I was told to come down to you straightaway.' He looked at me with a smile and said: 'Sara-Jane, your brother Fred has just been in to see me and told me this story about you finding a ticket in the yard and that you brought it to me and that I told you to go to each class to see if anyone had lost it. Now, Sara-Jane, is that true?' I was completely petrified; not only was this head brother going to cane me, but I was certain to get the hiding of my life when I went home. 'No, Brother Sebastian, it's not true.'

I then proceeded to tell him my sorry tale of how my mother had broken her promise to me and left me feeling upset at not being allowed go to the pictures and how I then came to see him and let on that my mother told me to ask him for the ticket. He looked at me again with a smile and said: 'Well, now, Sara-Jane I told your brother that that is what happened, but you must promise me never to do that again. Do you promise?'

'Of course,' I said, 'Yes, Brother Sebastian, I promise I won't do that again.'

He told me I was a good girl and gave me two lollipops, then sent me back to my class.

I felt euphoric and triumphant. I had just this once managed to withstand my mother's best and most determined efforts to get me to confess, waiting no doubt to give me another of her beatings around the head, coupled with the usual verbal abuse. But not this time, definitely not this time! This was to be one of those rare kindnesses shown to me during these tender years and I was grateful for it.

During the summer holidays, we would find so many ways to pass the time. We played soccer, street tennis, bulldogs, rounders, handball, etc. The smell of fresh Bitumen being poured between the splits in the concrete is something I loved, and still do. It made it so much easier to make calls in our tennis matches, as we could see the lines more clearly. We would go for long walks up to the canal and play in the graveyard inside the Lawns at Le Fanu Road. Often, I went away on my own, walking, collecting bees in a jar and cycling around the Kylemore industrial estate.

But through all of this, I was secretly going through my own intense agonising over who I was truly meant to be. Any chance I got to play with the girls, I took it. We played a game called 'piggies' in which we would hop and push a shoe-polish tin between chalked squares until we got to the square at the top. It wasn't as easy as it sounds. What I loved about it was that it was mainly the girls who played it, so I could play with them without looking conspicuous. Yet, in spite of these happy moments, I hadn't the slightest idea why I should feel so completely at odds with myself, save what my parents, siblings, schoolteachers and schoolmates made me feel: that I was utterly stupid, retarded and worthless. I felt all that they made me feel, and yet these feelings of disconnectedness were coming from a very different place. I think it was my emotional response to various life situations, along with a very non-male intuition which left me feeling that I didn't belong inside my body. This feeling of being disconnected from my body was to get much stronger over the coming years and was to become a serious life-and-death issue; something I could not share with another living soul.

Despite my conflicting feelings and the temptation to withdraw, I decided to join the altar servers, when I was eight years of age. I was completely devoted to being the best altar server I could be and was awarded a prize for being the 'star altar server on a few occasions. This was one of the upsides to the being an altar server. Another upside was serving at ten o'clock Mass, because this meant getting off school for a couple of hours each morning. Sometimes, it would be longer because some funerals and weddings would be held after 10 o'clock Mass. But the 7.0am morning Mass was a scary experience, especially in the winter when I had to get up before 7 a.m. and walk down dark cold roads to the church. I was really scared of the dark and my imagination always ran away with itself, imagining people I knew who'd died coming out of their gardens and grabbing me.

As altar servers we would be treated to trips to the theatre and to see films in the Plaza cinema. It was while I was with the altar servers I got to see Ben Hur and the Ten Commandments for the first time. It was amazing watching the chariot races in Ben Hur on the large curving cinema screen. It felt like the chariots were actually running over us.

Another benefit of being an altar boy was that my mother and brothers were less likely to give me a hard time once I was wearing my soutane and surplice. Wearing them made me feel very spiritual and close to God. The Tridentine Mass was still being said during my first couple of years as an altar boy, in Latin and with the priest's back to the congregation. The people were like mindless drones as they repeated verbatim the same prayers Sunday after Sunday, but that all changed after the second Vatican Council, which had taken place a few years earlier in the early 60s. The altar was moved nearer to the congregation and the priest now faced the people. However, the ceremony was still very grandiose in nature and clearly intended to create a feeling of reverential awe on the part of the congregation. It worked, of course, and people enjoyed the spectacle, although they rarely, if ever, understood the full significance of what they were actually participating in. It was years later that I found myself questioning the value of all these rituals and the church for that matter.

As an altar boy I had to attend numerous funerals; far too many for such a young boy. We would have to attend the receiving of the remains on the evening before the funeral Mass. The bodies would be kept overnight in rooms at the back of the church, and if there were more than two coffins at a time, some would be left at the front side of the church. There were times when we would have to close the church, normally around 9p.m, and when switching off the lights we would have to check some of the rooms in the dark. It scared the living daylights out of me every time. Then there were those occasions when coffin lids were removed in order to allow loved ones to say goodbye for the last time. I found this a deeply emotionally disturbing experience, to stand there holding the crucifix and incense burner while staring at the corpses. They had a deeply scarring effect upon my mind, bringing a terror of death into my life at a young age and adding to the darkness that was already engulfing my tender spirit. They made me far too serious and introverted

During these years, and for many years afterwards, I had waking nightmares. They consisted of the most vivid images of me being buried alive, waking to the sounds of soil dropping onto the lid of the coffin. It terrified me so much that I would curl up against my brothers in the bed, but they would push me away, telling me I was a weirdo, or they would ask me if I was 'queer or something?' I couldn't tell them why I was doing it because they would have just called me an attention-seeker. If I couldn't get comfort from being close to them then I would curl up like a foetus and snuggle against my pillow while sucking my thumb, while the tears streamed down my face. I had to turn my screams and terror inward where no-one else could hear them. Eventually I would get to sleep, only to go through the same horror the next night, and again the following night, and so on for years. The nights became weeks and the weeks became years. This continued right through until my early twenties, as did my thumb-sucking. There is a photograph somewhere of me sucking my thumb while sleeping. It was taken while I was on two weeks' camp with the FCA in Longford, of all places. The situation wasn't helped when we looked at horror movies late at night. I absolutely dreaded going to the toilet, because it meant going upstairs and expecting to see ghosts at the top of the stairs, or getting the fright of my life if the bulb had gone and I would have to look up and see the picture of the Sacred Heart on the wall, with the red light making it look very spooky. I really hated that bloody thing, it was always scaring the bejaysus out of me.

I was sitting with one of my friends recently and sharing my experiences of the nightmares with her, when it suddenly dawned on me that it was not the fear of my own death that I was afraid of, but the death of my female gender identity; my female personality was slowly but surely being buried alive; literally! There is no other way of describing it other than that it was absolutely terrifying. And I hadn't a clue how to cope with it.

It was also as an altar boy that I became convinced of my calling to the priesthood, but had to wait until I was seventeen before I could do anything about it. But I had a constant sense of spirituality from this time on. I had been so affected by my sense of calling that I engaged in religious role-playing in my bedroom with the help of some of my younger brothers and sisters. I would play the role of the priest saying Mass, using the dressing table as the altar and my brothers and sisters would act as altar boys. I guess they had a point when they thought I was weird. If I wasn't saying Mass then I would re-enact the crucifixion, using the bed as the Hill of Calvary. I even cried out: '*Eloi, Eloi, sabacthani.* My God, my God, why have you forsaken me?' These words were to prove prophetic.

Even at this young age I would enter the church on my own and stare at the crucifix. Everything else in the church seemed so meaningless and false by comparison. The only thing I could relate to was, the figure on the cross. I felt we understood each other, that we had something in common. I would ask if my sufferings were a preparation for a life of service, and if so, what kind of service that would be. Being a Catholic and having spent so long as an altar boy it seemed logical that maybe I was being called to the priesthood. My sufferings made some sense in this context. Maybe I had to learn to suffer in order to help others who were suffering. Maybe I was learning to separate from my family, I thought, because I would have to work with so many people that I wouldn't be able to commit to a family of my own in the future. Of course, I now know that I was preparing for a life of a different kind, but it would be many years before I was to be able to live it, and so, for a long time, religion became my preoccupation.

It was also around this time that I started to sense my femaleness in a more pronounced way than earlier in my childhood. It was becoming less vague, especially as I was beginning to feel increasingly physically abnormal. I couldn't understand why I still had a penis instead of a vagina, and then I noticed girls my own age developing breasts and wondered why I wasn't. I became increasingly distressed but never dared to express my feelings to a living soul, especially as they already considered me to be odd. There was no undue female influence upon my life that could explain this, and I tried really hard to be a normal boy just like my brothers and friends. In fact, just about everything I did throughout my entire life was aimed at proving to others that I was just as normal as they were. Yet even this was to bite me over and over again as people, especially my family asking me (always in accusative tones): 'well if you knew you were a girl all that time why didn't you say something?' It has always been very difficult to answer that question, especially against the background I grew up in. But it really didn't matter because I knew it was never a genuine question to begin with. But of course the answer should have been: "why in the name of god would I be telling you when you would use it against me and lock me up?

Apart from wearing my soutane and surplice in public at various religious events, the only other time I came close to wearing anything remotely girlie was a swimsuit during a Community Week fancy dress competition. It was held during the summer holidays and there was a variety of activities, including soccer tournaments, fancy dress competitions and a fair. Community Week was a really big deal, a real coming-together of the community. We all participated in cleaning our streets and putting up bunting. It was a time for taking pride in ourselves and in each other. Soccer tournaments took place in the Lawns. As much as I looked forward to it I was rarely picked for any of the teams, which made me feel left out, but I came into my own at the fancy dress parade.

In one particular year, 1970-71, I dressed as Miss World. Strangely it was suggested to me by my mother for some reason. But I jumped at the opportunity because it was in keeping with my growing sense of my own femininity. I was dressed in a diagonally striped swimsuit, tights, heels and a wig. The cups in were filled with nylon tights to give the appearance of breasts. The only thing that struck me after the initial nervousness was how natural I felt, for the first time in my ten years. It felt like I was in a state of bliss. It remains a fond memory of one day in my childhood when I really felt how I was supposed to feel, and in public! It was simply a wonderful experience. An incident occurred on the day, which though it didn't feel funny at the time does make me laugh when I remember it. We were at the top of the road waiting for the winners to be announced. I was leaning against the railings outside Hughe's house when a young fella from down the road came over to me and started squeezing my breasts, or what appeared to him as breasts! I was really embarrassed and lashed out by giving him a right slap in the face, as you do. My mother was very quick to have a go at me, but Mr Hughes came out and told her what had happened, which led to her backing off. Nerves aside, being able to wear a swimsuit in public, in tights and a wig was something of a red-letter day. Not a single person there knew of how much this experience meant to me. The breast pulling incident aside, it was quite simply joyful!

Nonetheless, there were times when I felt myself able to fit in with the other boys. During the summer holidays one of our favourite pastimes was to go up to the canal and play around the Seventh Lock. We liked to dare each other to walk across the narrow foot boards. This was a special thrill for me because I couldn't swim. I really did envy the boys who could be so fearless and jump into the lock and swim. I feel that the reason I still can't swim is because of the time that Joey Maguire pushed me from behind into the canal. I was about eight at the time. We were standing under the bridge and Joey was daring me to get into the water, but I was saying I didn't want to.

'That's because you can't swim,' he said.

'Yes I can,' I retorted, although it was a lie. I didn't want to be caught being a 'cissy'.

'I bet you can't.'

'Oh, yes I can,' I said, adamantly.

The next thing I knew, I was heading towards the water in a state of total panic. Jaysus! I can't swim, I can't swim! Get me out! For fuck's sake get me out, I can't swim!'

'I knew you couldn't bleedin' swim, you fuckin eejit!'

They pulled me out of the water, but not before they had a really good laugh. I never learned to swim after that. I was like a ship that was off balance and kept keeling over to the right every time I tried.

From time to time, we would go to the Gala cinema on a Saturday or Sunday for the afternoon matinee. We also went to the pictures shown in the playground hall. We saw all kinds of films, Westerns, war films and fencing films —as we called them. We would play out what we had seen in the films on the way home through the Lawns. We also watched Lassie, Flipper and the Three Stooges, to name but a few. We all wanted to be the Americans when playing out the war films and the cowboys in the westerns. Sometimes we went searching for vampires in the old graveyard. The graveyard was turned into a mound some years ago.

Another formative time for me was our holidays in Oakwood in Co. Wicklow and Coolure House in Co. Meath, organised by a local community group. We loved these holidays; I just loved being away from my parents and from all the stress and tension, the rows, violence and favouritism. I still remember our bedrooms in the cabins and the toilets and showers across the yard; the communal hall for our meals and the sitting room where we relaxed and had our dances. I loved Oakwood and still do. It was there I learned to love the songs, 'Matrimony' and, 'Nothing Rhymed' by Gilbert O'Sullivan and, 'Sylvia's Mother' by Dr Hook. I won a talent competition in Oakwood for singing 'Two Little Boys', by Rolf Harris. I loved the farm animals, the ducks and geese, the pigs and the donkeys, the slopping hills down towards the rushing river; walking across the river on the slippery stones. I envied the boys and girls who could swim in the deepest part of the river, and I especially enjoyed sitting by the riverbank watching them all jumping in and having such fun. It was all so lovely and relaxing and I really did feel free from the awfulness of my home life.

The last of my holidays was in 1973. The holiday was to be truly momentous. We were due to go to Coolure House in August and needless to say we were full of excitement and impatience. A few days before, I was trying to flush the toilet when the chain came away in my hand. I tried to put it back into its bracket, but while I was standing on the toilet seat, it split in two. My mother came home and discovered the broken seat. I was too scared to tell her what had happened and, as usual, she threatened us with another beating from our father. We were all under suspicion, but despite this I was just too terrified to own up. When we were summoned by him we remained silent. He then told us that we would not be allowed to go on our holidays. Still no-one came forward. He was relentless and we were all sent to bed without anything to eat. The next day we started all over again, after he arrived home from work. Needless to say we were disconsolate at the prospect of missing our holiday. Eventually, my brother Stephen went in and told him that he had done it.

'I fuckin' knew it was you, you little fucker!' my mother shouted.

When I heard this, I started to cry for Stephen and rushed in to tell them that I was the one who broke the seat and how it came about, but as usual they would not listen to me. Stephen got the most savage of beatings. He was beaten with fists, then an army belt and then my father kicked him around the floor. I was having flashbacks to the vicious assault on my brother Peter years earlier. My father was determined to continue with the punishment against us so he forbade us to go on our holiday. It was a completely petty and unjust act. We pleaded with our mother to ask him to let us go. He eventually relented and allowed us to go.

We travelled to Coolure in a Ford Transit minibus. I remember us driving up what seemed like a boreen into a wide opening at the front of the house. It was a mansion compared to what I was used to, with large rooms immediately to the right and left as we entered. We slept in a communal bedroom. No sooner had I arrived than I felt a strong sense of elation mixed with an immediate dread of going home in a few days. Anything was better than Ballyfermot and this place was paradise.

I went out to explore the grounds. At the rear of the house was Lough Derravaragh; to the right were the stables, where I met Angela. She looked after the horses and was very down to earth. I felt really comfortable in her company. We had discos in the big room to the left of the entrance and I enjoyed the dancing. It was wonderfully peaceful and stress free. I just loved it and hated having to go home.

One day, we were riding along the boreen and coming through one of the gates. Just as I had come through the gate, one of the boys hit the horse's hind leg. The horse bolted and the next thing I knew it was galloping along the boreen. Someone shouted, *'watch out!'* I stuck my head up and looked back to see who had shouted the warning then, I turned to the front, just in time to see the branch sticking out from the tree. The next thing I remember was waking up in Angela's arms in Our Lady's Hospital in Drogheda. I became unconscious again, for some hours in fact. And when I did eventually wake up. It was to the sound of Neil Diamond's Hot August Night LP. I still remember listening to 'Crunchy Granola Suite', 'I am, I Said', 'Canta Libre', but most especially 'Morningside', a song about a man who made a table out of oak wood, but no-one noticed the gift he had. He died alone. That made such an impact upon me. I recognised myself in the man who gave the best of what he had only to remain unwanted and alone. And then there was 'Girl, You'll be a Woman Soon'; except that I never did get to be a woman anytime soon! No prizes for guessing that Neil Diamond was, and remains, my favourite singer song writer, with John Denver a very close second. They sang to my soul.

I was the one who introduced the Bee Gees, Neil Diamond, John Denver and many others into our home. My brothers would let on that they didn't like them but when I wasn't at home, they would listen to my records; only for me to arrive home and catch them. In fact, we learned to gauge the state of each other's love lives by the music we were listening to at any given time. Peter was dating a girl from across the road and we could always tell when it was going well and when things were going badly. He would play my records until they couldn't be played any more.

Peter had this habit of rolling his head from side to side with the head phones on and singing at the top of his voice, while crying. We got a great kick out of this, especially when he would deny that he was doing it. Despite the fact that he did ruin my records, I hated to see him go through the pain of his break-up. He had been with the same girl for a number of years and he clearly loved her very much. I always had a soft spot for Peter and tried to get close to him, but it wasn't to be. The need for my mother's approval and that of his peers meant that he was more interested in belittling me at every opportunity than he ever was in being my brother. This was to be one of the greatest hurts of my life.

One of the most notable aspects of my childhood and adolescences was the complete lack of moral guidance from either of my parents. They issued their orders, but never felt it necessary to explain the reasons why we should obey their rules. It was supposed to be enough for them to tell us what to do and we would simply obey without question. It was a case of 'do as I say, not as I do'. It never occurred to them that we realised they were applying double standards. We were not permitted to ask even the most innocent of questions or to make any kind of comment or complaint. Most of us lived in fear while a small number of us lived in sheer terror. Virtually every one of my brothers and sisters learned to keep their mouths shut — it was far more important to fit in and avoid vicious beatings than it was to have their own thoughts and opinions, to have their own minds —and who could blame them, especially when they saw what happening with me. I just never believed that it was right for me to remain silent and I'm so glad I never did, despite the vicious beatings and other abuse I was to receive throughout my childhood and well into my adult life. I'm really glad I withstood all the attempts to get me to be something I'm not.

This phase of my life was to be marked by a growing sense of being disconnected from everyone around me but, more importantly, feeling disconnected from *myself*. Of course, I didn't know that it was really the girl inside me trying to live. It was also a time in which I began to develop a deeper sense of my being female, but without really understanding why it was happening to me. I began to develop the ability to relate to people on an unusually deep level and was able to see to the very heart of issues rather than engage in small talk; not out of arrogance or trying to be smart, but simply because of how things came to my mind. I was very aware of it at times but hadn't a clue where it came from or how to manage it. I also developed an ability to strongly empathise with other people's suffering, especially other children, all of which might be considered *female* attributes. But I received many put-downs, precisely because of the fact that I was so very different from everyone around me. So, the more they told me I was abnormal, the harder I tried to be normal. But the more I tried to be a normal boy, the more I felt like a girl; the more sensitive I was, the more they ridiculed me. Growing into adolescence was to be a very difficult and lonely period in my life. The only real glimpse of light I had was going out. My life was moving in such a way that there was simply no further opportunity to experience being a girl, even to the limited extent I once enjoyed.

In starting puberty, I was also entering an emotional wilderness, without any of the emotional or literacy skills which would enable me to survive; and yet somehow, I managed to survive. I was entering a phase in which my female identity became even more noticeable, which ironically was also around the time I was working hard to hide it. Another irony was, I didn't have the slightest hint that my parents and siblings had noticed that I had very strong female traits during my earlier years, apart from calling me names that is, the significance of which I never understood at the time. They would later comment on it when I disclosed my diagnosis; but at this stage, they ignored them or used them as a justification for putting me down, calling me a *'cry baby'* or a *'cissy'* and *'an attention seeker.'*

I spent the last six months of primary school working at home, cooking, cleaning, minding my younger brothers and sisters, changing their nappies, taking them for walks and entertaining them in whatever ways I could. I loved this role and enjoyed it immensely. I cannot adequately state just how much I loved my brothers and sisters or what I did for them, but this too was about to change. This change was to create a great distance between us, despite my best efforts to look out for them and seek their best always. Dysfunctional relationships are full of love and good intentions, and my relationship with my siblings was based on that, which is why it is so hard to break free of them, but I did finally cut all contact with them in 2008, following the publication of my book.

At this age I was experiencing the self-empowerment that comes from not following slavishly what others told me to think, say or do; whether they be my parents, teachers, priests. It really didn't matter who they were or what their authority, I was already asserting my right to question and to disagree. It marked me out as being a cheeky little bastard, but that was a small price to pay to have an independent mind and for speaking up for myself and others; both of which I was to do many times over the course of such a young life. It was very much out of the ordinary for one so young to be like this, but I was undeterred and remained determined to express myself in any way I could. It was not until later in life that I learnt about how much it had been noticed by others and how much it was respected. It was a pity I didn't know this at the time as it could have made such a positive difference to my self-belief and confidence. If I could send a message to parents today it is that these are some of the most formative years of a child's life, their character and personality. The parents play is vital in shaping their children into the kind of people they will become and it is immeasurable. I am the exception to the way I was raised, not the norm.

Chapter Three

The Child Adult

Which of us…is to do the hard and dirty work for the rest — and for what pay?
Who is to do the pleasant and clean work, and for what pay?
[John Ruskin]

1972 was a momentous year. On Sunday 30 January, 13 people were shot dead by the British Army and the incident was to go down in history as *Bloody Sunday*. There was the burning of the British embassy and the throwing of coffins against the burning building. It was also the year in which eleven Israelis were massacred at the Munich Olympics and Michael Jackson made it to number one with his song 'Ben'. It was also the year during which I started work, at twelve years of age. I was well below the legal age and my first jobs were very hard and the wages very low. As soon as we were able or showed a willingness to give up school, our mother made sure we started work and earned a wage to support our large household. Education was not a priority for my parents, and not one of my brothers and sisters was to finish school, but to their credit, this has not held them back when it came to finding work.

I have often described my first years of work as something out of a Charles Dickens novel. There were no rights for younger workers back then. No matter how sick I was, I was still expected to arrive at work and put in a full day's hard graft. But, more importantly, in order to survive in the workplace, it was necessary to become an adult of sorts; all the talk was adult talk, all the humour, adult humour; all of which I was expected to keep up with, but which went completely over my head. I was lost and out of my depth. To make matters worse, I was becoming more aware of the fact that I was not developing physically as I thought I should. In other words, I wasn't developing into the girl I felt myself to be inside. Everything was becoming a contradiction.

My first job was in a clothing factory on the Kylemore industrial estate. I started on a Monday and my wages was just £6.50p per week. All I got out of the £6.50p was about 50p.

My job was to press the hems of trench coats; an extremely repetitive and boring job. I had had a heavy infection by the Wednesday and spent a lot of time going to the toilet to blow my nose and clear my throat of phlegm. It was very embarrassing, and my boss noticed that I was leaving my post quite a bit. On enquiring into what was wrong I told him I'd had my appendix removed and that I was still in pain. Well, at least it sounded better than just having a heavy cold. It worked, but it resulted in losing my job after just three days. He told me I should not be working until my scar had fully healed. Of course, he was right, but my mother didn't see it in quite the same way. I really did have my appendix removed just weeks before I started my new job and I shouldn't have been working at all so soon after the surgery, but such were the times and the little regard my mother had for my health at the time.

My next job was Ryan's Petrol Station on the Rathmines Road. My wages there was £7.50p per week. I worked two shifts there, 7 a.m. to 3 p.m. and 3 p.m. to 11 p.m.; and I was still only twelve years of age. I had lied about my age. Because I was tall for one so young, I was able to pass myself off as a teenager of 14 or 15. It meant, of course, getting up very early in the mornings to get the number 18 bus from Kylemore Road, then walking from Rathmines Garda station to the end of the Rathmines Road, another mile or so away. I was given just 50 - 75p from my wages by my mother, and from that I had to pay my bus fares and for some of my lunches. Also, I would have to make my own lunches and do my own chores either before going into work for the three o'clock shift or when I came home from doing the early shift.

It didn't matter how exhausted I was, I still had to do them and often before getting anything to eat. I felt that this was terribly unfair given that my other brothers got away without doing them. But things were changing.

The more time I spent out of the house, the more remote I felt from the family and experienced a sense of genuine elation at not being under my mother's control. And there was no-one to squeal if I did something wrong or for making mistakes. For those few hours at least, no-one could give me a hard time because I was using my left hand. I could have conversations with adults without worrying about what they would say to my mother. And I would jump at the chance of doing overtime as it meant being out of the house even longer, and an extra 50p or so for my pocket money.

I met Marie who worked across the road in Martin's rental shop. She was about 17 and I really liked her. I would look for any opportunity to go over and have a chat. I always liked talking to other girls, though it always seemed strange to be doing this as a *boy*, or at least in a boy's body. But I had no sisters at this time that I could talk to, as they were all younger than me, which added to my ever-increasing loneliness and isolation. As awful as the isolation felt, though, it was still better than being in such a stress-filled house.

I needed to earn more money because of having so little pocket money — the little I had was being spent on my younger brothers and sisters and on buying my mother gifts for this that and the other — so I came up with the idea of washing cars in the garage. It was not being used for anything else and so I decided to make use of it. I started by asking the man who owned the rental shop across the road if he would like to have his car washed. He said he would and I was delighted. I told him it would be 50p and he agreed.

'Make sure you so a good job now.'

'No problem…'

'And make sure you wax it when you've finished washing it.'

'Okay.'

'Put plenty of elbow grease into it.'

'Okay, but where will I get the elbow grease?' Yes I really did ask that question.

'The lads in the auto shop two doors down will get it for you.'

So I confidently strolled into the auto shop. 'Heya Paddy, Martin from across the road wants me to use elbow grease for waxing his car. Do you have any?'

Paddy looked at me in disbelief, but never let on. 'I don't have any here at the moment. If you come back later, I'll make some up for you.'

'Okay, see you later. Oh, by the way, how much is it?'

'Don't worry about that.'

'Okay, thanks, see you later.'

And I did call back later, looking for the elbow grease. And when I found out that he had no elbow grease I was left puzzled at what to do next, so I went to tell Martin. He just smiled and said not to worry. It never occurred me that they were having a bit of fun at my expense. It was one of those rites of passage we went through then when starting a new job, and there was more to follow.

As the oil crisis of 1972 deepened, filling stations were limiting the amount of petrol to £2.00per car. The shortage was causing rationing and long queues. The queues for our filling station went all the way to the top of Rathmines Road. It was a very difficult job trying to explain to customers why they were limited to the £2.00. Needless to say, they weren't very happy and quite a few customers tried to pay us to give them an extra amount. One incident I remember well involved the singer Red Hurley. It was a Friday or Saturday evening and there was the usual long queue, which seemed to never end. There were two petrol pumps. I served at one and the supervisor Joe served at the other. Because of the queues it was very hard to take a break, so we were exhausted and hungry before we'd be half-way through our shift, and certainly in no mood for anyone skipping the queue. But that didn't matter to some people who tried to skip and tried to get more petrol than they were allowed. Red Hurley was one of those who tried to skip and to get more than the £2.00 limit. He arrived in a fancy jaguar (maroon in colour, if memory serves), which had two petrol tanks; if you don't mind. He skipped the queue and pulled up to my pump. He double-parked beside the customer I was serving and got out of his car. 'Fill it up for me there, I'm in a hurry,' he said in a fluster.

'No I won't,' I said. 'you have to join the queue like everyone else.'

'Do you know who I am?'

'Yes, I do, and I don't care, you have to join the queue and you you're getting £2.00 just like everyone else.' He started shouting at me, but I ignored him. Then the supervisor came over to see what was going on. I told him that I wasn't serving Hurley as he had skipped the queue and that he was looking for more the £2.00.

'I'll take care of it, you go in and make a cup of tea." I went into the office and put on the kettle, and I watched as the supervisor gave Hurley more than he was entitled to. I was livid. The Supervisor and Hurley came into the office. 'Thanks for that Joe,' Hurley said.

'No problem, could I have your autograph for me wife, she loves listening to your LP?'

'Sure, what's her name?' Joe gave him his wife's name and Hurley wrote his name on a bit of paper. Joe thanked him for the autograph and was about to give him his Green Shield stamps but was told to keep them. As Hurley was leaving he turned to me and said, 'you're a right cheeky little bastard.' To which I replied, 'I prefer to be a cheeky little bastard than a stuck-up pig any day!'

I then turned on my supervisor and called him a right 'lick arse.' Needless to say, he wasn't best pleased.

As more and more filling stations ran out of petrol they had to shut down causing people to lose their jobs. I was let go from mine, but I got another one just as quickly It was in Robinson's Butchers on Dunville Avenue, Ranelagh. I worked on the delivery van and travelled to various locations around the city and as far as Wicklow. I enjoyed working in the butchers, but I could have done without having to get the heads of the cows out of the freezer first thing on a

Monday morning. Another of my jobs was pickling the corned beef and bacon, while another was making the sausages.

A lady named Mary came in and did the canteen work and made sandwiches for our breaks. She would fry the freshest bacon and sausages and put them between slices of white bread and butter. They were fantastic. We could smell the lovely sausages and bacon and hear the sizzling as they fried. I looked forward to going to work, knowing what awaited me at my ten-o'clock tea break, especially as I rarely had a decent breakfast at home.

Working in Robinson's nearly cost me my life though. I had just started work on a Monday morning and was told to go into the freezer in the shop to take down a carcass and bring it into the shop. When I went to lift the carcass off the hook, I received the most awful electric shock. The lads knew the bars holding the meat were live and thought it would be a great laugh to see me get such a shock. Needless to say, I wasn't very impressed and let off quite a few expletives.

Later that same day I was cleaning the yard and decided to wash it down with water from the tap against the yard wall. I had forgotten about the earlier incident and never made any connection between the live bars in the freezer and the water coming from the tap. In fact, the first time I turned the tap, there was no problem. However, the second time I put my hand on the tap, the electric current went right through me. I could not get my hand off the tap and felt my life draining away as I was being electrocuted. I was only saved because one of the workers, Richard, who came out of the shop just in time, saw what was happening and grabbed a wooden bench, using it to wedge me away from the tap. I was in the most indescribable pain, yet no-one took me to the hospital to make sure I was okay, not even my mother when I told her what had happened. I was made to go to work the next day despite still being in a lot of pain.

The after effects of the electrocution have lasted me for the rest of my life in the palpitations I've suffered from ever since. The palpitations got worse by the day and came to a head on Christmas Eve, 1973. I was helping my mother clean the house and prepare for

Christmas morning. It was about 9.30 in the evening, when it felt for all the world like my heart had finally stopped and I was dying. I completely freaked out and kept screaming, 'I don't want to die, I don't want to die.' It was truly awful. My parents decided to leave me until the next morning and, if the problem persisted, to take me to Our Lady's Children's Hospital in Crumlin. Christmas morning came, and I was no better, as I had spent the night afraid to go to sleep for fear I would never wakeup again. My father saw that I was in a very bad way and so took me to the hospital. They diagnosed me as having palpitations and advised my parents to keep stress to a minimum: fat chance of that happening.

I endured a constant state of fear from that time on. It was to be many years before I could stop checking to see if I still had a pulse. Added to this were the waking nightmares, which were becoming more frequent, keeping me in a morbid state of fear. The palpitations still affect me up to the present time, but thankfully not to the same extent.

A short time after my electrocution I was let go from Robinsons, but I wasn't out of work for more than a few days having got another job in H. Williams Supermarket. I was there for about three months, after which I was let go because I was automatically due a pay rise once I'd completed my probation period. Having been laid off, I found myself looking for another job. It was now 1974 and I was fourteen years of age. I decided to look for a job closer to home, which would hopefully mean no more bus fares or travelling. I called into Weavex on Kylemore Road and asked if I could speak to the manager. They made curtain tape and clothing labels. I was led up to the production manager's office. He was sitting with his back to me and didn't turn around when I spoke: 'Excuse me, mister, do you have any jobs?'

'What age are you?'

'I'm fifteen,' I lied. In fact, I was still only fourteen.

'What's your name?'

'Sara-Jane Duffy',

'And where do you live?' I told him my address and he just said, 'Start on Monday at eight o'clock.'

'Thank you,' I said and left the office, before he had a chance to change his mind. I never let on that my father had worked there previously, because, even at fourteen, I wanted to get on in life on my own merit and not have to use other people's names.

On my first day in Weavex, I was a cause of curiosity as some of the other staff recognised me as one of the Duffys and remembered that my father worked there some time before me, so I was bombarded with questions.

My job was in the packaging and despatch department. Part of my job was to pack the finished roles of curtain tape into large boxes and write up the weights. I was told to lift some of these boxes and stack them; and my word were they heavy, so heavy I don't know where I got the strength to do it, but I had to, it was as simple as that.

Another job was to be the 'nipper', which meant doing the shopping for the staff. I had to make a shopping list and take it to the shops on Decies Road. I would leave a large order into Borza's, chipper, then go to the newsagents and finally Londis supermarket. I would make my shopping list out on pieces of cardboard, starting in the packaging and despatch department where I worked, then out to the department where they made the warps and quills and then to the weavers. It was an amazing experience to walk amongst all the looms with their loud repetitive clacking noise, so loud that you could hardly hear yourself speak and, so you would have to shout at the top of your voice. It was strange being in the very place in which I used to bring my father his lunch and to meet the same workmates who worked with him and to be asked if I was his son. I was to spend the next five years of my life here, which was my entire adolescent life and entry into adulthood.

On one occasion when I was doing the shopping I was asked to get Durex! Of course, I hadn't a clue what they were and so asked the guy who wanted them. He told me they were like a chocolate éclair! I put them on the shopping list and handed it into the girl in the newsagent's, then left for the chipper. When I returned to the newsagent's, the girl asked me out loud what I wanted Durex for? I was very surprised by the question and tried to explain that they were some kind of chocolate éclair cake. She said, 'We don't sell them here, love. You'll have to go to the chemist for them.' I did, and again much to my surprise, received the dirtiest of looks from the staff. 'We don't sell them here,' they said in scornful tones. When I returned to the factory, I told the guy who requested them, but all he did was laugh with his mates: 'Jaysus, Duffy, you're such a gobshite.'

On another occasion, shortly after I'd started in Weavex, I was told by one of the fitters to go into the steam house and ask Charlie for a bucket of steam. On this occasion I was certain they were having me on and confidently said, 'Yis are having me on. There's no such thing as a bucket of steam.' But the fitter replied, 'There is, if you put a cloth over the bucket.' So, off I went again like the proverbial turkey to the slaughter and asked Charlie for the bucket of steam and if he would mind letting me have a cloth to cover it. He said he hadn't got a cloth, but that the steam would stay in the bucket if I ran with it to the fitter's workshop. I did, but surprise, surprise, there was no steam left in the bucket by the time a got to the workshop; a mere twenty feet away! I displayed this kind of naiveté a few times before I copped on.

One of my jobs was to clean the canteen and later on the games room. The lads used to leave their unfinished lunches behind and I would eat some of them, because I frequently left home without any breakfast or lunch and had no money to get anything from the shops, having spent the little I had over the previous weekend, or having loaned it to my mother. This was only one step up from the times when I picked the sweets up from the ground on my way to and from school because I had no money at all and it was better than going hungry.

It was while working in Weavex that I decided to do something about my lack of education and the fact that I was semi-literate at best. It had bothered me for such a long time that I wasn't allowed to finish school and that I could barely read or write. This came to a head shortly after staring working in Weavex. I had to fill in the weights on the cartons for the curtain tape, but I didn't know what a Gross, Tare and Nett weight were. I asked someone very quietly which got me through a potentially sticky situation, but I knew there and then I could lose my job if I couldn't fill in forms and the weights on the cases. So I was determined to teach myself how to read and write, and from this prove to the people who had branded me a retard and stupid that I was just as normal as they were. This has been the second dominant motivation of my life apart from trying to allow Sara-Jane the right to live as nature intended. It was a huge mountain to climb but I was determined to climb it. I was resolved to teach myself to read and write and embarked on a journey that I've been on ever since. I love learning new things, new words, new insights; anything that enhances my understanding of life and the world around me.

The first thing I did was buy a dictionary and thesaurus, and the words I learnt were Gross, Tare and Nett! Because I felt I was so far behind everyone else, I thought I would have to read books at a much higher level than primary school, so I started to buy books that were at university level. This filled me with trepidation, but I was convinced that there was no other option. Along with reading was the need to have good handwriting, so I practised my handwriting every day and sought for reasons to write things down, especially taking notes and writing letters. I got down to some serious reading with books on psychology, sociology, history etc. It was really hard but I was determined. I didn't have a study plan. I bought books based on what subjects that interested me. No sooner had I started reading, when I realised I had a very poor vocabulary and that I wasn't making much progress because I wasn't able to understand a lot of the words I was reading, so I bought my first ever dictionary and thesaurus. Every time I came to a word I could not understand, I would go to the dictionary and, once I found the correct definition, would write it in the margin of the book and run a line under the sentence so that I could refer to it whenever that word occurred elsewhere in the book.

This is how I learned the importance of understanding things in their context. I would then use the words I had learnt in my everyday conversation. Once I got the hang of reading, I then started to develop a love for studying and learning new things and it has been one of my passions ever since.

I began to expand my reading interests and started to read more literature and developed a great liking for period dramas and documentaries and later in my teens I developed a love of classical music. This was a very unusual thing for someone my age to do, but it never occurred to me at the time and was another of the reasons offered by my siblings for finding me 'weird'. I was damned if I wasn't educated and damned if I was; a no-win situation. But it has held me in good stead ever since. Being self-educated went a long way towards helping me to become a good conversationalist and a good socialiser. Burying myself in learning and music helped me to suppress my conflict with my gender identity even further, but not so much that I could hide my very girl-like emotions, especially my crying at romantic films and sad situations.

At this stage, I was making my first tentative attempts at dating, without any success it has to be said. I met a girl in Weavex. To say I fell head over heels for her goes nowhere near to how I felt about her. I was absolutely and unashamedly besotted by her. She was quite simply gorgeous, and she had the most beautiful eyes. I could not stop thinking about her and longed to have her as my girlfriend. I was irrepressible in my efforts to get her to go out on a date with me, but it was to no avail. We did though become friends and I got to visit her regularly at her home on Ballyfermot Road. I would find out what music she liked and would make sure to bring along her favourite singers, Glen Campbell, the New Seekers and The Stylistics. One of her all-time favourite songs was, 'Honey Come Back.' I tried to woo her by singing it at the top of my voice, much to her annoyance. I can still laugh thinking about it.

It was at this time I started to write songs. It was my feelings for her which inspired me to write them. I can't remember them now, but there were quite a few and they were very intense. Alas, she remained unimpressed at my gallant efforts. But she couldn't put me off, and for years I wanted to date her more than any other girl I knew. It was much later that I figured out that I had been writing the kinds of songs that I would have wanted someone to write for me.

As much as I enjoyed working in Weavex, there were some awful experiences that I would have happily forgotten. One experience was being a victim of bullying. One example of bullying occurred on a very warm summers day in 1976. A work colleague and I were working extremely hard unloading and loading a forty-foot container in sweltering heat. No surprise then that we were sweating like proverbial pigs. When we needed to take a break, we went in behind the sewing machines where it was nice and cool. One of the girls called out to the supervisor at the top of her voice: 'Girls, can you get a terrible smell? Jean, Jean there's a terrible smell over here.'
The supervisor came over and started to sniff the air in an exaggerated manner. She then came over to where we were standing and proceeded to single me out from the others and sniffed me from head to toe. 'Jaysus, yeh smell like a smelly dog. Stay there until I come back.' She went up to her office, which was a good distance from where we were standing. While we were waiting for her to return, completely clueless as to what she was up to, the girls were looking at us and smirking. The supervisor returned several minutes later with a bottle of perfume and proceeded to spray it all over me; not the other lads, just me. 'Now,' she said, 'that's much better'. It does not fully express the awfulness and damage done to me when I say how I was made to feel humiliated that day.

A few weeks after this incident a strange situation arose which involved me being fired, then reinstated, and then promoted; and all in the space of a week! It involved the same supervisor, who clearly had it in form me and took every opportunity to have a go, including timing me whenever I went to the toilets. If I was any longer than five minutes, she would make life very difficult for me. In some respects, having this woman as my supervisor was like having to work with my mother.

The strange incident started on a Friday afternoon shortly before we were due to finish work. We were doing our normal big clean up and I needed to find a sweeping brush, but there was none to be found, so I had to walk around the factory to find one. It took all of about seven minutes, including looking in the canteen. I was coming from the canteen into the packaging and dispatch department where the supervisor was waiting in the middle of the floor. She demanded to know where I was for the past half hour. I told her it wasn't that long; that I was looking for a brush and that I was no more than ten minutes. But she wasn't having any of it. She deliberately shouted at me for maximum effect, telling me she would be taking me to the production manager's office first thing on Monday. And sure enough, that is precisely what she did. So, Monday morning came, and I was brought up to the manager's office where the supervisor was sitting against the manager's desk and facing me. The manager sat facing the window and never once looked at me. She repeated her bare-faced lie about me being away for half an hour and that I had back answered her and that she was fed up with my cheek. It was obvious that this was not going to end well, so I decided to let rip and tell him about the appalling way she had been treating me. His response was to tell me to collect my cards on Friday.

How do I describe how I felt? How do I describe the fear of having to tell my mother and father that I was sacked through no fault of mine own? How do I tell them knowing that I was going to be beaten to a pulp, especially as my father used to work there and my being sacked would have caused him embarrassment? Knowing I was guaranteed to get another massive hiding inspired me to get another job before saying anything, even if it meant pretending to go to work until another job came along. It was either that or pretend to be sick. I needn't have worried though, because the strangest event was to occur on the Wednesday before I was due to finish up. I was summoned to the supervisor's office, where I was greeted by one of the weaving department supervisors, the production manager and the supervisor who tried to have me sacked. The Manager started by saying that they were going to keep me on and that I was going to be moved to the weaving department where I would work as an auxiliary weaver. I didn't know what to do with myself. It was totally surreal. I was beyond delighted. I managed to keep my composure and tried to be matter of fact about what was happening. The supervisor was not best pleased at what was happening, but I couldn't have cared less; for once I was in a better situation and she could do nothing about it. Apart from not having to deal with her anymore, I was also getting a modest pay rise, so happy days! I was so glad to see the back of her. Talk about speaking too soon.

I was working as an auxiliary weaver about three months when I was summoned to the supervisor's office. To say I felt a sense of foreboding would be an understatement, but off I went to her office, where I was greeted by her, the production manager and one of the shift supervisors, another weaving department supervisor. The supervisor, who just three months earlier tried to have me sacked, said 'Listen Sara-Jane, I will understand if you say no, but I was wondering if you would consider coming back to the packaging and despatch department? I know we've had our differences, but the department is falling apart since you left. I know now that you were the one doing all the work. You were doing more than the other three put together. You can say no, but I am asking you to have a think about it." Wow! I hardly knew what to say, and before I did, the production manager chimed in by telling me that I was a very valuable worker and that he would appreciate it if I would at least think about it. He said I could choose my terms if I agreed to go back into the department. Don't ask me why, but I decided that I would go back, but on strict terms; firstly, I made it clear that I would not tolerate any of the supervisor's previous behaviour towards me, including making it clear that she was not to time me going to the toilet, and she was not to be shouting at me. I then insisted that I be given a £5.00 wage increase. They agreed to all my terms, and so I agreed to return to her department. From day one I was able to walk tall and feel some degree of confidence at having stood up for myself when pushed to it. But a few weeks after I returned to her department the supervisor started getting up to her old tricks and started shouting at me. I told her I was going to the toilet, not asking her permission as before. She shouted at me that I was not to go. Well, what can I say. I wasn't having it. I shouted back at her that she was never to talk to me like that again, and that if she did I was gone from there. She very quickly apologised and promised she wouldn't do it again. It was absolutely exhilarating and something that gave me every reason to feel proud of myself; much like I felt after standing up to my mother during the kangaroo trial over the ticket to see the film in the school.

It was now 1977 at the Christmas Dinner Dance at the Fitzpatrick Hotel in Portmarnock, where Bernie looked beautiful in her cream floral dress. My heart melted at the sight of her. But she didn't pay me the slightest notice. Nor would she dance with me. Sometimes words simply fail to express the feelings I felt that night. I still have such strong memories of that night and how I was affected by her, especially when they played Chicago's song: 'If You Leave Me Now' (I'm listening as I write). I can hardly describe the pain I felt as I finally accepted that she was never going to be my girlfriend. She had left Weavex shortly before this and it was to be the last time I saw her, or so I thought. We were to meet again in a most unexpected place, and with the most frustrating of surprises.

I loved to sing, and I did plenty of it while working in Weavex. The lads on the night shift would ask me to sing for them whenever I was working late. My favourite song at that time was 'Power to All Our Friends' by Cliff Richard and 'Red, Red Wine' by Neil Diamond. When I sang 'Power to All our Friends,' I did the same actions to the song that Cliff had done in the Eurovision Song Contest. I would stretch my arm into the air while bringing my knees together. The guys loved it and found it very entertaining.

It was a few months after my return to the packaging and despatch department when I was summoned by the production manager. It was about 8.30 on a Monday morning. I thought I was in trouble for some reason, but I needn't have worried. 'Sara-Jane, what age are you now?' I replied that I was seventeen. 'That's good. Would you be interested in training to be a weaver?' I couldn't believe it. Of course, I accepted immediately, especially as it meant leaving the packing and despatch department for good. It also meant a significant increase in my wages, which delighted me greatly, especially as I thought it would please my mother. But she seemed indifferent to my news and when I asked for a pay increase, she told me I could have an extra £1! I was so disappointed and angry, especially as around this time, I learned that my other brothers were handing up a great deal less than me. Whereas I was handing up over 90% of my wages, they were handing up as little as 50%. What made this even more unfair was the fact that I was earning far more than any of them and worked very long hours to do so. I wasn't quite sure at this time how I was going to change this, but I was absolutely determined to do it. I knew it was not going to be easy but one way or another it was going to happen. I thoroughly enjoyed my time as a weaver and it really was a positive time in my life, despite the difficulties with my gender identity. I was determined to get on with things as best I could in the circumstances. I also wanted to be nothing like my mother and some of my siblings who wallowed in their misery

One of the upsides of the long hours of work was that it meant spending a lot less time at home. This was helped further when I joined the Ballyfermot Peace Corps.

The one major downside to my promotion was, I wasn't able to have the same conversations with the girls. I did miss them a lot. I thoroughly detested the manner in which the men spoke to the girls and about them, it was so crude and vulgar. I was also mortified by the pictures of nude girls in the Mirror and the Sun and the calendars on display in the maintenance workshop.

One of the most embarrassing experiences I had was when one of the weavers asked me if I ever had wet dreams. I had heard about them but wasn't sure what they were, so, rather than display total ignorance, I replied that, 'I do wake up sweating sometimes!' That was a cause of great mirth as was my speech impediment — I had a lisp. I would be in the canteen or the rest room when someone of them would say,' Sara-Jane, say "chlicken and clchips".' There was no malice in it, though it was embarrassing. Many years later I was to regret losing my lisp after being told that it made me sound very feminine; just another of those ironies, I suppose.

The experience of the wet dreams made me more determined than ever to pin my parents down and get them to tell me the facts of life. I went home from work having spent the day preoccupied with how I was going to broach the subject with them. I decided to ask straight out: 'Mam, would you please tell me the facts of life? I'm seventeen now and still don't have a clue, and it's getting embarrassing with the fellas at work asking me questions about wet dreams and stuff. And I still don't know how to ask girls out.'

She just told me to speak to my father, that he was in the shed and that it would be the ideal time to catch him, especially as he was in a good mood. So off up the garden I went to the shed, with my stomach in knots, unsure of what his reaction would be. I asked my dad the same question. Here I finally was ready to receive my father's wisdom on women and how to treat them: 'There are just two things you need to know about women. First, make sure you never get VD, and two, make sure you never get into a joint bank account with a woman.

That's it? I thought. I was dumbfounded. Talk about a revelation of my father's views on women. I remember making a conscious decision to never be like him, and I despised the very idea that I would have to go on in life being his son. With my ever-growing sense my female identity and my longing to be detached from this god awful male body, I couldn't relate at all to what he just told me, particularly given my innate dislike of living as a male. There was also the awful realisation that this was not a man I could ever consider to be a positive role model or someone in whom I could never confide. How many times did I hear this man unashamedly say that men who badly treated women should be castrated; only to be proven guilty of that behaviour himself. Hypocrisy, it seemed, was to be the norm in adult behaviour. I left him in his shed, and as I said before, I was determined never to be like him, or any man who talked about women the way he did.

Chapter Four

Puberty: Not What I'm Supposed to Be

Heavenly hurt, it gives us —
We can find no scar,
But internal difference,
Where the meanings are.
[Emily Dickinson]

There was nothing on my body that would ever let you think I was a girl, except maybe the missing Adam's apple. There were no scars that would in any way indicate that I was wounded and there was nothing on the outside to show that I was in the most excruciating mental and emotional anguish and constant internal conflict, but I was, and it really did hurt. Heaven knew and did nothing, at least that's what I thought. Now, I realise and accept that this simply is not true. Heaven did indeed have its purpose, but waited a lifetime to reveal it, and all the while I had to cope with being different, very different.

Puberty and adolescence can be traumatic at the best of times but going through adolescence with a conflicting gender identity is so much worse, it is beyond comprehension for most people. It is very difficult for most of us to admit to being confused about sexual matters while we go through this phase in our development, but the constant uncertainty surrounding who I am and what I am, made it extremely difficult to know my sexual orientation and it was to be many years before I was to understand the complex process I was going through. I had a growing awareness of being alienated from my own body and at times even from my own mind. I became increasingly conscious of being double-minded, or double-gendered in the way I viewed the world around me. It was very much a case of how I was being socially conditioned versus how I really knew myself to be. My obvious preference for all-things female, especially female company and friendship was becoming much more pronounced and causing me no end of problems socially.

It never really occurred to me that I was wrong to expect to grow breasts and to have my periods along with every other girl. I genuinely believed that I was sooner or later going to start entering into womanhood with a body to match how I was feeling inside. But as time went on and the wrong parts started to grow and expand then I truly did freak out, albeit internally. I was absolutely terrified by what was happening and could only scream back into my own being because it was simply impossible to explain this to anyone else, and I do mean anyone. Had I cried out for help then I am absolutely certain I would have been put into a psychiatric ward.

I was utterly certain that I was living and would eventually die in the wrong body; that instead of having a penis I should have had a vagina and that instead of having a flat chest, I should have had breasts? How was I to explain just how freaked out I was at having facial hair and chest hair, when I knew I should not have had either? I became obsessive in comparing myself to other girls, wondering if, just maybe, things would suddenly change, that the dreadful mistake would be finally realised and that my body would be put right of its own accord. But it never did and I was left bereft of hope and to obsess and fantasise about how my life might have been had my body developed as it was supposed to. I can safely say that this preoccupation with my body was never about having sex at this time. It was all about wanting my body to match my gender identity and feeling like a normal girl. This has always been the case and remains so to this day.

I wondered how on earth girls could complain so much about their periods when, to me, it was one of the greatest affirmations of their womanhood. I cried at the thought and grieved over it and the fact that I would never have that experience; that I would never get to complain about my own periods, to take them for granted and feel so complete and so completely normal. I, Sara-Jane, was denied my right to live as I should; as a beautiful teenage girl sharing all the same apprehensions about entering womanhood with all my teenage girl friends. It just never happened for me.

It was only when I researched my condition that I understand why my body didn't develop as I had always expected and longed for it to do. Mine was a male body containing a female gender identity and the two were completely irreconcilable. Although there were still some indicators that things should have been different. For example, not having an Adam's apple; my voice being very soft, along with my hands and getting pimples around my face and mouth regularly on a monthly basis, which I was later to learn was female acne. I was often questioned about why my hands were so soft and feminine looking, despite them being large and used to the same hard work as the guys I worked with. Then there was my distinctly feminine posture and hand movements, which, though I tried desperately to hide over the years, they were still spotted by some and even raised some questions about my sexuality. Even then, looking back, there was evidence that my body was not as it should be.

Just like any teenager, I became more naturally inclined to worry about my body and personal appearance, including my clothes, personal hygiene and social interactions, especially as some of my features and mannerisms were becoming decidedly more feminine. But because I was afraid of being mocked and called a 'cissy', I became quite adept at hiding some of my instinctively feminine traits, especially my body language and deportment; or at least that's what I thought.

The most marked development at this time was in my emotions and communications. My emotional development was definitely shifting more towards the feminine rather than masculine. It was also during my teens that I began to experience what can best be described as out-of-body experiences, during which I became more detached and divided from myself. There was a girl screaming from within my body, trying desperately to fight her way out of years of conforming to her male upbringing. But scream as I might, things were not going to change anytime soon. It was going to take many long years before I, Sara-Jane Cromwell could claim the right to live as my true self and to assert my natural birthright, regardless of how I looked on the outside. But for the time being, it would be more about mini skirmishes rather than full-blown battles. Winning the battles and the war was still a long way off.

I had very few opportunities, if any, to dress during my teens and that caused me much distress. The truth is that I felt like a complete freak living in a boy's body. Others never noticed, due to my ability to *act* the teenage boy, but I certainly felt that there was nothing about me that fit into the society in which I was raised. What felt particularly freakish and unnatural to me was how my body was developing male, rather than female, features. I continued to hold onto the hope that at some stage I would get to have a vagina. I genuinely thought that my male genitals would shrink and turn into a vagina; honestly! And I thought I would develop breasts and have my periods. I was so looking forward to them and how they would make me look and feel normal. And it meant that I could wear pretty girl's clothes rather than those horrible boys' clothes I'd been made to wear all my life. I was excited to think that I would finally get the body I should have had when I was born. But it never happened. Instead, I started to grow hair in places where girls shouldn't have hair and my voice started to deepen, though it was to be very soft for a teenage boy. All of the things I was most afraid of.

As I watched all these changes and realised that there was nothing I could do about them, I became terribly sad and depressed. I felt completely helpless, with not a single person to turn to. The best I could hope for was that it would in some miraculous way change of its own accord. Yes, despite all the evidence to the contrary, I still held onto the forlorn hope that my miracle would come. It never did. So, I tried to deal with it as best I could and spent a lot of time making sure I was properly groomed, especially when attending social occasions. It is ironic that this was the one thing about which my mother was most complimentary!

There is no getting away from the fact that I felt utterly cheated, and helpless to do anything about my situation. This was made so much worse by not being able to tell anyone about what I was going through. It was bad enough that I was already being bullied for being left-handed, tall, for reading books, and working with the Peace Corps and for being 'retarded'. So, imagine my difficulty even thinking about telling others that I felt I was a girl living in a boy's body! It just didn't bear thinking about, and so I really tried not to and just got on with being the best teenage *boy* that I could be. It didn't work.

It was during my early teens - thirteen to fourteen, that I first bought my own clothes. I remember my first ever suit, which I bought in Weavers to Wearer in Henry Street. Even from that age I loved shopping, even if it meant getting into debt to do it. My mother's response to my complaints about my low wages was to give me 'credit notes', which took the urgency out of giving me a proper wage. The downside to shopping was that I couldn't go to the boutiques, which was where I really wanted to shop. It was the greatest strain trying to walk past all those beautiful clothes and shoes. Sometimes, I was mentally exhausted from the effort.

I tried to find a way to buy clothes that would look and feel feminine but would not give the game away, so I bought orange, pink and purple round-collared shirts and flared pants with stripes running down the legs. I even tried to buy unisex nylon underwear that at least looked like it could be worn by girls. Nonetheless, despite my best efforts, I was unable to act in the same way as my brothers and other boys my age. For example, I simply could not identify in any way with the manner in which boys treated girls, especially their vulgarity and rudeness; the way they would speak of 'touching them up' and 'dropping the hand'. Just listening to them made me sick; and it didn't go unnoticed. At least some of my brothers and sisters were curious about this and reminded me of this after hearing of my being misgendered. They were also curious about my difficulties in chatting up girls and the way that I became increasingly withdrawn. Some of them admitted to calling me a cissy and some wanted to know if I was 'queer'. Interestingly, they would also attribute my search for spiritual answers as a search for my true self. Strange how they could recognise these things yet treat me so badly at the same time.

I was particularly revolted by the way guys spoke about girls having their periods and referring to them as having their 'flowers'. If a girl did not want to dance or go on a date, she would be called 'frigid' a 'homo' or a 'lezzer'! And if she was having a bad day she was said to be 'in her rags'. These were common insults used against girls who spoke up for themselves or who were having a bad time. Other comments would be made about girls developing breasts. My own brothers teased my sisters quite a bit and it made me extremely angry, though whenever I spoke out against them speaking that way, they, along with my mother, would tell me to shut up and mind my own business. But there can be no doubt that these comments did hurt my sisters, despite their best efforts to laugh them off. Some of them admitted as much to me years later.

I really did identify with them but was completely excluded from their company, especially when they were hanging out together. I so wanted to be a part of their group. I was very tuned into my sisters' feelings whenever they were having boyfriend problems and some of them would confide in me, one sister in particular. And yet we never really became close. This was impossible given their need to be accepted by their mother, and it was her disapproval of me that, I believe, ensured we (my sisters) would never be close. This remains one of the greatest sadness's of my life. Whatever about the estrangement I feel from my brothers, not having a relationship with my sisters is infinitely worse. There were so many times I would love to share things with them, or to be able to meet up for coffee or lunch, and all the other things sisters get to do.

By now, it was 1976 and I was sixteen years old, desperate to escape from my pain, feeling misunderstood and rejected by my family and colleagues, and increasingly disconnected from my true self. My life had barely even started when began to think about trying to end it. I felt that I didn't belong to anyone and I didn't belong anywhere. In all honesty I felt more and more like a Foundling. Everything was closing in on me and I felt as if I was being sucked into a black hole and seeing nothing but perpetual darkness. The most obvious thing to do, it seemed, was to remove myself from this life, and from being the inconvenience I was made to feel by my family, and above all, to put an end to the excruciating torture that was my daily life. So, I tried. One night in March, I hauled myself up onto the railing over the canal on Kylemore Road, and leaned over, staring into the black watery abyss below. All I needed to do was to jump. I was just seconds away from that final leap of fate, when something stopped me. It suddenly occurred to me that there might be another way. It was a long shot, but it might just work. What if I left home and changed my name, so I couldn't be found? The very thought of it was enough to make me change my mind. Yes, that's what I'll do, I thought. I'll leave home and change my name. I didn't know how to do either, but at that pivotal moment it was enough to give me a reason to go on living.

Having made that decision, I immediately tried to imagine a life away from my family and how best to achieve it. The idea alone gave me some sense of control over my life — a feeling I had never had until this time. It felt truly liberating. I walked away from the canal bridge that night with an overwhelming sense of joy and determination, resolved to find a more purposeful way of escaping the terrible situation I had been bound to for so many years. It was a fateful decision for another reason; that although I didn't get to change my name at this time, it planted a seed that would one day eventually blossom into the beautiful name I now own, *Sara-Jane Cromwell*.

My attempt to break free from my family proved to be not only naïve, but an inevitable failure. I tried to find a place to stay but was unsuccessful. I tried the Salvation Army, across from the Royal College of Surgeons and Sarsfield House at the end of Ballyfermot Road, but was found unsuitable, so I had to stay put and to find other ways of escaping. One of the ways to escape was to spend as little time as possible at home and instead to spend as much time as possible at my job and get involved in voluntary work.

Ultimately, I did what I was expected to do, which was to find a girl and get married.

Later that year I decided to join the OLV on Sarsfield Road to see if I could get involved. I passed as older and more mature because of my height and the way I spoke, so I was able to slot into leadership roles quite easily. I had been doing this since I was about thirteen and involved in running street soccer tournaments. I wanted to encourage youngsters and teenagers to spend their time productively and not be hanging around with the wrong crowd. I organised a number of competitions including five-a-side, table tennis and Badminton. They were very successful. This encouraged me to continue being involved in some form of community work, which I did afterwards by joining the Ballyfermot Peace Corps.

At seventeen I joined the FCA and stayed there for eighteen months. I felt that it was the right thing to do in my continuing attempt to further *normalise* my life and to help me fit in. In truth, I enjoyed the experience and felt I was serving my country in some way. I joined the 11th Motor Squadron in McKee Barracks and was in Troop 3; Trooper Sara-Jane Duffy (not my first name at the time of course). On the night I signed up I was under-age by a few months. I never let on that my father was one of their colleagues and that he had served with them over the years. I hated name-dropping and wanted to get by on my own merits. I attended barracks every Thursday night. I learned how to use various kinds of weapons, including the Lee-

Enfield, the FN and the Gustav. All the weapons were designed for right-handers and, being left-handed, I found it difficult to use some of them, which was a cause of great merriment when I was at the firing range during shooting practice. Some of the officers took bets that I would either not be able to hit my targets or would score very low. In fact, I consistently had above-average scores and in the Gustav. I scored the second highest on the day. Quite an achievement for a left-hander!

I felt very proud to wear the uniform and kept myself immaculately dressed; so much so that I regularly won the prize for best-dressed soldier! And believe it or not this happened despite my blatantly breaking the rules for how the legs of the trousers were supposed to be tucked inside the boots. I couldn't get it from a fashion and style point of view, so I persisted in leaving mine over the top of my boots. There was just no getting away from the girl inside of me!

We would go on camps to the Glen of Imaal and Gormanston. And in the summer, we went on an annual camp to Longford. On one of the days during camp in Longford, I was assigned to work with the cook in the Officer's Mess. He had a major gripe against the officers because they had lost his discharge papers. He clearly did not believe them and so carried a grudge, which he exercised against them on a daily basis; without their knowledge of course. When he was cooking for the them, he would take their steaks, throw them on the floor and wipe them across the floor with a filthy mop. He would leave the vegetables in the cupboard to go off for several days before using them and with great relish he would spit phlegm into the teapot. It was utterly disgusting. I didn't know what to say or do about it.

It was while in Longford that a photograph was taken of me sucking my thumb. I had returned early from a night out at a local pub. The lads came back and found me asleep sucking my thumb. I never got to live that down afterwards. I was in my early twenties before I finally managed to overcome the habit. Sucking my thumb and listening to music were the only comforts I had whenever I was distressed.

I requested a discharge from the FCA after I had made my decision to sign up for the priesthood in 1978, but not before I had learned of my being promoted to an NCO. I'd requested my discharge before going onto the NCO's course as I felt that staying with the army was incompatible with preparing for the priesthood and my ongoing commitment to the Peace Corps, which I was still involved with during that time. They granted my request and so I left in the autumn of 1978. Just weeks before my Nan died.

I had finished the night shift in Weavex and had gone to bed. I was awoken from my sleep to the sounds of my sisters' screams: 'Nana is dead, Nana is dead!' I instinctively jumped out of bed from the fright and got dressed and went straight down to see Nan. I'd wished I hadn't. What I saw horrified me. She was lying in my uncle's arms, her eyes staring in terror at her impending death. My mother had always told us how terrified she was of dying.

That night we held the wake and I stayed up all night looking after my uncles. One of my uncles refused to go and see his mother and had to be coaxed up by his brothers. I told him that he would probably always regret it if he didn't go up and that it would probably prevent him from getting closure later on. He eventually went up to see her and, as expected, he fell to pieces. It was strange to see the same uncle who a while before had spat on the ground and said: 'my mother isn't worth that spit to me' now grieving for her in that way. It was a shocking experience and brought home to me that there were others who were prepared to be honest about their feelings towards their mothers. This was a major taboo at that time, and still is, to a large extent.

My uncles asked me to sing during the wake. They told me how much Nan loved me and that I was one of her favourites and of how she enjoyed my visits late at night on my way home from my work with the Peace Corps. She also appreciated my bringing her bottles of stout and Gold Bond cigarettes. She especially appreciated that I continuously ran the gauntlet of my mother's fury, defying her insistence that I keep away from Nan. I don't know what happened between Nan and my mother, beyond my Nan calling my father a 'bastard'. But it was enough to leave my mother feeling embittered towards her until just before her death, when something changed and brought them to some form of reconciliation.

They reminded me that Nan thought of me as that 'lovable little fucker', as she had called me just a few months earlier. My Nan was my oasis, I could confide in her without fear of things ever getting back to my mother, and, whereas my mother seemed to hate the sight of me, my Nan was always delighted to see me. She was the only one I felt I could truly trust.

On the following night Nan was removed from the house to the church of the Assumption. We walked behind her coffin. The next day was the funeral mass after which she was later buried in St Fintan's Cemetery in Howth, near where she once lived. It was extremely hard saying goodbye to my only ally.

By the time I'd left my teens behind I had developed a very intense personality and was strongly committed to whatever I believed in. I was also very loyal to those I cared about and who showed kindness towards me (few though they were). And I'd already learned the importance of a well-rounded education, coupled with an open mind and tolerance towards those who happened to be different. And why would it be any other way; after all who knew more about what it meant to be different than a young woman living in the wrong body, who had the misfortune to be left-handed and was regarded as mentally retarded? It cannot be any surprise then that I become so intense, overly- sensitive, feeling myself to be unworthy of people's love and acceptance and the need to constantly prove myself to be normal. That was how life was to be for me during the 70s. Busy, busy and even more busy; that was how I drowned out the sound of Sara-Jane's cries for help and how I tried to rid myself of those ever-present nightmares of her being buried alive.

During my time with the Peace Corps, I sang at twelve o'clock Mass every Sunday and for the patients at the Cheshire Home in the Phoenix Park. Every year we held our peace concerts, which were always a sell-out and extremely enjoyable. Folk Group practice was every Thursday evening in the Dominican girls' school. I also worked for Welfare Action, another unit of the Peace Corps, which was dedicated to helping the poor and elderly. We did this a couple of nights a week. I liked the idea of helping others less fortunate than myself. We visited peoples' homes to do painting and decorating, shopping, gardening etc. We also arranged delivery of goods donated by members of the public to poorer families, which could be televisions, furniture etc. I later became the leader of the Welfare Action group, and later still became the Coordinator of the Welfare Cadets, which was established in May 1978.

Ever since surviving my first suicide attempt and my ever-growing desire to get away from my family, I found that my job and voluntary work gave me great solace. But nothing could make up for the loss *being* my true self. It is fair to say that my alienation from my family was copper-fastened during this period, as was my alienation from Sara-Jane. What I didn't really appreciate then was just how much of a weirdo my family considered me to be, especially because of my helping others. They simply could not understand why I would join the Peace Corps and be such an intellectual. They were forever slagging me off, because of my vocabulary and my taste in clothes and music. They let on not to like my taste in music, but when I was out of the house, they would play my records and wear my clothes out on their dates; all the while saying that I could not accompany them to dances in the TV Club and the Apartment. Apparently, I was cramping their style and I was too boring. It is entirely true that I was not the best of company when out with them. This was because I was finding it increasingly difficult to converse with my peers as a boy, when all I felt inside was this girl wanting to find her own voice and be among other girls, doing what girls do.

It was during this period that I began to be excluded from an increasing number of family functions. My mother and brother Damian made sure that I was excluded. Every time an invitation was issued for some function or other, this brother would say, 'I'm not going if Sara-Jane is going'. To which request my mother always acceded, while pretending to do her best to change his mind. She never did, and the reason was increasingly clear: he was the undoubted favourite. Everyone towed the line and ignored me at every opportunity; so much so that when their own birthdays or other celebrations came up, I was either completely excluded or given a token invitation, in the hope that I would refrain from attending. I was getting the message and so found reasons not to attend, but this never stopped me from helping them whenever they needed me; and need me they did, many, many times.

Happiness is not a word I would have used to describe any stage of my life prior to my going public about my gender identity. Were there times when I was happy? Of course, but they were so intermittent and too often accompanied by an immediate sense of dread as to render them difficult to remember. It was simply the case that acts of violence could occur at any time and at the least provocation. One example of this is an incident between me and my brother James. I had had words with his my mother about an injustice I felt had taken place. James arrived in shortly afterwards with his wife. I was sitting on the sofa when he arrived in with his then wife. When my mother gave him her version of what happened, he came into the sitting room, dragged me up by the shirt and slammed me against the wall smacking my head. But before he had the chance to beat me to a pulp, I told him to go ahead, because that is all he and my father and brothers had to offer. This stopped him dead in his tracks. He just stared at me for a few moments then dropped me. Years later, he mentioned this and the impact it had had on him at the time. This incident and others included here were to be corroborated by my former sister-in-law, after the book was first published.

Aside from these types of incidences, there were those special moments when I found cause to be happy and content. This would happen for example whenever I discovered a beautiful piece of music or heard a song that went straight to my heart. I thoroughly enjoyed playing my music loud and singing along; it was a great therapy and a wonderful way to escape the bad stuff that was going on around me. I would also go for long walks through the fields off Le Fanu Road and up and down Ballyfermot Road; going to the church to pray for direction. These were just some of the ways in which I tried to get time for myself to get answers to my questions: like making sense of my life and my family's behaviour towards me. I couldn't fathom why they were so persistently cruel to me. But the divine was always too abstract and inaccessible. I tried to find God directly through my own prayers. I was never able to understand why such an intelligent God would have me pray to him in mindless repetitions. Of course, I was to discover later that he doesn't want us to use mindless scripted prayers, chants or mantras. He wants us to talk to him intelligently. But that was for later, for now I had to be content with asking questions about why he had allowed me to go through so much turmoil. Of course, I didn't know that, even as I was going through all these difficulties, my sisters were going through their own traumas; something I could never have imagined possible.

Some of my greatest fun moments were the Peace Corp's trips to Glencree. I went on quite a few of them and always enjoyed them immensely. We also travelled up to Corrymeela on the Antrim Coast, near Giant's Causeway. These trips were part of the North-South exchange, in which we were attempting to get a better understanding of the different cultures and their feelings about the *troubles* as they were euphemistically called then. At the time, there was hardly a day or week went by without a bomb going off or someone being shot. Then there were the massacres; such as the Miami Show band. There were moments during this period when I thought the world was going to end, such was the darkness of the clouds that hung over this country. It was hoped that through these North-South meetings we would create a common understanding and tolerance towards each other and that this would help towards a more peaceful society within Northern Ireland; or as we called it, the *North*. It was quite an experience driving through the border checkpoints and seeing all the British soldiers with their weapons and armoured vehicles. It was a mixture of awe and fear.

I remember the first trip up and trying to understand the Northern Ireland accent. It was so hard. During our meetings there was a lot of laughter around the fact that our accents could be so difficult to understand. They kept telling me they could not understand a word I was saying, especially that I talked very fast. So, I decided to speak with a Northern accent, and they understood me perfectly. It was mad craic altogether.

Looking back to a time when the world viewed being *normal* as being heterosexual, male or female according to our reproductive and sex organs only, being right-handed rather than left-handed, knowing one's place and not answering back and always conforming to societies expectations etc.; I can see why I was universally viewed as being abnormal, because, judged by these appallingly ignorant standards and expectations, I was anything but. However, I can truthfully say now, that despite all the pain and distress over many years, I am delighted that I wasn't their *normal*, and despite the untold damage done to me, I never succumbed to their best malevolent efforts to make me so! They did not break my spirit then nor has anyone since!

Chapter Five

Finding a Girlfriend

Love has the power of making you believe what you normally treat with the utmost suspicion.
[Mirabeau]

I was at least seventeen before I managed to get my first date, which by the standards set by my brothers made me a late starter. My brothers had been dating at a much earlier age and they were beginning to wonder about me. I was hopeless with chat-up lines and couldn't ask a girl out to save my life. I was far more interested in good conversation than chatting up girls, which, under the circumstances, should come as no surprise. I'm sure it must have made me very boring, but I simply never got the 'chatting-up' bit.

When I was dating, I found it extremely difficult to think of girls sexually and I found it equally difficult listening to boys talk about them in that way; and yet, at the same time, I wasn't attracted to boys either. For me, friendship was always far more important with girls than anything else and I found myself able to love them in that way; most probably because I was overwhelmed at the mere thought of having a girlfriend as opposed to a girl-friend. This led me to getting carried away at times and coming on too strong. By too strong I mean that I was too intense in how I expressed my feelings. This was another of those signs that I was not your typical boy. Try as I might to get it right, I was simply incapable of being a competent dater, and this was to show itself in so many ways; not the least being my inability to draw a clear line between being a 'boy' dating 'girls' and *being* a girl, even when trying not to be! I wanted to talk about girl's things and not the things boys would talk about, which I'm certain must have been very disconcerting for the girls I dated.

I remember doing a Personal Development course in Newcastle West in 1998. Many of the women were surprised at how much I knew about women and about being a woman. But they were also extremely doubtful when I told them I'd never made a single pass at a woman (maybe they'll believe it now!) and that I always felt extremely uncomfortable having to be the one to ask women out on a date. I told them I never once used a chat-up line on a woman, which again they refused to believe. And of course, why wouldn't they, after all they saw me as a man and not as a woman. Looking back, these encounters, which grew in number and frequency over the years, were to become my unconscious way of trying to integrate as a woman, despite my best efforts to consciously suppress my feminine traits.

Given the choice between my male colleagues at work and my female colleagues, I much preferred the females. If I had to choose between talking about sports, cars, machines, war films etc. on the one hand, and relationships, children, fashion, makeup, socialising with girls on the other, then there was no competition. I would certainly opt for the latter. But of course, I was stuck trying to fit in with my male colleagues, which I found intolerable. Nonetheless, I did try my very best to fit in and to prove I was as *normal* as everyone else. There's that bloody word *normal* again.

My attempts were frustrated by the fact that I was getting absolutely no feedback from anyone. I can well understand why people would have felt confused about where I was coming from and what my motives might have been, as I was experiencing so much confusion myself and was desperately trying to come up with answers that would set me on the path to 'normality'. This was especially a problem with my efforts at trying to determine my sexuality; something I felt ambivalent about for most of my adult life. However, none of these realisations were to be of any help to me during my teens and even during my twenties and thirties.

When I eventually managed to get a date, I really wished I hadn't. The girl I asked out was a member of the Peace Corps. It was my brother's 21st Birthday party. It was due to be held in the Green Isle Hotel on the Naas Road. I asked her out on a normal date first, but she turned me down, so I resorted to impressing her by inviting her to my brother's party. I decided to pluck up the courage to ask her during the week of our peace concerts in the Dominican Covent. She turned me down flat, but I wasn't giving up that easily. It just so happened that my eldest brother was also having an engagement dinner in the Green Isle Hotel, so I asked her a second time if she would go out with me to the Green Isle, and this time she agreed. But the dinner was cancelled for reasons I can't remember, so I had to come up with a plan B. I told her I would take her to the La Dolce Vita Club on Mary Street. It was a new club and *the* place to go to in the city at that time.

I was all dressed up in my best and full of excitement at the prospect of having a nice date. However, when we arrived at La Dolce Vita, we were refused entry on account of us not being members. I suspect that the real reason was that we were both under-age, but the doorman was very discreet and clearly didn't want to embarrass me in front of my date. The problem now was that I didn't have a plan C! But she came to the rescue by suggesting that we go to see Gone with the Wind. I was only too happy to agree and, so we went. While we were watching the film, I did the usual boy thing of trying to put my arm around her shoulder. I was so slow about it that I made snails look like sprinters! When I finally managed to get to the other side, she was completely unresponsive, so I discreetly removed my arm while I cringed inside.

During the intermission, she asked me go buy her 20 Rothmans and I duly obliged, in spite of having to leave the cinema and go across the road to get them. As I passed the ladies' toilets on the way back in, I saw her with her sister and her friend giggling and when they saw me they quickly re-entered the toilet and closed the door. It took her ages to return to her seat and when she did, it was obvious that she wasn't at all interested in the date. I brought her home and when we got to the gate, I asked her if she would like to go on another date. She said she would let me know. She gave me a kiss on the cheek. That was the first and last date I had with her.

I had much greater success and was to make a firm friend with my second date. Small and bubbly, she had joined the Welfare Cadets some months earlier and really seemed to enjoy working with me. She was very enthusiastic and committed. She was also much fancied by many of the guys and they were forever trying to chat her up, but to no avail.

The Peace Corps, who were associated with the Welfare Cadets, were having one of their many nights out bowling in Stillorgan and I invited her along as it would be an opportunity for her to socialise with the folks from the Peace Corps, which she was keen to join. We were all waiting at the bus stop outside Trinity College when it started to rain. The bus was at the stop and the driver sat there and wouldn't let us get on, even though it was pouring rain. I thought that he was being stupid and inconsiderate and so took it upon myself to open the door and let everyone on. Because of this, the driver refused to allow me to get on, so they all left for the bowling without me. She decided to get off the bus, which surprised me greatly. She said that if I wasn't going, then neither was she. I was absolutely delighted with myself, as I fancied her like mad. The problem was, I didn't have any other plan. She suggested we go to the pictures, so we decided to go and see Saturday Night Fever at the Savoy. It was wonderful. As we sat there watching the film, I plucked up the courage to put my arm around her shoulders. She was very responsive, and the feeling was truly electrifying. I was way above the proverbial cloud nine. So much so that I ventured to kiss her, and again she reciprocated. I can hardly describe just how completely wonderful she made me feel; words cannot do it justice; suffice it to say I felt completely exhilarated.

Of course, I had to spoil it by telling her sometime later that I loved her. I allowed myself to get completely carried away and scared the living daylights out of her with my intense feelings. She was, after all, just fifteen and I was just seventeen. There are moments from this time in my life which still can make me feel tearful and this is most definitely one of them. She will never know how truly amazing she made me feel then and how grateful I have always been for the joy she brought into my life.

Convincing myself that I wasn't meant to date girls and that I should once again consider my vocation, I finally resolved to apply for the priesthood and went to see the Director of Vocations, at Ringsend. I spent about two hours with him, going through all the reasons why I thought I had a vocation. He was convinced that I had and so got me to fill in this enormous form. I signed it and, in signing it, agreed to attend the local VEC for two years to get a formal education, which was vital if I was to study at Clonliffe College.

Once I had made my decision, I decided to tell my parents. My mother was delighted and said she would do everything she could to help me, including getting a job if necessary. For the first time ever, I thought she was proud of me. And why wouldn't she be, thinking I was eventually going to be the first in the family to join the priesthood, a huge thing in those days. A family's prestige increased greatly after the ordination of one of its own. My father on the other hand was utterly indifferent. Once I had told my family, I felt my resolve grow even stronger and so began preparing myself in every way I could while waiting for the school year to begin.

It was at this time that I told my former girlfriend of my decision to train for the priesthood. I could see that she had very mixed feelings about it. On the one hand there was an obvious disappointment and on the other, she said that she was pleased for me and would help me in any way she could, and she did. On my eighteenth birthday she bought me a Bible. It was a Roman Catholic Revised Standard Version and carried the Imprimatur and Nihil Obstat. These were to be crucially important for me later on, especially when confronting some very difficult discoveries I would make while reading this particular version of the Bible.

These discoveries were to do with the Church's teachings on the Mass, Mary Worship, celibacy and divorce etc., which were contradicted in their own translation. These were just some of the fundamental teachings of the Church contradicted by their own Bible translations, including the Douay and Knox versions. This discovery was to challenge me on a profound level. It made me question whether I could enter a priesthood that was so much in contradiction with the teachings of its own authorised translations of the Bible, and it challenged me on whether I could preach against divorce when I knew it was allowed in Scripture under certain circumstances. There were other issues, too many to mention here, which caused me to reflect on whether I should go ahead. I gave these matters very serious thought over a few months before finally deciding that to go ahead would make me a hypocrite. How could I possibly hold to and preach on teachings I knew were a complete contradiction to what I held to be a higher authority than the Church's teachings, namely, the Bible? I made the decision to withdraw my application to Clonliffe College and later still, I formally resigned from the Roman Catholic Church; much to the chagrin of my parents, even though they were not fully practising Catholics themselves. Immensely difficult though the decision may have been, it is one I have never lived to regret. I made the decision to leave when I was just twenty years of age and at a time when it was seriously frowned upon; not in a time when it is easy or even popular to do so. How things have changed in that time.

I went to see my then priest Michael Cleary; he was popular at the time, especially as part of the singing priests show, which was very popular at the time; and girl did they lap it up. They could do no wrong and were a law to themselves. No one would ever dare speak up against the church or the priesthood in those days let alone actually go to a priest to request the removal of their name from the church's registry; yet that is exactly what I did. And what an experience it proved to be. I called to Fr. Cleary's home on Colepark Road. I brought along my Revised Standard Version of the Bible so that he couldn't dismiss what I was saying if I used a Protestant translation.

He was friendly enough and allowed me to talk quite a bit. He even pretended to agree with some of the things I'd said, especially about the role of Mary in Salvation and the pagan titles given to her by the Church over the centuries. Things changed though when I spoke about the Mass and the doctrine and practice of transubstantiation, and the claims about the Pope and papal infallibility. It was at this point he asked to be excused and went to another room, only to return with a large volume of the Catholic Encyclopedia. This stunt was clearly designed to impress and intimidate me and to put me back in my place. It failed dismally. He asked me how long I'd been studying the Bible, to which I replied I was studying it for nine months. He then said that he was studying the Catholic Encyclopedia for seven years and that I should do the same before discussing these issues with him. I retorted that it was not what was in the Catholic Encyclopedia that Catholics should believe and practice but rather it should be what is contained in their own translation of the Bible. Anyway, I said. I'm not here to argue with you. I'm here to resign from the Catholic Church and to ask you to remove my name from the Church's register. As expected, he refused to do it, but I made it clear I was effectively resigned from that moment, regardless of what he decided to do thereafter. To say I felt empowered from the experience would be such a huge understatement. The feelings of courage and exhilaration left me shaking from head to toe, but only in the most life affirming way.

Hardly had I made the decision not to go ahead and join the priesthood than I met Barbara, my future wife. It was this fateful meeting that was to overshadow my struggle with my gender conflict for the next twenty years.

PART TWO
Adulthood

Chapter Six

Marriage, What Marriage?

Many marriages are first announced, then denounced and finally renounced
[Anonymous]

Call me an idealist, call me a romantic, call me naïve, desperate even, but I really do believe in love; so much so that I could never contemplate living without it, or at least the hope of finding it. And this despite the many hurts that loving can bring. The problem was I was so desperate to find love, or what appeared to be love that I allowed myself to enter into a disastrous relationship and an even more disastrous marriage.

I met Barbara in the autumn of 1978. I was coming down Ballyfermot Road one evening after a night spent on Peace Corps work. I had just made my decision not to go ahead and study for the priesthood and it was only days after my nan had died. I passed two girls talking, when one of them called after me, saying, 'Don't say hello then'. I had met Barbara a couple of times on the street but had never got further than 'hello'. That night, I went back to her and we started chatting. She said goodnight to her friend, and I walked her to her gate. I plucked up the courage to ask her out on a date. To my amazement she said yes, so we arranged to meet the following Thursday.

I was like a giddy child going home, hardly able to believe my luck. I spent the next week between a state of delight and utter mortification. Delight at having a date, mortified at the fact that I couldn't remember her name! I spent the entire week stressing and calling myself all sorts of names for being so stupid as to forget the name of my date. I could only hope that when I called to her house, that she might answer the door herself, because if one of her family answered, then I was going to be in a right pickle. I would have to say something like, 'Hi, I'm here to see the girl with the glasses.' No, I'm not joking, that is what I was thinking at the time.

Thankfully, one of Barbara's friends came to the rescue. I bumped into her on the way to Barbara's house and, when I told her about my predicament, she very kindly offered to go to the door for me — though not without having a good laugh first, which was fair enough.

The first date amounted to nothing more than going for a walk, chatting and a kiss goodnight. We arranged to meet and go to the pictures the following Sunday. I arrived for our date only to find Barbara house-sitting and looking after her grandparents. Both her parents were out, as were her three sisters and two brothers. When her grandparents eventually left, we sat and looked at the Muppet Show, amongst other things. Her father arrived home about 10.30pm. We were sitting in the dark, so he couldn't see me. The first words out of his mouth were, 'Is that that long bastard?' I was shocked and rooted to the sofa, but Barbara was quick to reassure me that her father was not referring to me, but to her ex-boyfriend, Colm. Needless to say his arrival and abrupt tone put an early end to our date.

We began to see each other most nights. She brought me to stay with her sister Lily and her family in Tallaght after just two weeks. While there I met Lily's two children Aaron and Linda. We went to the Waldorf in the city centre for some drinks and dancing. When we came back, we were given the sofa bed to share. We stayed up most of the night, and around three in the morning, I proposed to her, and to my surprise and delight, she accepted. I was astonished because I never really believed that anyone would actually love me, never mind marry me. So, I took the first chance I got. How foolish and immature I was. And I was to pay a most terrible price for this act of desperation.

We were walking from the bus stop on Kylemore Road on our way to visit her sister in Bluebell when Barbara gave me my first, and very nearly my last Christmas present. It was a silver chain and medallion with my name engraved on it. No sooner did she hand it to me, when she told me she was calling it off! I was completely shocked and didn't know what to do. I cried my eyes out. I was distraught. She was shocked by my reaction. I pleaded with her to tell me why. She said that she did not think it would work out. I told her I loved her and that I didn't want to finish with her. Then, as cool as you like she said, 'I was just testing you.' I was too relieved to be annoyed. This was just the first of many tests she was to put me through. Nonetheless, as I was so desperate for love and support, I stuck with it.

Being honest about it, I had always felt much more comfortable having women as friends rather than lovers. I have loved them more as companions than as prospective wives and, though I'd asked Barbara to marry me, I was still extremely uncomfortable with taking the initiative, especially when it came to matters sexual, but that is what I was expected to do, and I had enough problems without people thinking I might be gay. The great issue for me was one of surviving my family, and my relationship with Barbara had all the promise of delivering me from them and bringing me to a place where I would feel loved for the first time ever.

As stated earlier, there were some readers of the original version of this book, who took exception to the comment I made about my struggles with my sexuality and mentioning that I had enough to deal with without people thinking I might be gay. Such people clearly had a *context* bypass. Back in the 70s, being gay was a huge problem for people. We were in the dark ages then and to be mistaken for being gay or being gay was an extraordinarily difficult thing to cope with. Throw gender dysphoria into the mix and it would be more than anyone could handle; and a great many didn't. In fact, many went to their graves; as I nearly did. My whole focus throughout this period was with trying to prove I was *normal* even if it meant suppressing my true gender identity and sexuality. Thank God for context! So yes, sexuality and sexual intimacy was a hugely difficult challenge for me throughout this period, as it was for countless others.

I didn't tell my mother about my proposal to Barbara until after I was engaged, because I knew she would never approve. My mother was against everything I did apart from the time I intended to train for the priesthood, doing the house cleaning and giving her most of my hard-earned wages, which at that time was more than eighty per cent of what I earned, including overtime. But now that I was engaged, that situation would have to change. It was a few weeks after I told her of my decision to get engaged that I decided to do something about my wages. It was a Friday evening, after getting home from work I told her of my decision to hold onto most of my wages as I would be saving to get married, and that it was high time I had the same percentage as my brothers. I attempted to placate her by buying her a box of chocolates and trying to reason with her as to the rightness of my decision. She was unmoved, except of course to try her usual antics and attempts at emotional manipulation with her usual crocodile tears, but I remained unmoved and equally steadfast. I had prepared myself for this confrontation, even to hardening my tummy and not being overwhelmed by my butterflies. As bad as our relationship was up to this point, (and it was bad) it was to get much worse. However, I was above all this and was so proud of the fact that I did not seek her permission to hold onto what I had earned; I was acting on my decision and showing some adult maturity and resolve. The elation I felt was amazing. There were other times when I would have to show the same resolve, but this was one of my better moments.

On a very cold and icy January day, just two months after our decision to get engaged, and her calling it off, I went to Gerard Bradley, at Weavex, who ran the savings club in Weavex, and asked him if I could get my club payment earlier than I was scheduled to, as I wanted to buy an engagement ring for my girlfriend. I felt so fantastic at the prospect of surprising Barbara with an engagement ring. The following Friday night we went to the pictures. I couldn't concentrate on the film because I was bursting to tell her the news that I was buying her engagement ring the next day. Suddenly, I blurted out, 'We're getting engaged tomorrow'. She never heard me; the moment was lost.

The following day, we went to visit her sister Mary in Bluebell. I told her I had to go to the city on some important business and off I went to the jewellers in Henry Street. I found a beautiful and unusual ring, a set of six rubies with a diamond mounted above them. I just felt it was the perfect ring for her. The woman serving me was amazed that I even knew her finger size.

I returned to Bluebell with the ring and oozing with excitement, so much so that I was fit to burst. When I entered the house, I asked Mary if I could have a minute with Barbara on my own as I had something special to give her. I went into the sitting room where Barbara was sitting by the fire. I knelt in front of her and handed her the ring box. She opened the box, looked at the ring and said, 'Oh, that's lovely. Who's it for?' I was gobsmacked and deeply embarrassed at the same time. 'It's for you,' I replied 'Oh, that's nice,' she answered, and put the ring on her finger. She then called Mary in to show her. Mary congratulated us and made us a cup of tea. I felt totally deflated: it felt like an empty and meaningless experience after such an emotional build-up. This was to be another sign of things to come.

Over the next two-and-a-half years Barbara was to call it off on numerous occasions. Each time, she would tell me that she was testing me, while on other occasions she said I was being too possessive. She was right, because I couldn't handle the idea of her being with anyone but me. I never realised just how terribly insecure I was and how desperate. I don't beat myself up over it, because I know that I was incompetent when it came to relationships. In fact, the psychiatrist who would carry out a later assessment for the courts as part of my application for nullity described me as being 'socially inept' at this time. I must admit to having felt aggrieved at this, but he was right. How could I have been otherwise? It was as if I was more the girl and Barbara more the boy when it came to how I expressed myself in the relationship. And as it proved later, the relationship was always far more important to me than to her.

Barbara and I went to see our local priest, Father Hughes, in March 1979 to inform him of our decision to get married. But when I told my mother, she said it would be over her dead body. My attitude at that time was, then so be it. She resented the fact that I had chosen someone she did not approve of, and that I was making my own decisions for my life. When we tried to discuss the matter with Father Hughes, he simply stonewalled us, telling us that he was not going to marry us. It transpired that my mother had been to see him, expressing her dissatisfaction at our plans: I was dumbfounded and very angry towards them for what they had done to us. I was nineteen at the time. It was to be another year and a half before we finally married.

Over the coming months, my relationship with my mother would deteriorate even further. I came in from work one evening and found nothing but hostility towards me because I had gone to see Father Michael Cleary. I went to see him to get some advice on how to deal with the situation. I mentioned to him my mother's opposition to my marrying Barbara. He told me I was very mature and had given him excellent reasons for getting married. He promised he would talk to my mother and try and get her to see sense, but that is not how things transpired; at least not according her. She told me that Cleary told her I was nothing but a troublemaker. I think she was lying. Either way, that really was the beginning of the end in terms of my very dysfunctional relationship with her; if one could call it a relationship.

Things reached an all-time low when I was knocked down in a hit-and-run accident in October 1979. I was working in General Motors in Tallaght when the accident occurred. I was with Barbara before heading in to work. Just before I left she called it off with me, for the umpteenth time. I was extremely upset over what happened and cried much of the way to work. I was cycling up Ballymount Road, crying and preparing to turn onto Airton Road when I was struck from behind. I knew nothing about it and was unconscious for some time. When I regained consciousness, I found myself in a field surrounded by passengers from the number 77 bus. Apparently, the bus had been behind a van which had hit me and sped off. I was taken to St. Stephen's Hospital with some internal bleeding and cracked ribs. I was kept in for four days.

When my mother came in to see me, she had the most awful expression on her face. She never asked how I was. What she did say was that she was going to 'sort me out' when I got home. The reason? I had confided in my sister (a typically girlie thing to do) that I was having a sexual relationship with Barbara. The situation between us became irretrievable after this (despite many vain attempts on my part afterwards to get along with her). When I came home from hospital, she tore into me about what my sister had told her. I was completely unapologetic and stood up to her about her obvious double standards and favouritism towards those brothers whom she knew were also having sexual relations with their girlfriends but did nothing about it. I made it clear to her that I was not going to stay and suffer her injustice and hypocrisy any longer. I went upstairs to pack my clothes. She followed me, and, to my horror, she went for me with a knife, telling me she would 'fucking kill' me. I knew then that I must leave the house. I packed all my belongings into a black plastic sack and was carrying it downstairs when she blocked my way. She told me I wasn't leaving. I told her to get out of my way that I wanted nothing more to do with her. She followed me all the way up Ballyfermot Road, to Barbara's house, telling me I was nothing but a 'fucking troublemaker' and that I would marry Barbara over her dead body. I tried my best to ignore her, which seemed to make her even worse than she already was. My family really didn't like it when people stopped arguing with them and remained composed despite their onslaughts. This silence was to hold me in good stead in the following years.

When I knocked at the door, Barbara came out. I told her I'd left home and that I was hoping I might be able to stay with her while I found somewhere to live. But once she saw my mother standing outside the gate, she told me I should go home, that she didn't want any trouble. I felt like the ground had opened-up and swallowed me, the only thing that made me feel worse was that I now had to turn and face my mother and go home while watching and listening to her smugness and her obvious feelings of superiority over me. What hurt more than anything, was the fact that I felt I could not depend on the very person I was marrying. My mother had been so enraged by my efforts to leave that she had tried to stab me, and my fiancée failing to support me; talk about a double whammy.

My mother told my father about what had happened. His response was to be so self-righteous and so far beyond hypocritical as to be nigh impossible to believe it actually happened. He told me in no uncertain terms that if I got Barbara pregnant that I was to get the fuck out of the house. Really? That is precisely what I had just tried to do! I wanted to leave the house but couldn't, and here he is telling me I will be kicked out. This was before he headed to Lebanon for six months, with the UN. The situation just went from bad to worse over the following months. But, just as I had promised – and ironically it was my father who was instrumental in making it happen – I did finally leave. While he was in Lebanon, my mother asked me about the times he gave me lifts to McKee Barracks while I was in the FCA. She wanted to know where he was going. I told her I didn't know, except that I understood he was doing nixers on the North Circular Road and that his car was there when I was coming home from the barracks. A few weeks after this I received a letter from him telling me he was disowning me and wanted me out of the house before her returned from the Lebanon. He did this on the pretext that I was causing trouble at home. This was a flagrant lie. His real reason was he thought I'd betrayed him in some way. I'm certain it was my mother using the information I gave her and added her piece to it, which was that he was having an affair with a woman on the North Circular Road. She was putting these words into my mouth. This was also a flagrant lie. But at least I finally succeeded in leaving home; staying first with Barbara's sister Lily, and then a house in Clondalkin for a few months, before moving into the mobile home which we had bought in anticipation of getting married. We bought it from a mobile home site on the Killeen Road. Barbara's parents were reluctant for me to move into the mobile home, but I made the case for moving in by stating we could save more for the wedding and for buying a house if I didn't have to pay the rent for the room in Clondalkin.

It was while living in Clondalkin that Barbara called off our relationship for the last time, before we got married. It was yet another of those distressing experiences that was to test my commitment to her. I remember it especially on account of the foolish I'd made of myself by getting palatic drunk during the daytime. I knew her work coach would be stopping off in the village of Clondalkin, so I made my way down to where I knew it would stop. When the doors of the coach opened I called out her name and told her I wanted to talk to her. She reluctantly got off the coach, and when she did she made it clear that she was not impressed. I didn't mind that too much really, as I was intent on trying to win her back and succeeded in doing so. She told me some time afterwards that she was impressed by the state I'd gotten myself into as it showed her just how much I really cared, even to making a complete fool of myself.

One of the issues we discussed before we married, was the number of children we would like to have. When she asked me how many children I wanted, I said that I would like five. Her reaction was to give me the most awful clatter across my face. 'I want at least twelve', she said. I replied that that was okay with me so long as we could afford to have that many. It was on the strength of this I thought we were all set for building a loving, happy and fulfilling family, despite the many problems we'd had along the way. At least there was the prospect of having children. This made me immensely happy.

We finally got married on 27th March 1981 at St. Matthew's Church on Ballyfermot Road. It was, to say the least, a lacklustre affair. Just two weeks before we were due to get married, my family announced that they were not coming to the wedding. My mother cried and said it was sad that they would not be there. I reminded her why they weren't coming - because of her attitude towards Barbara and my break for independence - and that this was never the way I wanted it to be. She relented and determined that she would be there, even proposing to have the reception in her house. For the sake of a possible reconciliation, I agreed.

How do I describe the wedding reception? Not great is putting it mildly; farcical, most definitely. It started with a power cut. This was due to the power being cut while a mobile home was being lifted into one of our neighbour's back garden. This meant that the reception meal could not be prepared for at least a couple of hours, which resulted in quite a few guests heading to the pub and not coming back in time for the meal; when it was eventually prepared. There were guests there who I would never have invited, in fact I wasn't properly consulted on the invitation list. I kept my counsel on the matter as I wanted the day to go off as peacefully and pleasantly as possible. I felt compelled to express my thanks for the efforts my mother made and presented her with a bouquet of flowers. This did not go down well with the in-laws. A good many of the guests including my siblings went back to the pub as soon as the meal had finished. And I couldn't wait to get out of the house and go to the hotel.

We stayed in the Ormonde Hotel on the quays. While we registered, I overheard someone saying, 'There's another Mr and Mrs Smith.' I was mortified. What they were referring to was that we were just using the hotel to spend the night together for sex. This was obviously something they were used to seeing and because we were so young they assumed we were doing the same thing! Cheeky beggars. We headed for the Silver Springs B & B in Killarney the next day, Saturday, to begin our honeymoon, which was remarkable for the almost complete lack of enthusiasm on Barbara's part; I knew that she didn't want to be there with me. I tried all manner of things to generate some interest in our honeymoon, but it was to no avail. I had surprised her with a long blue satin nightdress. She looked really lovely in it, but that is as lovely as things were to get for me that night, or most of the time since. I was completely clueless as to the real reason why. That was to come later. I later came to realise that we were both marrying for the wrong reasons. Barbara was desperate to get out of the house and away from her parents, and I was desperate to be loved – hardly a good foundation for marriage. The following week we headed to Cork to stay with her brother. What an awful time that was, one I am happy to have forgotten, for the most part.

Overall, and despite the forgettable wedding day and honeymoon, the first few weeks of our married life were reasonably okay, though a little fraught. But the following months were to see a significant deterioration. It started with Barbara not wanting to do any kind of housework and on the occasions when she did, it was with the minimum of effort. It fell to me to do the cooking, cleaning, ironing etc. despite working long hours in Gilbey's. I had started working there after leaving General Motors in 1980, which in turn followed my being made redundant from Weavex in 1979. I was to stay in Gilbeys for the next twelve years, until 1992.

The marriage deteriorated to such a degree that we had little or no sex life. And the rare times we did, it had to be with a condom. This was quite simply awful, especially given the fact that she had pretended for so long that she definitely wanted children.

Shortly after our honeymoon, we started saving for a house of our own, as we wanted to get out of the mobile home as soon as possible. I took on a part-time job in the Lawrence Bar at the end of Ballyfermot Road. I only lasted about two weeks though. I hated it so much I didn't even go back to collect whatever wages I was due (I wonder if they still have my wage packet!).

It was on a Saturday afternoon that I received one of the cruellest kicks in the stomach anyone could ever experience, and it was to affect me for a long time. I was resting in the sitting room of our mobile home. Barbara came in and started screaming at me: 'I hate you and I don't love you. I'm sorry I ever married you and I'm never going to have your children!' Words can barely describe the hurt and devastation I felt. I later learned that Barbara's outburst was due to her anger at having made a terrible mistake in getting married. She loved and cared for someone else and preferred to be with him. But she was not prepared to take responsibility for her mistake and tried on numerous occasions to bully me into leaving, which I steadfastly refused to do. It was clear to me that she did not want to be seen as the one who had walked away. On the matter of her never having children, it was my father who gave her the cruellest of all excuses for not wanting to have them with me. This was the revelations of what he did to my sisters. It was impossible to focus on anything after this. Going to work was especially hard. I was reduced to tears thinking about what was happening at home, but was unable to explain why; after all, *men* are not supposed to tell their troubles to anyone. I opted to get on with things and live my life as purposefully as possible and spend my time on some worthwhile projects.

Chapter Seven

The Worst of All Betrayals

Do ye hear the children weeping, O my brothers,
Ere the sorrow comes with years?
They are leaning their young heads against their mothers —
And that cannot stop their tears.
The young lambs are bleating in the meadows;
The young birds are chirping in the nest;
The young fawns are playing with the shadows;
The young flowers are blowing toward the west —
But the young, the young children, O my brothers,
They are weeping bitterly! —
They are weeping in the playtime of the others,
In the country of the free.
[Elizabeth Barrett Browning]

I was still struggling with the devastation caused by Barbara, when another devastating event unfolded. I had just turned twenty-one in June and received Barbara's bombshell a few weeks later in August, and then came one of the most awful events of my entire life. It was a balmy evening and I was coming home from work at around 10.30 p.m. after doing the evening shift. I was cycling towards the Church of the Assumption on Ballyfermot Road, when I saw my father standing outside with a suitcase. Of course, I went over to him and asked him what was up.

He said, 'That fucking mother of yours causing trouble again. Can you give me a pound, so I can get the bus into the barracks?' I knew better than to pry and left him off with a couple of pounds. My next stop was the house to find out what on earth was going on.

No sooner had I reached the sitting room when my eldest brother James took me into the kitchen and told me that I was not to breathe a word to anyone of what he was about to tell me.

'Dad has been interfering with the girls.'

'What!? What do you mean he's been interfering with the girls?'

'He's been having sex with them…' Silence. What else could there be but silence. 'How many of the girls?'

'As far as we know, four.'

'Where's Mam?'

'She's down talking to Brenda and Martina and the other girls.'

Shocked, bewildered, devastated, appalled, sickened, dumbfounded. None of these can adequately describe the feelings that were running through me. The envy that I carried towards my sisters because of their closeness to my father evaporated as the images of them on his lap became utterly horrific.

The more I thought about it, the more one of my sister's later actions began to make sense to me. She would come and sit on my knee from time to time and she would allow her hand to run down between my knees. I would be acutely embarrassed, but without ever realising where it was coming from. Now I realised its meaning and I was just distraught.

My mother came in and called us all together. She threatened every one of us with the direst consequences if we attempted to tell anyone about what had happened. And after the previous incident in which she attempted to stab me, I knew she meant what she said. She proceeded to intimidate us against telling even our own wives and husbands. My immediate thought was, how dare she do that to us? In the name of God, what were we supposed to do? According to her, it was none of our business and we were to stay out of it.

I could not believe that she could actually think that this devastating news would not have repercussions, which would go far beyond our house and would last for decades — for the rest of our lives. Whatever limited information we received then, our imaginations took over and ran riot. It was to be many years before my family were to face the full impact of what our father had done and the lengths our mother and my siblings went to in order to protect him; to protect this villain.

I went home in a complete daze. I was in a state of shock and bewilderment, to the point where I thought my head and my heart would explode. I tried not to say anything but how could I not say anything? I went to bed. I kept tossing and turning and kicking the sheets as I often did when distressed over something or other. Try as I might I could not stop playing the images around in my head; images of what he was doing to my beautiful little sisters; my innocent little sisters. How dare he do that to them. Try as I might I could not stop the tears any longer, my breathing quickened and was shallower. I was hyperventilating. The tears came in floods and I kept crying: 'No, no, no, no, no, no, no, no!' Barbara kept asking me what was wrong. I tried not to tell her. But how could I not tell? Needless to say, I slept very little, if at all, that night and for many nights after. I realised that, ironically, had I been born in a girl's body as I so much wanted to be, I would have been subjected to the same abuse. This thought meant I was able to feel what my sisters must have felt at being so terribly violated by our father.

Later on, Barbara would use the revelations about my father's abuse of my sister's as an excuse for not having children, despite the fact that she had already made it perfectly clear that she never had any intention of having them. And she did this, knowing the deep hurt it was causing. In fact, it got to the stage when it was hard to tell which of the two I cried for the most; that I felt so acutely the pain of my sister's abuse, or the fact that I would never be a mother to my own children. This, with a strong sense of being trapped in a loveless relationship, was proving to be more than I could bear, and I felt I needed to do something drastic to help me cope.

It seemed to me at least, that we needed to deal with the revelation of my sisters' abuse as a family, and that we should all give them the fullest support and reassurance of our love. It is a shameful fact that this never happened and for years afterwards my sisters were to suffer alone, with the fear and guilt of hurting their mother if they dared to have their father charged, as he should have been. The only thing more disturbing than this was the lengths they and my mother went to keep things quiet. The situation was so bad for my sisters that some of them were terrified to seek counselling for fear of how their mother would react.

Because of my refusal to keep quiet about the abuse that had taken place, I was no longer welcome in the family home. And my sisters wanted to avoid any mention of what had happened, despite the fact that they were still hurting because of it, this was easier for them to bear rather than the guilt of getting justice and hurting their mother in the process. It was after these revelations and my reaction to them that I believe I lost my sisters forever; not that we were ever really close.

Of course, secrets like these can only be hidden for so long, and ours was to come to light despite my mother's best efforts and threats against us. The catalyst for the abuse being disclosed was an act of violence against my sister Sophie's boyfriend Stephen, which resulted in the boyfriend and Sophie, going to the local Garda station to make a complaint. He had been assaulted by James, who pinned Stephen against a lamppost and beat him. During the interview with the gardaí, Sophie was asked why she wasn't living at home. She broke down in tears and proceeded to disclose the sexual abuse she'd suffered by her father.

The first I knew of this was when she knocked on my door at noon on the following day, which was a Sunday. She was clearly terrified and came to me for refuge. She had obviously realised the enormity of what she had done and was in fear of her life. I promised her that I would stand by her if she was telling me the truth. I knew I would pay a high price for this, but she was my sister and there was no question of abandoning her at a time when she needed me. I went to the Garda station the next day to enquire if she had made a statement. Once it was confirmed I was asked if I would be willing to make a statement about what I knew. I made a statement, confirming what I knew up to that time, which was not very much, but it was enough to confirm what my sister had told them.

Word had gotten back to my parents that Sophie and her fiancé Stephen were staying with us. They were too frightened to return to their flat. A brother and sister came to our home and tried to speak to Sophie, but she was too terrified to talk to them, so I refused to let them in. My brother became quite aggressive while my sister waited by the front gate. He pushed past me screaming at my sister to come down and talk to him. I ordered him to leave my home immediately, He refused to go, so I told him to leave or I would call the gardaí. He just screamed at me 'call the fucking guards, I don't give a fuck. I'm not leaving here until I talk to Sophie. I repeated my warning and as I did, I started dialling the local Garda station. He came up to my face and said 'go on, ring the fucking guards. See if I care.' I did and as I was talking to the Garda my brother left the house. He and my sister eventually left, leaving us very upset. A few days after this Sophie fled to Dingle with her boyfriend, thinking they would be safe. They were wrong. About five of my brothers and sisters went to Dingle to bring her back and to 'close off' the situation. In other words, they terrorised her into keeping her mouth shut. They also got her to lie about me putting her up to going to the gardaí as I would be the obvious scapegoat, and in their estimation the easiest to discredit. How wrong they were. This fact was to come back to haunt them in 2010 during their father's sentence hearing. I say their father, after I finally disowned him and them in 2008, because of their appalling behaviour following the publication of Becoming Myself. I was not in court to hear my sister's victim impact statements to the court, but I did get to read them in the newspapers, who reported the proceedings. I can safely say I punched the air with delight at the vindication it brought to me; not that anyone else got to see it or understand its full importance at the time.

In the meantime, however, two garda detectives called to see me, looking for a fuller statement. I duly obliged. They then told me they intended to go to my sisters' place of work in order to get statements from them. I was appalled and told them that that was completely unacceptable and that it would be too much of a traumatic experience for the two sisters involved. I proposed that I would accompany them and go into the supermarket where they both worked and have them both released by their supervisor. The detectives thought this was a good idea and asked me to accompany them. I did. I went to the supervisor in the supermarket and asked to speak with her privately. I explained that I needed to speak with both my sisters urgently and could she please have them come and speak with me. The supervisor made a right song and dance about the situation and it took her an age to do something that should have been so simple. My sisters were finally released and allowed to speak with me. But before I had a chance to tell them why I was there, the two detectives, having gotten fed up waiting, came into the store. As soon as my sisters saw them they automatically assumed that I was responsible for them being there. Between the supervisor's mishandling my request and the impatience of the detectives, they managed to create the very distressing situation I was trying so hard to avoid. I was left trying to explain the situation to two very distraught sisters, who instantly blamed me for bringing the detectives at my own instigation. They were not for listening to anything I had to say. It was truly beyond belief and like some horrible scene from a film. This situation was finally cleared up some years later, but the damage had been well and truly done. This whole god-awful experience, and my family's reaction to my support for my sister Sophie, served to reinforce the fact I was not wanted as a member of their family.

On the strength of my sister Sophie's brave actions, my other siblings were compelled to finally confront all that had happened and how it was affecting them. A meeting was held in my brother's house in Palmerstown where they all attended. I was excluded, of course. During the meeting my brothers expressed the feelings I'd been encouraging them to express since the original disclosures had been made. And all, except one, openly admitted to being very badly affected. They revealed how they never saw their own children in the same way afterwards; how they were afraid to bathe them lest they too, be accused of abusing them. I knew exactly how they felt.

One of the more disastrous consequences of my father's abuse of my sisters was how it affected my relationship with my nieces and nephews. I used to babysit some of them, which was the nearest I ever got to having my own children. Of course, it never came anywhere close being a mum in my own right, but it meant so much to me to be able to babysit them, much as it did when I looked after my younger brothers and sisters. I had every reason to believe that I would be able to enjoy a wholesome and happy relationship with my nieces and nephews, so I was utterly heartbroken and genuinely terrified that I might somehow be accused of doing anything to hurt these lovely children. The fear was so great that I stopped babysitting altogether and have never done so since. Words rarely fail me, but they fail me utterly when I try to describe the loss and grief I felt, and still feel at not having any kind of relationship with my nieces and nephews.

In the meantime, the detectives went to my father with the allegations made against him. He admitted to the allegations, but out of fear of their mother and her blatant and cruel manipulations, the girls relented from pressing charges against him. That remained the case until 2006, when the case was reopened following the death of their mother in 2005. One of the reasons offered by the girls for not proceeding with the charges was their mother telling them that if they went ahead with having their father charged, they would be responsible for breaking up the family and that they would become orphans; and did they want to be responsible for doing this to the family? Other incidents followed from this that are too shocking to disclose here but are now part of the court records which formed the case for his conviction in 2010. I hope that my sisters will someday feel able to tell their own stories. I only share the above incidents as an illustration of the lengths their mother went to in order to cover up the abuse and silence her own children; the very ones she had a god given duty to protect. I was sickened by the way she went to such great lengths to protect our father at the expense of her children, but there wasn't a single thing I could do about it, much as I had tried to. But even more so, I am ashamed of those siblings who stood by them both knowing full well what they had both done. The one saving grace now is that this is all a matter of record and the girls got to confirm these matters in their statements to the court.

Chapter Eight

The Marital Prison

Marriage is like life in this — that it is a field of battle,
And not a bed of roses.
Virginibus Puerisque [Robert Louis Stevenson]

When I look back on those days and the events that were to unfold, I feel like such a complete idiot. I mean really, how many times does a spouse have to tell someone that she doesn't love them before they get the message? People who are desperate for love will do desperate things to be loved, even tolerating the most terrible behaviour and cruelty. In this respect I was very much the weak one in the relationship, but given my history and my sense of worthlessness and unworthiness, what else could I do?

I stayed in this hopeless marriage because I was convinced, on the one hand, that I could do enough to get Barbara to want to stay married to me; on the other, it was the absolute fear that if I left this hopeless relationship, I would be held responsible for something that was really not my fault. But there was also the plain and simple truth that I loved Barbara very much and simply could not countenance life without her, despite the overwhelming evidence that she never really loved me; the worst kind of unrequited love in the worst kind of situation. Later on my loyalty would be complicated by my being a committed evangelical Christian and all that that entailed in terms of the duty of a husband to his wife. But even that could not resurrect a marriage that had never really been a marriage to begin with.

Nonetheless, in the early 80s, we struggled on. We started to look at a few houses in January through April 1982 and finally settled on a house in Tallaght. We decided to make an offer for it. It was £19,500 and we could just afford the deposit. Barbara was so intent on getting the house that she promised to start a family once we got out of the mobile home. This, of course, was all the motivation I needed to expedite the sale as soon as possible, which I did, and we were ready to move in July of that year. I genuinely thought that our marriage was going to work, and that Barbara would keep her promise to start a family. I was totally elated, gleeful even at the prospect of being a mother (I cannot bring myself to say *father*, as all my instincts were that of a mother), and would imagine what it would be like giving my love to my children, just as I had years earlier with my brothers and sisters. I really didn't care whether I had boys or girls. What was most important was to be a mother, and to help my children to become whole rounded human beings who would make a positive contribution to the world. This is just one of so many difficulties I've had in expressing myself as a woman. I should have been able to simply say how much I longed to be a mother, but that simply wasn't possible back then. Anyway, whatever the case might have been, it was important to me that my children's upbringing would be the total opposite of the way my parents had raised me, or rather, how I would have turned out had I not consciously withstood their years of abuse and bad example. I believed then and now that no matter how much others may make things difficult for us, we can choose how to respond, and that we can make better choices about how we treat ourselves and others.

We moved into the house on a Saturday. Our next-door neighbour came out to greet us, giving us some salt to throw over our shoulders on account of the superstition that it was bad luck to move into a house on a Saturday. I didn't know about the superstition, but it is certainly true that the time we spent there was an unmitigated disaster. It was there that Barbara was to leave me for the first time and it was there that I was to experience some of the worst violence of our time together.

I never needed to be told that it was wrong to hit a woman. Violence of any kind was already abhorrent to me and I felt it should be used only under the most extreme circumstance; to the point that I would allow people to beat me stupid rather than fight back, I would not hesitate to use violence to protect those I loved, just like I did in defence of my younger brothers and sisters, but rarely for myself. This view predisposed me to allow myself to be beaten and verbally abused by Barbara without ever retaliating, except that is, to express my hurt and frustration at the way she would treat me. It started with clatters across my face, then having shoes thrown at me and used to pound my face: on one occasion she beat me with a Bullworker while I was still in bed. All I had done was say 'good morning'! I succeeded in not retaliating, but this just made her worse. She used the death of her mother and missing Ballyfermot as her excuses.

Eventually, Barbara decided to return to Ballyfermot, to her parents' house, for a break. It was while she was there, that that I experienced a strong need to dress as a female and of being unable to cope as a man. This had been a long time in coming and when it did, it never left me. On the contrary, it was to become more pronounced as the months and years wore on, despite my very best efforts to suppress it. It was during this period that I found myself unable to deny that there was a different *self*, longing for expression; a deeply vulnerable, gentle, tender and sensitive *self* that needed above all to feel loved and wanted in my true gender. But there was nothing or no-one to help me feel this way. The loneliness was sweeping over me in waves and my health was suffering because of it. I resented having to be strong all the time.

Barbara came back after a few days, telling me that she was only doing so because her father had told her that she had made her bed and had to lie in it.

During our time in Tallaght, I threw myself more fully into my studies with the Jehovah's Witnesses, with whom I began studying while living in Ballyfermot. Not the right place to go for any kind of spiritual insight, as it transpired. It was also in Tallaght that I became a born-again Christian and would remain one in one form or another for the next twenty or more years.

Looking back, I can think of several reasons why I became so intensely involved in religion at this time. One reason was that I could use it as a mask to hide my true *self*. I thought that I could use religion to explain why I felt the way I did. By accepting my gender conflict as part of my 'sinful nature', I could repent of it and, through much prayer and fasting and confessing it to my pastor and some of my brethren, I could finally rid myself of it and get on with living a normal Christian life. Yet again, I was wrong. I continued to repress my true gender identity from myself and, I thought, from everyone else. It never occurred to me just how many people were already questioning this, but never letting on to me that they were. It was to be many years before I finally realised that my gender identity had absolutely nothing to do with me being a 'sinner', and the mental and emotional burden I had placed on myself which by then had become increasingly intolerable and certainly contributed to my later breakdown. And yet it was all so unnecessary.

It was in April 1983, that I became a professing Christian, around the time Barbara's mother died. She was just 57. She died from emphysema. Barbara never really got over the grief of her loss and she completely shut me out and would not allow me to provide her with any comfort or support. Her father died three years later and again she was plunged into grief and again she shut me out. There was nothing I could do for her. Despite our many difficulties I wanted to be there to support her in any way I could. It was heart breaking to be in a situation where I was neither wanted nor allowed to be the support, I longed to be for her.

In 1987 things looked up briefly when Barbara found out that a former neighbour on Ballyfermot Road, Mrs Daly's, house had come up for sale. I never saw her so enthusiastic about me buying a shirt before! We were living in Goatstown at the time having given up our house in Tallaght. It was a Friday evening when she encouraged me to go shopping in the local Pennys, where I saw a lovely silky shirt. She encouraged me to buy it, telling me I deserved it. On the way home, she told me about Mrs's Daly's house coming up for sale and that she would be so much happier if I would go and speak to Mrs's Daly about it. She also made a fervent promise to have children if we went back to live in Ballyfermot. Of course, I was so desperate to have children (which she knew all too well), that of course I agreed and went over to see Mrs Daly. The price for the house was £19,500, which we couldn't afford at that time. But I was not to be deterred and came up with an idea I thought might help us to work towards buying it. I asked Mrs Daly if she would be willing to rent the house to us to give us the chance to save for a deposit. She agreed, and we managed to save for the deposit and buy the house outright less than a year later. I learned some years afterwards that Mrs Daly thought very highly of me and always appreciated the way I continued to visit her long after we had bought the house.

I now turned my attention to starting a family and asked Barbara if she was going to keep her promise. Her response was utterly devastating. She told me she never had any intention of having children but only made the promise so I would buy the house. This was the third time she had refused in the six years since we had got married. The devastation I felt was compounded by the realisation that I would never be a mum and added to this was the realisation that I was stuck in a marriage that I was not prepared to leave her because of my faith. This meant that there was virtually no hope of me ever having children; unless by some miracle she would change her mind. Of course she never did. I had to carry this loss in silence and amidst continuous queries about when I was going to start a family. To compound my misery, I was frequently jeered in work by some of my workmates because I still had no children after eight years of marriage. They asked if I wanted them to come up and show me how to make Barbara pregnant. Words fail me to express how this made me feel. There is a most remarkable footnote to this, and it comes from one of my former colleagues in Gilbeys. In or about August 2013 I received a message on my Facebook page in which she apologised on behalf of herself and her colleagues for the manner in which they treated me and the very crude things they had said. They were devastated at the idea that for all the years I was there, I was carrying these burdens and that they were completely unaware of them. She also stated that some of them felt ashamed. The first they knew of the damage caused to me was on reading this section of the book. She also went on to say that even after twenty plus years since I left Gilbeys, I was still highly regarded as the best union representative they ever had, and there were times when they wished they had me back, but that they left it too late to show me any appreciation. I was very affected at hearing this and it means a lot to me still. I really did enjoy being the Senior Union Representative in Gilbeys and am immensely proud of all I achieved during my time in office.

It was 1988 when I noticed that Barbara was spending more time with our friends Helen and Pat. At first, I didn't think much of it given that we they were both present whenever we would meet up. But then I noticed that she began wearing more revealing tops when we went around to their house. She would ignore me while we were there. It was on a sunny Saturday afternoon in June when we went to visit them. Barbara wore a white satin blouse. She started to mess about with Pat in the back garden. He sprayed her with the hose soaking her blouse. The blouse became completely see-through and looked really sexy, which I'm certain was the whole point of him spraying her in the first place. She never batted an eyelid. On the contrary, her enjoyment of it was all too obvious. I was seething with jealousy and did nothing to hide it. I told her that it was inappropriate for her to be going around with a wet see-through blouse. She told me to mind my own business!

A few weeks later we had a row over the way she flirted with Pat and I told her that I was not prepared to tolerate it. She responded by giving me the most unmerciful slap across the face and tearing my skin with her nails. I reacted by thumping her on the shoulder. A couple of days later, she left me and moved in with Pat and Helen. She stayed there for three weeks. I called to see her one evening to see if I could talk her into coming home, but when I got there I saw her wearing some of the clothes I'd bought her for Christmas, but which, until now, she'd steadfastly refused to wear. Now she was wearing them while sitting alongside Pat. He was in his seat while she was sitting on the floor. Again, I pleaded with her to come back. She made her disdain obvious and told me yet again that she did not love me and wanted me to leave her alone.

I returned home where my brother Graham had been waiting. I told him what had happened. And, as I recounted what happened, I felt a resolve to move on and felt a rush of elation at the thought of what life might be like if I separated from her. It was during the following week that Helen called to see me. She came to tell me that I had every reason for being suspicious of Barbara. The reason? Helen's daughter found Barbara and Pat in bed together; not once, but twice! I came to the realisation that I could not allow her to continue treating me like a piece of shit under her shoe. I resolved to get myself together and move on. Regrettably my resolve was short-lived. She returned home a few days later, but in doing so made it abundantly clear that she was coming back for the house, that she had no intention of giving it up, and that I could leave if I wanted to. That was never going to happen given that I was a very committed Christian; something that was of little help during this whole period. If anything, it was a huge burden and only made matters more difficult to deal with. I can say with the utmost confidence, that if I hadn't been a Christian, I might have been able to end my unhappy marriage much earlier.

The only time Barbara and I ever really got on was after we attempted to live separately in the same house, which we did from 1984 until our separation in 1995. We came together physically no more than three or four times a year. This, however, did not stop me from initiating counselling in the hope that the marriage would work. I asked several pastors over the years to counsel us with a view to saving our marriage. In every single instance Barbara stated that she had made a mistake marrying me and that she regretted the hurt it had caused me. She told them that she was beating me and verbally abusing me because she resented my persistent efforts to make the marriage work when she didn't want to. The problem for me was that I fully accepted this in my head but not in my heart. I could not cope with being rejected by someone to whom I had given so much of myself. It was wrong for me to keep this up, but keep it up I did, though only intermittently. From around 1990 onwards, Barbara encouraged me to find someone else to love. I knew that my marriage could not be saved, but it would take time and more difficulties before I could fully and finally resign myself to that fact.

It was somewhat ironic that, years later, my mother would confess to me that she felt guilty about the way she had pushed me towards Barbara by being so resistant to us being together. She also confessed that, had she brought me up to think more of myself, to have greater self-worth, that maybe I would not have tolerated Barbara's abuse for so long. She stopped short of admitting that her own and my father's abuse of me contributed to how I allowed myself to be treated by others. It was absolutely true, but neither of them was prepared to admit to this; though that was to change some years later.

Looking back at the numerous times I encouraged Barbara to come shopping with me and the vast amounts I spent on buying clothes for her, I realise that on at least some of those occasions, I was really buying the kinds of clothes I would like to have worn, had I been able to do so. I loved shopping and especially looking at the latest fashions. I also loved the new choices of ladies' lingerie and how it was becoming much more feminine. I would use my purchases for Barbara as a cover for buying my own bits and pieces, mainly skirts and blouses, along with some lingerie. The sense of achievement and satisfaction I got from buying my own clothes bordered on the ecstatic. But that was short-lived as I would be hit with bouts of guilt and acute shame and embarrassment. This would lead me to pray and fast, asking God to remove the urge to dress as a woman. I was convinced that He would. And there were times when it appeared to be working, as I would get these mad bursts of peace and contentment when I would throw my lovely clothes into the rubbish bin. But these feelings were always short-lived, and my efforts didn't work in the long-term. The need to be Sara-Jane would come back again and again, only more intensely than before. My response to this was to throw myself deeper into my religious activities, especially praying and fasting more frequently, attending church, theological conferences, visiting members of the church and work colleagues; anything and everything that might help me to suppress who I truly was and how I was meant to live. And, the more I did all this and failed to get the deliverance I so desperately wanted, the more preoccupied I became with it. It became an intolerable vicious circle.

Chapter Nine

Time to Grow

The spirit of self-help is the root of all genuine growth in the individual.
Self-Help [Samuel Smiles]

It is amazing how we can develop and grow and never see it happen until we look back from where we came. That is what it was like for me in my twelve years working in Gilbey's. The things I would learn there, and the opportunities I got to develop as a professional, gave me some comfort at a time when my identity was in crisis. Although much of my time there was boring and unpleasant, there were quite a few reasons to look back and be grateful.

My first job there was as a general operative, or, roughly translated, a general dogsbody. I worked on the back of 'A' and 'B' production lines, loading bottles and cases onto the lines. I also had to sit in the crow's nest, opening the flaps on the cases to allow them go through the packer, which dropped bottles into the cases and then sealed them before they moved along the conveyor belt to the palletiser in the warehouse. Another job involved feeding the Sig packing machines with flat boards, which were then made into cases for the bottles coming from the Jones machine.

We changed jobs every hour, but every one of those jobs was the most boring imaginable. I mean, how many cases can you load, how many pallets push and pull, how many boards can you feed into the magazines without getting stupid? My promotion to the position of relief operator was not much better. Watching thousands of bottles of

Baileys Irish Cream going by day-by day, week by week and year by year was not my idea of an interesting and purposeful occupation.

The longer I stayed at it, the worse I felt, to the point where I developed serious anxiety attacks every morning before going work. Some were so bad that I curled up into the foetal position and stayed in bed. I could not face the pointlessness of the work I did and craved something that would be interesting and challenging.

After several years as a relief operator, I'd had enough and went back to being a general operative, mostly for the exercise. To overcome the boredom and to stimulate my mind, I began reading. The more I read, the more I wanted to read. I also looked out for opportunities within the company that would get me away from the machines, so I volunteered to train as a first-aider and a safety representative for the bottling-hall staff. I was sent away on courses and this became a catalyst to go on and do more courses and to look for opportunities to use my newly acquired knowledge and skills. Things were definitely looking up. I also sought out every opportunity to chat with my female work colleagues, which would be the high point of my day.

It was shortly after I started in Gilbey's that I became interested in the Jehovah's Witnesses. It was whilst I was with them, that I acquired the discipline to sit and read with a purpose other than just learning to show I was *normal*. I was passionate in my interest in learning and personal growth. Indeed, it is fair to say that I was somewhat impatient during this period. Reading gave me a view of life and people that enabled me to show discernment when dealing with difficult circumstances and it gave me the vision and strength to be different, which was very unusual for someone of my age. It did mean becoming rather serious-minded but never morose. It was during these years that I would seek out places where I could sit over a cup of coffee and a good book and just while away the hours, filling my head with new knowledge and new ways of looking at not just my own life, but the lives of those who had gone before. I was in heaven.

It was while I was in Gilbey's that I faced one of my biggest fears and challenges, not having any formal education since leaving school at eleven years of age. I had a growing interest in industrial relations matters and very much wanted to become involved with the union; and later still in politics. I was so keen to get involved that I decided to go to the National College of Industrial Relations, on Sandford Road, Ranelagh, which was up from the number 18 bus route. I did my first year in 1981-82 and got my First Year Certificate. But I pulled out after getting involved with the Jehovah's Witnesses and their false teachings about the end times. I believed this nonsense so much at the time that I thought it pointless to continue with the course. I left them after eighteen months, after I became a Born-Again Christian in 1983. It was to take another nine years before I went back to restart my studies.

Of all the Union meetings I attended in Gilbeys, the general meeting held around 1988 was to be life changing. The Union had been negotiating a wage agreement with the company and held a meeting in which they were recommending acceptance of the deal. I was convinced that it was a really poor deal and that we would do better to reject it and go back to the negotiating table. I went to the meeting all prepared with my calculator and notes. I had it all worked out in my head as to what I was going to say, but when the time came for me to speak, I was like a blunderbuss. I got up and just blurted the whole thing out, making a complete mess of what I wanted to say. It sounded perfect in my head, but it could like a complete mush. It was a cause of great merriment to everyone present but it left me feeling hugely embarrassed and humiliated. My message was lost because of my inability to speak slowly and calmly. I vowed not to attend another meeting until I worked on my communication skills. It became obvious that I was okay in one to one situations, but rubbish in front of groups or crowds. I was determined to change this, and with it the bloody awful standard of industrial relations within the company.

The deal was voted in by the members. However, my prediction about the wage settlement proved to be correct. This had a positive effect in that it encouraged me to make a very important decision. The experience showed me that I was capable of analysing complex issues and coming up with the right conclusions, solutions and recommendations, even if I found it difficult to articulate them verbally. So, I resolved to do something about it. It made me even more determined to return to college and finish my diploma course in Industrial Relations, and to learn to speak effectively in public. I was prepared to start over again if necessary. So, I plucked up the courage to phone the college to speak with the course administrator. To my astonishment he not only remembered me, he told me I had made quite an impression (take that whatever way you will!) during my time there. I restarted the course and in doing so was invited to go directly into my final year! In 1990 I graduated with a Diploma in Industrial Relations, with Merit. Attending the conferral ceremony was a fabulous experience. It made me feel competent and confident in my subjects, and confident in myself, which in turn encouraged me to return to the union meetings I once dreaded so much, and to get even more involved than I had been previously. And oh girl did I!

I joined Lifegate Bible Baptist Church in 1983, not long after I left the Jehovah's Witnesses. I had great ambitions for going into the ministry and training to become a pastor. I made it my business to attend every meeting and learn as much of the Bible as possible. I truly loved the studying and learned to study in a systematic way. I also acquired some new study skills that I hadn't acquired on my Industrial Relations course, especially the importance of context, literary criticism, polemics, ethics and the importance of forming a world view. This has stood me in good stead in the years since. I setup my own study in the box room at, which became much bigger when I moved to Ballyfermot, and began building quite an extensive library which attracted the admiration of many.

My library consisted of several thousand books and included subjects such as Theology, Biblical and other Encyclopedias Bible Commentaries, Sermons, Church History, Philosophy, World Religions, Counselling etc., amongst others. In the Baptist church, I felt that I had truly found a place where I belonged, where I fit in. There were opportunities to teach and preach and I did so with great relish. I became a Sunday-School teacher, street preacher and door-to-door evangelist. It meant being out of the house quite a bit, which, under the circumstances, suited me very well. It did have its downside, though, in that I received a lot of slagging and ridicule but, such was the strength of my beliefs and my genuine enjoyment at what I was doing and how I was living, that I was well able to cope with it all. In fact, it hardly cost me a second thought. Barbara was not anywhere near as interested in religious or spiritual matters and though she was encouraged by our pastor to come to church, she was indifferent for the most part.

It was during this period that Sara-Jane once again sought to assert herself and her right to exist. In fact, her need for expression became increasingly more intense to the point that whether consciously or unconsciously she was going to live and slowly but surely, and come what may, she (I) was not going to be denied any longer. But for now, I was acknowledged as having the call to enter the ministry and it was this which preoccupied my every waking hour; for a while at least, but it was inevitable not to last. It was to take another few years before I would learn that personal growth plays a part in the development of gender dysphoria, and vice-versa, in that as your personality changes, your gender identity becomes more pronounced. So, I started wearing women's clothes again and, despite my best efforts at resisting, I was unsuccessful in my attempts to overcome the need to dress. It still had not occurred to me that this was my nature at work rather than a mere compulsive fetish.

The problem with my gender identity and the need to express it, became so great it prompted me to confide in my pastor. His response was to tell me that we sin instinctively as children but that we get better at sinning as we get older. What this had to do with my problem I had no idea, other than to realise that he hadn't a clue how to deal with my situation. I was alone yet again in my efforts to understand and cope with my female gender identity. I not only had a wife who preferred other men to her husband, but I also had to cope with the guilt of being a sinner and the guilt of wearing women's clothes; something that is condemned in the Book of Deuteronomy. Of course, this prohibition does not apply to people with gender dysphoria, but I didn't know that at the time, and clearly neither did any Baptist minister.

Much to my disappointment, this next section and others, were omitted from the first version of the book. They were included in the original manuscript but for reasons best known to the publishers they left them out. It is important they are included here as they are a record of a major turning point in my life for which I want to acknowledge those involved, especially as the people included had such a positive impact on my confidence and how they encouraged me to go on to better things. It is no exaggeration to say that the several trips made to Leeds in the mid to late eighties were to have a profound impact, which in later years led to my changing my name by DeedPoll. And whilst I no longer share their theological position, I will always have the utmost respect and gratitude towards them. I hope that what I recount here will do them sufficient honour; they thoroughly deserve it. I also hope that those who read this will look up Caring For Life and see for themselves the fantastic work they do for those most vulnerable within their community and beyond.

It was in 1987-88 when I first met Peter Parkinson, Pastor of Leeds Reformed Baptist Church and co-founder of Caring For Life. I was introduced to Peter by Chris Robinson of Ranelagh Christian Fellowship. I began attending Ranelagh Christian Fellowship after I left Lifegate Baptist Church. I was involved in similar activities to those at Lifegate, but with no opportunities to preach or teach. I also attended the Bible studies in Chris's home where I met his wife Helen and daughter Ruth. This was a place where I got some opportunities to share my thoughts on what I had been learning, but they were few and far between. Chris was not anywhere near as enthusiastic about my calling as was my Pastor at Lifegate. Chris's ministry was more in the form of teaching and evangelising rather than on anything pastoral. This lack of pastoral ministry was to influence my later decision to move to Evangelical Church Fellowship, at the Dublin Christian Mission. But I was committed to Ranelagh for the foreseeable future and in doing so gave myself wholeheartedly to supporting Chris's ministry. Chris's teaching and those of Leeds Reformed Baptist Church were of the Calvinist Faith, and the Five Points known as TULIP; whereas Lifegate Baptist Church were of the Arminian persuasion.

It was in the Spring when Peter would bring a team from his church in Leeds for a week of evangelism and special meetings. I still remember the first names of the first team: Esther, Lesley, Wendy, Graham and Russell. We would gather in the room on Ranelagh Road for prayer before going out to the street to invite people in to the meeting. Peter would give his talk and afterwards we would have tea and coffee. It was during his first visits that I was introduced to him, and we hit it off immediately. What resulted from this meeting was both very strange and wonderful; and it must be said, in retrospect, not a little ironic. He invited Barbara and I to Leeds and to Crag House Farm, which is the home of Caring For Life. It is a charity that was formed in order to provide homes for teenagers who had been turned out by family and social services. Some were drug addicts, others were homeless, and some were prostitutes. What they all had in common was their need to be given a home; a place to belong, and a new chance at life, which no one but Caring For Life was prepared to give them. The meetings were a great success and we said our farewells, with a commitment from me to travel with Barbara a few weeks later.

We arrived in Leeds on a Friday around lunchtime. We were staying in Crag House Farm, which was the home of Peter, Judith and their sons Jonathan and Tim. We were sitting at the dining table, where opposite me on the wall was a picture of Oliver Cromwell! I was amazed to see it, and the truth be told uncomfortable. This was no surprise given his history in Ireland and the inveterate hatred we Irish had towards him and the English in general. But we held a particular hatred for him, which stemmed from the historical accounts of his time in Ireland from 1649-1650. My reaction took me completely by surprise, especially as I had prided myself on being more objective than most in my attitude towards the English. Clearly this was not the case. I was quickly reminded of one of the songs I sang in my teens, "The Men Behind the Wire, in which there is the line *"and Cromwell's men are here again."* I remember singing this line with great gusto and satisfaction as I heard the applause from those listening. Little could I have known then how much falsehood there was, and indeed remains in the history of this country, and of Oliver Cromwell in particular. But I was about to learn, and what a lesson it has proven to be.

Peter noticed my discomfort while looking at the picture and said he could understand why I would feel that way. He then asked me if I was open-minded enough to hear a different version of what occurred during Cromwell's time in Ireland? I said I was, and I did. After we had lunch Peter invited me into his study. It was wondrous to see all his books. I was especially taken by his vast array of Puritan writers, whom I'd learnt about from my studies in church history. While browsing the shelves I came across several books on Oliver Cromwell, of which two in particular stood out: one was Antonia Fraser's "Cromwell Our Chief of Men," the other was Thomas Carlyle's "Oliver Cromwell's Letters and Speeches." While I was browsing the latter book, Peter called me over to have a look at a facsimile copy of the original Death Warrant of King Charles I. Cromwell's signature is third on the warrant. I was enthralled. The next thing was Peter giving me a video to look at. It was the movie "Cromwell." The irony of this film is that Cromwell is played by our own Richard Harris, who is brilliant in the role. It is set around the time of the two Civil Wars in England from 1641-1649, culminating in the execution of King Charles I. And to cap it all off, Peter insisted that I bring Carlyle's book back to Ireland with me. I was amazed at his generosity and trust. I read the book and returned it to him, then spent the next ten years trying to find a copy, which I eventually managed to do.

Why all this is so important for me is the shocking facts I learnt about our false history and the way in which Cromwell has been maligned for over three centuries. Of course, there are still those who will never be open to a different account of the history of Cromwell's time here; that must remain with them, but their refusal does not change the facts as we now know them to be. The truth is, I found myself having much in common with my namesake, which led to me making some life changing decisions. It is a sad irony that a country that has for so long condemned injustice in its many forms, should be so unwilling to conceive of the possibility that our history has been unjust towards Oliver Cromwell. I know that for many this will be hard to stomach, but it's true.

It was during this trip to Leeds that I got to see the work of Caring for Life first hand. I visited Carey House and Tyndall House where I met some of the residents. The first people I met were Gary, Owen and Colin, and a young teenage girl named Mandy. Mandy was a prostitute and had HIV. She had been thrown out of her home by her mother for no other reason than that she was in the way. I felt that I could relate in some way to her vulnerability and rejection. All my preconceived ideas about the homeless, drug addicts and prostitutes were to be challenged through the time I spent with these young people. Being amongst them brought out my nurturing instincts, which led to me volunteer whenever I visited Leeds. Anytime I visited I would be roped in to be a relief house parent, which I was delighted to do. It meant staying over in the houses while the house parents took some well-deserved time off. It was in Tindall house that I first saw that ghastly film Rawhead Rex. It was set in Ireland, about a creature unearthed after the removal of a sacred stone from a field. The less said about it the better!

An amazing thing happened as a result of my involvement with Caring For Life. I was asked by Peter Parkinson to consider moving to Leeds and work for them as a House Parent. This was astonishing and so very exciting. I discussed it with Barbara, and to my delight she said she was up for it. So, plans were put in motion for us to move across, starting with giving up our house in Tallaght and moving to Goatstown on a temporary basis while we waited to make the move. Unfortunately, the move never happened as Barbara changed her mind and refused to go. This was to be one of many times she would impact my career in a negative way.

On other trips to Leeds I would attend the family conference held at Leeds Reformed Baptist Church. I was asked to speak at one of these conferences, the theme of the conference was on evangelising several different religions including Roman Catholics, Mormons and Jehovah's Witnesses, amongst others. I was asked to submit a paper on evangelising Roman Catholics. I did, but it was found to be unsuitable for a family conference, though not for any bad reason. It was deemed to be at too high a level for the conference, and there wasn't enough time to prepare a second paper, so it didn't happen. The paper did eventually become what is technically my first published work, it was published around 1990 under the title "Evangelising Roman Catholics: It's Necessity and Justification;" heavy stuff indeed. I understand it did quite well for what it was, but I never received any payments from the publishers.

Peter also gave me a book assignment to complete. It was on the life of the 19th century Baptist preacher, Charles Haddon Spurgeon. I read the two volumes of his biography and wrote the paper, which left Peter very impressed. This was a very challenging project, but oh my, was it a great experience in exercising my critical thinking, learning and writing skills!

There is no doubt that Peter Parkinson and all the folks at Caring For Life and Leeds Reformed Baptist Church had an extremely positive effect on building my confidence and ever increasing desire to enter the ministry. And although we have lost contact over these many years since, I am forever grateful to them all and to Peter in particular for everything they did for me.

While I was busy developing myself spiritually, things were

deteriorating in Gilbey's. It is fair to say that I'd set myself up for the many wind-ups I experienced during my time there. I was undoubtedly devout in my beliefs, but I was also a royal pain in the arse in that every conversation was about religion; and if they weren't, then I manipulated them so they would be. I was all enthusiasm and no balance during those early years of being a Christian. But that was about to change and change dramatically.

The company was hugely successful in making large profits and had experienced rapid expansion, but morale within the workforce was appallingly low. It seemed that, the more the company increased its profits, the meaner they were to their employees. People felt they counted for nothing and that there was nothing coming from the company that would enhance their work experience and motivation. There was little or nothing by way of acknowledgement by the company for the workforce who had helped it to get to where it was. We had managers and supervisors who were becoming increasingly draconian, especially towards temporary workers, who were treated as second-class citizens by both management and other workers. I felt extremely angry about their treatment and vowed to do something about it. I decided to seek election as senior union representative to represent their interests. This, of course, meant doing something far more substantial than just preaching about what was wrong.

The shop stewards' committee had in my opinion, not been doing a good job. This led to a serious fall-off in attendance at union meetings. Morale was on the floor and there was nothing to be done, or so it seemed. It was during this period that I had been learning about Christian philanthropists and missionaries who brought the Gospel to the less fortunate in very practical ways and who brought about a great many changes and improvements in peoples' lives, including the abolition of slavery and so on. I also learned that there were quite a few religious people involved in setting up the various trade unions. I learnt that I could be spiritual *and* give a practical example of a living faith at one and the same time. 'By their fruits ye shall know them,' became a personal motto and made me determined to preach less and to practice more.

I had seen enough to know that all my predecessors had no formal training or qualifications for the position they held in trust. Rightly or wrongly, I held the view that it took more than good intentions and being Mr Popularity to represent those who would depend on me to act in their best interests. So after I had received my diploma in December 1990, I determined to put myself forward for election to the position of senior union representative, but how was I to achieve this when so many union members showed a dislike of my preaching? This really was going to be an uphill battle, but I was determined. I decided to force the first election in over twenty years, which created a major stir, not just amongst the SIPTU membership but throughout the entire company. I managed to get over a third of the vote, which was absolutely amazing given how difficult it had always been until now to get any kind of genuine election and the fact that all those who voted for me were aware that I was a practising Christian. This gave me the encouragement I needed to stick with my goal. I was elected soon after as shop steward for the bottling all members. I was on my way. I had determined that a year from this date I would be elected senior union representative and I started working on it the morning after the AGM. I wrote the following on a piece of paper and kept it in a safe place: *'On this date next year I will be senior union representative.'* And I was. The following year I was elected by a majority of six votes. This is still one of my proudest achievements.

One of the things I am most proud of during my period in office was increasing my majority from just six votes to a unanimous desire for me to stay in office, including amongst them my arch-rivals. I was taken aback by the level of respect I received from all areas of management. Their respect for me made it much easier to resolve industrial relations issues and disputes, with some of them seeking my advice before holding interviews with employees who had to be disciplined for one reason or another. At least here I was in a good place.

In order to make a significant difference as senior union

representative, I determined that I would have to take a very unorthodox approach to how I fulfilled my role and how the shop stewards committee would function. I decided to think like a company director and line manager. I'd always had a hatred for confrontation and so sought to bring an approach that emphasised our mutual interests rather than the old divisive mentality that had caused so much confrontation and distrust in the past. By doing this I was in a better position to understand the company's thinking and how to negotiate effectively with them, but without compromising on my loyalty and commitment to the people I represented. I wanted to change the way in which both sides viewed each other. I never accepted that we were always right, and they were always wrong. One of my strategies was to deal head on with the psychological disadvantage experienced by union representatives when attending management union meetings, so I introduced a policy for shop stewards to be released fifteen minutes before meetings in order to freshen up and change out of their overalls and work coats. This was essential to prevent them from being self-conscious during meetings, especially when it came to body odours and odours from working on machines etc. The other purpose for the early release was to allow the committee to meet before meetings, in order to discuss strategies and to assign who could and could not speak at the meeting. I also banned all profanity and personal remarks and insults. These innovations caused quite a stir and a few raised eyebrows, especially during the early management union meetings; but my oh my, did it work. This marked the beginning of very real change in the way industrial relations was to be carried out from this point on.

One of my proudest achievements as senior union representative was to initiate the coming together of the craft unions and the staff association to enter into discussions on my proposal to create an inter-union group that would combine all our resources and strengths in dealing with our common interests. This was a complete break from the old divisions that had existed. We set the group up and it was a great success. I was nominated as the senior spokesperson of the group which meant being the principal negotiator on behalf of the group. This meant that I was now the chief spokesperson for the entire workforce. It created a very positive atmosphere in which people felt hopeful for the first time in many years. It was truly ground-breaking, and I was proud to have been a part it.

Another reason to be proud of my achievements as Senior Union Representative was saving the jobs and distribution depot at Little Island in Cork. This was possible only because I'd done the course in Industrial Relations, which included a module on financial management and financial statements. The directors responsible for overseeing the closure of the depot did not see this one coming, neither for that matter did the Personnel Director. As far as they were concerned the closure was a fate accompli. I begged to differ. What makes this achievement so worthy of mention is that I was only three weeks in my new role and was already having to deal with the kind of issue that would normally be at the apex of a union representative's dealings on behalf of members, i.e. dealing with redundancies and closures. It is an extremely difficult issue to deal with, with years of experience required, but after just three weeks; that was a big ask for anyone. And yet that is what I had to do.

I was called into the Personnel Director's office on a Monday morning. He read an announcement that was being read out to the workers in Cork at the same time. It informed them that the company was bringing in an outside company to operate the depot and that all the jobs would be gone as a result. Their justification for doing this was the cost of distribution per case to their customers. They said it was not financially viable and that it would be more cost effective to bring in an outside transport company to do the storage and distribution for them. Needless to say I was utterly opposed to this move and made it clear that we would fight their decision. I insisted on being provided with a financial statement and the costs of delivering stock to customers. They said they needed to be delivering at a cost of 90p per case but that it was costing the company around £1.10p and per case. They claimed that they had tried different ways to bring the costs down but without success, and that giving the depot over was their most viable option. Again, we told them we were going to resist any move to give over the depot and any resulting job losses. One of the company directors told me if I could bring the cost per case down to 90p then the depot could remain along with the jobs. So, with the financial statement in hand I travelled up and down to Cork for nine days in a row. This was long before the motorways were built and driving up and down could take as much as eleven hours! It was exhausting, but so worthwhile in the end.

On the last day of my time in Cork I finally figured out what the company had been up to and what they had done to justify closing the depot. To cut a long story short, I found a way to bring the costs down to 90p as per the company's requirement. We were overjoyed and extremely hopeful. However our hopes were soon dashed by the same director, who told me they never intended to keep their promise. He said they were shocked that I had figured out a way to bring the costs down, along with a change in work practices by the staff that would contribute towards the long-term viability of the depot. We were all feeling very happy with what we had achieved and fully expected the company keep to their word. Unfortunately, they had no intentions to do so and I was told to get back to Dublin and enter into negotiations on the redundancies. And my response? I simply told them to "watch this space." I did return to Dublin, and in the following week I put a strategy in place that made it impossible for them to go ahead with their plans. They relented and decided to retain ownership of the depot and to retain all the jobs. One member of staff decided she wanted to leave, but that was entirely voluntary. This set a marker for what my members could expect from me during my tenure as their senior representative.

It was also during the eighties that I developed an even greater liking for arts and culture and reading a broad range of literature. I frequented the National Concert Hall to see the National Symphony Orchestra and other performances, including Handel's Messiah,

Beethoven's Pastoral Symphony, Rachmaninov, Phil Coulter etc. I went to the theatre to see plays and to various concerts in the Gaiety and Olympia. I tried to share all these interests with Barbara, but she wasn't that interested in them, which made them rather lonely at times, but still enjoyable. One of my most enjoyable ways to relax was to sit in the parlour listening to music while reading and having a glass of wine. Socialising was also enjoyable. This normally meant inviting friends for dinner and a few drinks. There were a good many enjoyable evenings to be had with friends and members of the various churches I belonged to over the years.

But despite all this positive union activity and finally having a role that allowed me to express a wide range of abilities, and enjoying a wide range of interests, I still had to deal with a certain issue: I refer of course to my continual struggles with my gender identity. Working in Gilbey's caused me huge frustration that sometimes became quite distressing. This was caused by working closely with so many women, and by my need for female friendship, which was never easy to achieve. Their sense of style drove me crazy and reinforced the growing tension I was feeling on a daily basis. It is fair to say that I felt quite envious and resentful at times. Fridays and special days were the worst. The girls would make great efforts to look their best, and they succeeded. The problem for me was that I was so envious of them being able to dress as they wanted and to be so comfortable in their femininity. It was quite stressful at times and extremely difficult not to make comparisons between them being themselves on the one hand, and my being denied the possibility being the woman I was meant to be on the other. This wasn't helped when my feminine body language and demeanour were becoming more pronounced, despite my best efforts to suppress them.

I made great efforts to befriend the girls, which I did with some success; until that is, they became curious, even suspicious about how I knew so much about women's feelings and being able to give them such good advice, especially in relation to the way some of them allowed their male colleagues to behave inappropriately towards them. In some cases, this was misinterpreted as me fancying them, or that I was just trying to get inside their heads for the purpose of getting them interested in me. It wasn't true, but how could I prove otherwise.

Chapter Ten

The One Constant is Change

Tempora mutantur, et nos mutamor in fillis.
Times change, and we change with them.
[Harrison]

Graduating from the National College of Industrial Relations was such a great experience that it motivated me to go on and do other courses, this time through correspondence. I took two diploma courses with Kilroy College, one in business communication skills and the other in business administration. Between my spiritual growth, academic achievements and wide and varied life experience, I was becoming a more rounded person, but despite all of this and my successful tenure as Senior Union Representative, I still hadn't fully developed confidence in myself or my abilities. This is paradoxical but nonetheless true. This was no surprise given that I was so far short of being my true self. Even in my twenties and heading towards my thirties everything I did came from that same determination to prove I was just as *normal* as everyone else. However, there was one important factor in everything and that was my innate desire to make a positive difference in the world. This has been the situation since.

In 1989 I began attending Grosvenor Road Baptist Church in Rathmines. It is the most affluent Baptist Church in the south of Ireland, and it showed. I got involved in the Thursday Club, which was run for local children. They would come in and play games and receive Bible lessons. I enjoyed the work and had some good fun with the children. This was the extent of my involvement though, for the most part I simply attended church like everyone else. I stayed with Grosvenor Road for a year and then moved on to the Evangelical Church Fellowship at the Dublin Christian Mission, across from the Four Courts. I was very well received by the pastor, Liam Joyce, and his wife Sheena. Liam immediately recognised my potential as a future pastor, and he did everything he could to encourage me in my studies. I had lots of opportunities to teach and preach, which caused envy amongst some. But there was something else Liam recognised in me, although he never let on. It did affect the way in which he interacted with me over the years, but he never told me what he had seen in me until after my diagnosis of gender dysphoria.

In order to get to know each other better we went for a walk around the Phoenix Park. We walked and talked for about four hours. I shared a great deal of my life story with him, especially the abuse and bullying from my family and others. I was very open with Liam, telling him some very painful things about myself, but not about my struggles with my gender and dressing, I didn't know where to start with that one; it took a particular kind of trust to tell anyone about it and I just wasn't ready for that. I was twenty-nine at the time. It was to take another several years before I would share my gender struggles with him. In the meantime, Liam assured me that I had a very special purpose for my life and that God was going to use me in ways I could not even begin to imagine. He wasn't wrong there. I told him of my previous aborted attempt at sixteen to write my life story and how my mother discovered my notes and destroyed them. Liam told me that I should write my story and have it published. In fact, he was unusually insistent upon my doing it to the point where he made me promise that I would do it. He told me that he saw me as a 'pathfinder' and that this would mean treading a very lonely path, but that I would come back and show others the way forward. I could not have imagined just how accurately that prediction would come to pass. It is fair to say that I am profoundly indebted to Liam and Sheena, not just for their friendship, but also for their significant contribution to my personal growth and development.

My work as Senior Union Representative in Gilbeys continued until early 1992. At which time the company announced that they were downsizing the business, closing the Naas Road plant and moving the entire manufacturing operation to Nangor Road. They were making 57 people redundant, preferably on a voluntary basis. This announcement exactly coincided with my being accepted into the Evangelical College in Wales. This was turning into a very exciting time as I was on the brink of fulfilling a long-standing desire to attend theological college and begin my training for the ministry. And, after some months of counselling with our pastor, it seemed that Barbara was actually becoming interested in us having a marriage after all. She even went so far as to commit herself to coming to Wales with me. With the announcement by Gilbey's, it seemed as if God was placing His seal on my plans. I was on a spiritual and emotional high and was feeling extremely positive about the future. But dark clouds and shattering disappointments were not far off.

The first of the dark clouds to overshadow the positivity was the tests Barbara had had done in February, just after I'd taken voluntary redundancy. She was being tested for possible Multiple Sclerosis. While she was not too troubled about it at the time, because she had no idea about the seriousness of this bloody awful condition, I did know something about it. Two of my colleagues in Gilbeys had been diagnosed with it and one died soon after his diagnosis, being in his early thirties. I remember our GP's surprise when I asked him if the tests were for multiple sclerosis; he had been doing his best to avoid using the term, preferring to use the initials MS instead. On 30th March we received the devastating news: 'Barbara, you are MS positive'. That is exactly how it was said and was followed with a phone number for the MS Society in Sandymount. The doctor who delivered the diagnosis was Australian. She made no attempt to explain the diagnosis, or, for that matter, to give any kind of prognosis. She said

Barbara could get counselling from the MS Society. And that was that. Needless to say, nothing was ever going to be the same again.

Regardless of how difficult things had been between us, my caring and protective nature kicked in immediately and I put plans in place to help Barbara deal with the situation. It is fair to say that Barbara was almost entirely passive throughout this whole period. I felt that it was imperative that she learn as much as possible about her condition and what she could do to manage it. I made an appointment for us to meet with the MS Society and attended within a couple of days. It was here we learned about the true nature of the condition and what we had to look forward to as the condition progressed. Again, Barbara remained passive, almost nonchalant in her attitude. I got her to join the MS Society and I joined with her and made it my business to learn everything possible about the condition. I discovered that there was a small steering group in West Dublin and made contact with them. We worked together to set up a new branch of MS Ireland. I was given several roles, i.e. Vice-Chair, PRO and Fundraising Coordinator.

So it was, that I threw myself into the work of the MS Society with my colleagues on the newly formed committee. We were hugely successful in establishing a branch that was second to none. One of our favourite activities was the social evenings. We booked a function room in one of the local hotels and brought members out for the night. They were very enjoyable events and extremely popular. I made it my business to visit members of the branch in their homes on a regular basis to see how they were and how we could help them. I was in a privileged position as members would take me into their confidence and share many of their intimate problems; some of which were quite shocking and very sad. I can say in all truthfulness that it was my work with the MS Society which prepared me in later years for my own diagnosis of gender dysphoria, and the transitioning process.

One of my first decisions on learning Barbara's diagnosis was to withdraw my application to the evangelical college in Wales. At this stage, Barbara told me that she had changed her mind before I left Gilbeys and before her diagnosis, that she never had any intention of ever going to Wales, and that she had decided this before I had been accepted. I was devastated at this news and went into a depression. Not only were my hopes of going into the ministry almost destroyed, but now I was faced with looking after a woman who neither loved nor respected me. It was too much to take, but take it I had to, because I still loved her and was determined to do the right thing for her, and because I took my commitments as a Christian very seriously.

The situation looked bleak. I had no job and was facing the future as a carer for someone who did not love me and did not want to be married; and who had already had one affair and tried to leave with an old boyfriend for England; and despite my standing by her at this very difficult time found it in herself to resent me for my constant efforts at trying to make the marriage work. What in the name of Jesus was I doing putting myself through all that? Why could I not have more respect for myself and leave before it got any worse? The answer is, I genuinely believed that God wanted me there and that he would turn it all around. I truly believed that God would help me through, to the point where I sought an alternative to going to Wales. An opportunity came to go to the Irish Bible College in Thurles, where I travelled to attend an interview. The interview went on for quite some time along with a tour of the college. I felt really positive about the possibility of being offered a place, but this time I watched my hopes and dreams completely destroyed. I was devastated at not being able to go to Bible college. I knew that my dream was well and truly over and that there would never be another opportunity to go to Bible College, or to train for the ministry. I was not given the real reason at the time for why I was not going to Thurles. It took over a decade before I discovered the real reason for not being offered a place, and it came from a most surprising source and for a very unexpected reason. In the meantime, my faith was coming under severe strain, and it wasn't long before it was tested to breaking point.

I found it near-impossible to find another job after leaving Gilbey's. Going back to doing manual work was not an option after being diagnosed with the muscular disorder fibrositis. I was registered as disabled by the National Rehabilitation Board around 1993. It was time to learn new skills and get new qualifications. So, it was that I signed up for a FÁS course in business management. The course was run in Finglas, so it meant a lot of travelling, but it was worth it. I remember my tutor, Joe Chaney, with affection. Joe took a shine to me and once told me that he had a soft spot for me. He told me that I would never be a millionaire but that I would be very successful in whatever I did. It was really nice to have someone believe in me like that. But I don't see why I shouldn't be a millionaire! Unfortunately, though, the course was doing very little for my job prospects and I was knee-deep in debt. I tried applying for innumerable jobs and got the same reply each time: 'We don't have a position suitable for someone with your qualifications and experience' or, 'you are over-qualified for the position.' It was dismal.

The redundancy money had run out fast and it was imperative that I find something soon as our debts were mounting, and the dole money was seriously inadequate. Barbara was eating up a substantial part of our income on drinking and smoking which added hugely to the pressure. This was happening while I was her carer; spending a good deal of my time on looking for her entitlements. It also meant that along with looking for a job I was looking after the cooking, cleaning, and collecting her Ensure energy drinks, her incontinence pads and so on. It also meant sitting around waiting to see local representatives to get them to fight for her benefits and to get her a home help who could assist her while I was at work. I also got her two dogs for company as she had been saying for years that she would love to have dogs around the house. One of the dogs was an English Springer spaniel called Charlie, the other was a cross breed called Dino. They were both adorable. The dogs helped us to get out and about more as we needed to bring them for walks at least twice a day. They were quite a handful to start with but they eventually settled down. But they were utterly useless as guard dogs. When they went asleep they stayed asleep, even while three motorbikes were being stolen!

With all the stress I was under, I came very close to my first serious mental breakdown, in April 1994. I was having an epic struggle with my gender and cross-dressing, as I understood it then, and my faith seemed utterly useless to help me with it. No matter how much I prayed, fasted, attended church, prayer meetings, conferences, preached, did street and door-to-door evangelism, Sunday-school teaching, had quiet times and so on, nothing could deliver me from this increasing need to be a woman, to be my true self. I was so desperate for God to deliver me from this gender conflict that I would prostrate myself on the floor of my study and, with outstretched arms, cry my eyes out to God, begging Him to deliver me from this great sin. I cried so much and spent so much time pleading and begging that I left myself an emotional wreck from it. The last time I did this was in 1993. I had been in terrible convulsions and crying my guts out, all the while trying to keep myself from having a breakdown. I managed to phone Liam and asked him to come and see me, that that it was urgent!

Liam arrived about an hour after I'd called him. We met in my study, where I had earlier picked myself off the floor (not for the first time), and where I was now about to open up to him for the first time about my cross-dressing. When I mentioned it to him he stunned with me with what had to be the most unexpected reply ever: "what's the problem?" he asked. He went on: "did it ever occur to you that you might be fifty-fifty?" I was astonished on the one hand yet not at all sure what he was referring to on the other; so I asked him. "Well, did you ever think you might be a male on the outside and a female on the inside?" Was I really listening to my pastor saying all this to one of his congregation and being totally serious about it? I told him that that was exactly how I was feeling. This astonishing development encouraged me to tell him of how I was struggling with my sexuality. Again, he surprised me by telling me that it was okay so long as I did nothing about it. I interpreted this as him understanding on the one hand but following the Bible's teaching on the other, which was perfectly understandable under the circumstances; not that he needed to worry about it, as it could not have been further from my mind. It was more than enough for me to be able to confide in him about it. This tied me over for a while at least. My taking him into my deepest confidence brought us closer to each other. It was to be years later before I learnt just how much and how soon he realised I had issues with my gender identity and what he did to prevent me from making one of the greatest mistakes of my life.

The low point of that whole period in terms of money problems has to be the day I went to the city to buy myself a much-needed pair of shoes. Nearly all my shoes were completely worn out, with holes in the few pairs I had. There was a closing-down sale in a shoe shop on the corner of Mary Street and Henry Street. I saw a pair of boots for just £10 and decided to buy them. I felt some relief at the thought that I'd been so prudent, but it only lasted as long as it took me to get out of the shop and into the street. I stood facing the shop and agonised about whether to return the boots and use the £10 to pay off a bill. I decided to keep the boots and live with the guilt.

I finally got a job as a financial advisor with Canada Life. I joined them in June 1994 and committed to giving them one year before deciding if I would stay permanently. I had turned them down three times before relenting and taking up their job offer. The problem was that it was commission only. I had turned down numerous sales positions prior to this but felt I could not turn Canada Life down given how many times they came looking for me. Like so many other people I had a serious aversion to sales and tried everything I could to avoid it, but they were the only jobs available at that time, and Canada Life was quite persistent. However, much to my surprise I was very successful in my role as a financial advisor and at generating new clients.

It was a few months after I started with Canada Life, November to be precise, when I was given a much-needed boost to my confidence. I received a phone call from my former tutor from the FAS Entrepreneurial Course, Tony Walsh. He told me I had been nominated for a Trainee of the Year Award. He needed me to send on a copy of all my course work and assignments for assessment by an adjudicating panel. I went onto the course after I'd designed a Debt Management System for families, and afterwards wrote a book called Family Money Matters. The Debt Management System was designed to help people to work through their debt problems. I did the course in the FAS Training Centre in Ballyfermot. A few months later I received a letter from FAS informing me I was to receive the award and invited me to an awards ceremony to be held in March of 1995. I was allowed to bring two people to the awards ceremony, so I asked Barbara and my regional manager at Canada Life. My manager told me he was honoured to be asked and I was thrilled he felt that way about it. But as was so typical for me at the time, and many times since, I underestimated the significance and importance of the award and many of my other achievements since (of which there was a great many). I kept thinking that it couldn't be that big a deal or that important an award if someone like me was receiving it. This no doubt was due to my continued lack of self-belief and self-confidence. Gladly, I was wrong. On the day of the awards ceremony, we were escorted around the side of the presentation area, which was closed off with large screens. But through a gap in the screens I could see the scrolls and plaques laid out on tables. It suddenly began to dawn on me that this was serious. When we reached the presentation area we were greeted by a lot of people, including some dignitaries and members of the press, along with photographers. I was called up to receive my scroll and plaque. I received a Trainee of the Year certificate and an Award for Excellence. I was beside myself with delight. All the recipients were asked to pose for photographs and to give an interview to the papers, especially the Ballyfermot People, who highlighted the fact, that of the 1800 trainees that went through the various courses that year, only two from Ballyfermot were considered to have excelled. This really was a red-letter day for me and one I remember with great affection and appreciation.

Winning the awards gave me the confidence to keep working on my Debt Management System and the book. One of my local representatives at the time was Joan Burton, who just happened to be the Minister of State at the Department of Social Welfare. I had met her a couple of times previously. She was helping me fight for Barbara's entitlements. As it also happens, Joan was also a Chartered Accountant, so she was the perfect person to speak to about my ideas on debt management. I thought long and hard on it before I plucked up the courage to speak with her about the idea and show her the system I'd designed along with the manuscript. She was highly impressed with the idea and said the timing of it was perfect. She was so impressed with it that she set up a meeting with officials in her department a few weeks later. I went to meet them, and they too were impressed and committed to helping me in any way they could. I told them that maybe a foreword by the Minister and taking out an ad in the book would be a big help. They agreed. They also suggested that I contact Bord Gáis, the ESB and An Post among others to also take out ad space in the book. I did, and they also agreed to take out ads! We were fast heading towards 1995 at this stage and the book had progressed to the point where I was in discussions with printers about design work and printing costs. There would have been plenty of money to pay for the printing of the books and enough to promote it. Everything was looking up for me. Even at home things were settling down; not that we were in any way behaving like a loving couple, but I had been hopeful that things might go that way as a result of Barbara's receiving counselling from our pastor. If only it had all worked out.

Liam called to collect me one evening for church, and as we were heading to church he asked me how I was but did not ask after Barbara. At first, I thought he'd simply forgotten, but it happened repeatedly over the following weeks, so I asked him about it. His reply took me completely by surprise and left me in a complete quandary. He told me that whilst he could not break confidences with Barbara, he had heard things from her that left him seriously unimpressed with her and he was convinced that she had absolutely no interest in making the marriage work, that she was happy to keep using me for as long as she could.

It was in the summer of 1994 that I finally decided on resolving the question of my sexuality and whether I might be gay or bisexual. I knew I had discussed it earlier with my pastor, but it kept nagging away at me, so I felt I needed to find out for once and for all. I was also in desperate in need of meeting others who were in the same dilemma with their cross-dressing and sexuality. Apart from The George on George's Street, a place I'd never been to and where I had no inclination to go at that time (because of its reputation), there was only one other place I'd heard of that I could go to, and that was a nightclub at the Ormonde Hotel called the Temple of Sound. I had heard that it was a safe place for those who dressed as women. I went along to see what was happening and whether I could answer some of the questions that had been vexing me for so many years. This was the first time I had ever kissed a man. It felt okay, probably due to being so bloody nervous about the whole thing. But as the man was dressed as a woman, it still didn't answer the question about my sexual orientation. It was very obvious to me that the vast majority of the transvestites were there to pick someone up for sex. It was hugely seductive and to an extent I fell into it, because it felt like a safe place to be and they felt safe to be with. But the guilt afterwards was simply awful. What the whole experience did do was, help me realise that I definitely was *not* a transvestite or cross-dresser, and that my problem was something completely different. The difficulty now was that despite what my pastor Liam had said to me months earlier, I really hadn't a clue where to go to get the help I needed.

However, other events were to take over and distract me. It was during 1994 and early 1995 that I made my last efforts to salvage something from my marriage, but to no avail. I know, I know, when was I finally going to get the message? I did. It was on Christmas Night 1995 that I accepted that the marriage was dead, but it was to be a few months more before I finally did something about it. No doubt, there will be those who will say, "about bloody time!" And they'd be right. But wait for it, there's more! But that is for later.

In the meantime, apart from Liam, it was nigh impossible to share with anyone what was happening in my life at this time. All my Christian friends were interested in doing was quoting passages from the Bible and reminding me of my duties to attend church and to take care of Barbara. Prayer was to be the answer to everything. But it wasn't for me. Everyone knew where I lived and how to contact me when they wanted my help with preparing CVs, job interviews, advice on Bible study preparing their sermons and Sunday School preparations etc, but not with providing me with the warmth and support I needed. I was desperate to go for a drink, or meet for a coffee, or just to go for a walk, but to no avail. All of which made my sense of isolation and loneliness harder to bear, especially as living with Barbara was making me desperately unhappy and causing my health to deteriorate. The loneliness was consuming me, in the way a black hole consumes everything that comes into its orbit. It seemed that there was no one to help me, not my family, not my wife, not my church, nor my so-called friends. I simply couldn't communicate my distress to anyone and felt myself entering into an irresistible downward spiral. I was deeply depressed, but couldn't see it, because all my focus and energy was outward; it was about trying to protect Barbara, it was about trying to earn a decent living; it was about being the best Christian I could be. But despite all this, nothing was coming back the other way; and still there was the wretched fear of what everyone would think and say if I finally plucked up the courage and do the right thing and leave this god forsaken situation, and damn what others would think or say about me.

I began to feel that the Christian message was irrelevant to the needs of people such as me, suffering all manner of trials and tribulations, unemployment, financial difficulties, family problems, health problems, struggles with gender identity and sexuality. What mattered more to Christians was, that you had the right theology, the right doctrine of salvation the right position on the end times, the rapture, the new earth, maintaining church attendance, that you hung out with only the right brethren, that you went to the right sort of conferences and seminars, and that you remembered your place as a miserable, unworthy sinner. Only Liam and Sheena Joyce and Chris and Helen Robinson were the exceptions to this. They showed us immense kindness and I am forever grateful to them for all their support. I had a major issue with Helen afterwards, but more of that anon.

There was no support from either of our families. The exception was Barbara's sister, Mary. Mary had a terrible life herself and continually lived on the fringes of poverty. She had separated from her alcoholic and abusive husband and was raising three children alone, two of whom were teenagers. Their financial situation was dire to say the least. Yet Mary was the one who provided us with the most practical help and was by far the most generous and supportive. When she went shopping she would bring some food items for us as a gift. She would call in and spend several hours at a time keeping Barbara company and helping out around the house. The trouble with this help was that it wasn't always the kind of help I needed.

There was no emotional support, no friendship in the way I needed it. I needed to have a best friend and confidant, not just a counsellor. I needed friends with whom I could go for a meal, walk and talk about other things apart from the Bible. I needed people who would call me on the phone to see how I was and not just to talk religion. Nor did I need people constantly reminding me of my Christian duty to look after Barbara. Of course, they were not to know about her behaviour or for that matter the affairs, nor the violence and verbal abuse. If I was to leave her, I would simply be that 'bastard' who left his disabled wife.

All the strenuous efforts I had made to make our marriage work were brought to a final halt on Christmas night 1994. Our neighbour, Ryan, who had been a regular visitor over a period of months had been invited in to have a Christmas drink with us. The evening was pleasant enough and there was no sign of anything being amiss; nothing to arouse my suspicions. In fact, it was strangely nice to have Barbara being so civil to me. But all that changed around midnight when Barbara went to the kitchen with the dishes to do the washing up — an unusual act in itself — and Ryan offered to help. She insisted on doing it, seeing as I had prepared the food. They were away for a considerable length of time and for some reason I became suspicious. I felt more and more that something wasn't right, so I went into the kitchen to see if everything was okay. As I walked towards the kitchen, I could hear them muttering and clearly heard Barbara telling Ryan that she really did fancy him. He told her he felt the same. I then heard the ruffle of clothes. My heart was pounding as I realised, they were fondling each other. When I put my head round the door, and sure enough, they were kissing and had their arms around each other in a tight embrace. Her hands were fondling his bottom.

There was a strange feeling of elation and vindication as I confronted them while they were still cuddling each other. Ryan was mortified about being caught and tried to let on that there was nothing between them, making himself look absolutely cowardly and pathetic in the process. Barbara, on the other hand, was quite brazen and made no attempt to disguise how she felt about him. The game was well and truly up for us. As elated and vindicated as I felt at the time, this marked the beginning of my subsequent emotional meltdown.

Here was the final intractable proof, if proof were needed, that she really didn't give a shit about me. It couldn't have been clearer. This was now the third man she preferred over me. How much more could a person take? Something had to be done, but what to do about it next was the problem. In the meantime, Ryan stopped coming in. Barbara made her resentment towards me obvious. She even had the gall to blame me because he wouldn't come in to see her.

Over the coming days I had to come to terms with the whole ugly situation. Added to this was the fact that all my faith and commitment as a Christian came to naught. It proved to be utterly useless. Aristotle's words were to taunt me: 'good deeds shall not go unpunished.' From this point on, my life was to enter into what I call the 'winding-down' phase. By that I mean I developed a deepening depression and an overwhelming sense of despair, compounded by a growing crisis of faith. All my years of believing and serving the gospel, of church-going and witnessing, of prayer and fasting and the ridicule and rejection I faced constantly because of my public profession of faith all came to nothing. I really did have nowhere to go and no-one to go to for comfort and support. I was absolutely alone.

I would like to say that at the end of all this I finally came to my senses, that I found my dignity and self-worth and walked away. If only. It was my health that became my final call to action, and which led me on what was to become the most amazing journey imaginable!

Looking over these many years a number of important discoveries have been made and valuable lessons learned. I realised that I had been using various coping tools and strategies but without any awareness on my part that this is what I was doing. Nor had I any awareness during this whole period that these tools and strategies would one day become such a huge asset and help me in helping others succeed in their own lives.

I am especially proud though of the fact, that I never allowed myself to be a perpetual victim of my horrible circumstances, and that I managed to maintain my grace and sense of humour (most of the time!). And as important as all these other things undoubtedly are, I am especially delighted that I managed to remain hopeful and to keep smiling. As this story continues to unfold, it will become increasingly obvious that all these positives would be tested to breaking point and beyond. But for now, it is important to state that they worked for me and they certainly helped me to survive in ways I never would have without them.

PART THREE
Letting Go

Chapter Eleven

Why Won't I Just Leave?

And who can tell but heaven, at last,
May answer all my thousand prayers,
And bid the future pay the past
With joy for anguish, smiles for tears?
Farewell [Anne Bronte]

I first got to know Maria O'Connor through a phone chat line in early 1995. The conversation I had with her was to prove the first life-changing event in a life-changing year.

No doubt there will be those who will smirk at the idea of my using chat lines, but given the circumstances I was in, it was either do that or drink and drug myself into oblivion. It wasn't ideal and under normal circumstances I would never have done it, but these were far from normal circumstances. I felt so isolated, so rejected, and so lonely, and the irony is that using a chat line and getting to meet Maria most likely saved my life; in fact I'm certain of it.

The more I shared with Maria about Barbara's MS and its debilitating effects, the more she demonstrated her concern. When I had shared with her the very difficult financial situation that we were in, Maria vowed to help us. When I confided in her that Barbara was drinking and smoking our money away, Maria sent us £80 and one hundred cigarettes, which Barbara accepted without showing even the slightest gratitude. In fact, she had to be shamed into phoning Maria to thank her.

It was in April of 1995 that I noticed a serious deterioration in my mental health and emotional wellbeing. The panic attacks were getting much worse and my depression was deepening, to the point where I was no longer contemplating suicide as a thought only, but was now considering how best to do it, including when and where. The frequency of my panic attacks was increasing and with this came a very noticeable increase in pains in my head. On one occasion the pain was so bad that I was convinced I had a brain tumour. Once, I was driving from my office along the South Circular Road, towards the junction of Clanbrassil Street. The pain was truly overwhelming, and my vision was blurring. It was very difficult to drive. I stopped the car in the middle of the road and got out and walked around for a few minutes while other cars had to drive around mine. I eventually got back into the car and drove home.

Barbara had a dinner ready for me, but I could barely look at it never mind eat it. 'What's the matter with you?' she asked, in her usual indifferent tone. I was unable to answer. My head collapsed onto the plate of hot food. I remained like this for a few moments and then made my way to bed. At this stage the pain worsened, and I was feeling very nauseous in my stomach. As I lay on the bed I curled up into the foetal position and swayed back and forth.

Barbara eventually came into the room and sat in the chair by the window without saying a word. After a few minutes, she asked if I wanted a doctor, but I was unable to answer. She then said that I could suit myself and left the room. A few minutes later she came back in, at which time I was in floods of tears and convulsing. She looked at me and asked for money for dog food. She never called an ambulance. I could hardly believe my ears.

The next morning, I went to see my GP in order to get some help. He promised me that he would get me into counselling and prescribed Prozac. He never got me the help and I came off the Prozac very soon after, because I was having bad side effects. This meant trying to cope without any medical intervention whatsoever. It was indescribably difficult trying to function on a day-to-day basis. Work was also becoming more and more stressful and I was getting ever nearer to my breakdown.

It was around this time that we were accepted into membership of Grosvenor Road Baptist Church. It was extremely important for me to find some spiritual fellowship after leaving Evangelical Church Fellowship. We had been attending Grosvenor for a few months before applying for membership. I very much regret the charade I participated in regarding Barbara's membership. It was nothing but a front, and was enabled by my inability and unwillingness to deal with the reality of our situation. The simple truth is though, I was caught between a rock and a hard place, which placed me in an intolerable position.

Maria contacted me a couple of days after our conversation about my difficult situation and asked how we were getting on. I told her about what had happened over the past few days, she was genuinely shocked and concerned. So much so that she travelled all the way from Limerick to lend her support. She stayed with us for a couple of days, in the spare room. It was while she was with us that she invited us to Newcastle West for a much-needed break. She felt a change of scenery would do us both the world of good. She had no idea how bad our relationship was at the time and all she knew from me was that I was trying to be as loyal as I possibly could under very difficult circumstances. I hadn't let on about the events which had taken place at Christmas and how they were affecting me.

We both accepted Maria's invitation, but as was so often the case, Barbara changed her mind and suggested that I should go on my own as I needed the break more than she did. I had mixed feelings about this, but I was happy at the prospect of getting away from Dublin and the whole situation.

Maria lived in a cottage which was just up the hill, off the main street in Newcastle West. It was very quaint, and it was definitely designed for shorter people! I lost count of the number of times I banged my head going through the doorways and coming up and down the stairs. I loved the house and the back garden, where we spent some time talking and getting to know each other better. As I got to know Maria better, I could not help liking her, but I also learned of how sad her own life was and how she had been through the mill herself. She had recently had an operation on her womb to remove cancer. The cancer eventually took her life some years later, at just 48 years of age. As I would later discover, Maria was also mentally ill, and this illness led her into actions that were not normal and caused a great deal of distress and hurt for other people. Maria suffered from multiple personalities and it was under this influence that she did many strange things. That said, there is absolutely no doubt in my mind and the minds of others who knew her that she genuinely did not know she was doing the things she did. Maria was also the first person who had been a real friend to me, and for that I am truly grateful.

While I was on this weekend break I felt the enormity of how damaged I was and how my life had been one unbroken stream of abuse, bullying and rejection, and the feeling that they were the root cause of my lack of confidence, and why I felt I must always prove myself to everyone. For the first time since being a teenager on holiday at Coolure House, I felt unable to cope with going back to Dublin and the life I was now convinced was destroying me. I was dreading the return so much that I told Maria I could not cope with the thought of going back. She told me I didn't have to and so I phoned Barbara to say I was staying over an extra night. She was her usual indifferent self. But ultimately, I knew that I had to return to Dublin and to reality, and so braced myself for the trip. Before heading back, Maria and her husband Doney said they hoped we would both come down for the holiday in August, but that even if Barbara opted not to come that I should still have my holiday. They felt that I really needed the break. They were right.

As I approached my 35th birthday in June Maria sent me a gift token of a meal for two in the Green Isle Hotel. Of course, I asked Barbara to come with me. She looked the best she had for a very long time and the evening was genuinely pleasant, no doubt helped by the fact that I had now accepted that we no longer had a marriage and never would have; that we were to be nothing more than friends thereafter. But inside, I was burning with the pain of rejection and was at a complete loss as to what to do next. I had to come to terms with the reality that I was never going to experience any meaningful love from Barbara and that she had, in fact, made a momentous mistake in marrying me. I also had to face the equally difficult truth that I had married her for the wrong reasons. I was so terribly desperate to get away from my mother and father that I would have done anything and loved anyone in order to escape. This was wrong, just so, so wrong in every way.

And yet, even though Barbara and I were no longer 'married' in the true sense of the word, I persisted in putting on a front, especially for the church. This, too, was wrong, but I was at a loss as to what to do. I was a practicing Christian and I had a duty to God to be a good witness in every aspect of my life. I was prepared to do my duty as a Christian, no matter how high the price. This meant carrying the cross of suffering which was my false marriage, and every other difficulty I had to deal with. I did not fully appreciate this at the time, but I eventually came to realise that this was the stock response of Christians for any situation where they have no answers or solutions to life's problems. It's their way of saying the Bible has an answer for everything in life. I found this to not be the case at all, and in fact it is quite irresponsible and dangerous, but that's for later.

It was also in June, a Wednesday afternoon to be exact, that I came home from work early because I had been feeling very low energy and was in a heightened state of distress, and with my concentration all over the place I was getting nothing done, so it made no sense to stay there. I arrived home to find Barbara sitting in her rocking chair. I went over and stood by the window and asked her how her day went. She said that she was feeling fine and asked how I was. I told her I felt very depressed was reaching the end of the road; that I simply could not go on for much longer and that I truly felt I was dying inside, and that it was only a matter of time before I ended my life. Her response summed her up and our hopeless empty relationship. She simply rocked back and forth in her chair and said: 'Well, you know I don't love you, don't you?' There really was nothing more to say after that.

I travelled to Newcastle West for my holiday, knowing on the one hand how bad my depression was, but on the other, I did not know just how close I was to having a breakdown, how little it would take to finally push me over the edge. I never saw it coming, and when it did, it was truly horrific.

It was on the first Thursday after I arrived in Newcastle West when the horror began. It was on that morning that Maria was out of sorts. For some strange reason she started going on at me about my family and railed at me because I wasn't getting on with my parents. She would not accept that my parents could have been so cruel towards me. I was completely shocked by this, not realising that that was to be the straw that would break the camel's back and become the catalyst for what followed. She left the house to go up to town on some errands. I was alone and was thinking about what had happened earlier. The more I thought about it, the more foolish I felt at having taken her into my confidence and telling her about my childhood and the abuse experienced from both my parents. The more I did this, the more stupid I felt and began calling myself names. The rush of memories and feelings that overwhelmed me was like a tsunami. I was caught in a barrage of voices shouting and screaming at me: '*You stupid fucker! You stupid idiot! You useless bastard! You fucking spa head! You're nothing but a fucking troublemaker! When will you ever learn, you bleeding retard?*' All of these voices were screaming at me while I punched myself all over my face. I tried to stop and pull myself together, telling myself to cop on, but it was to no avail. The voices became louder and more contemptuous. And the louder the voices the more vicious the punches became. And then it happened, the blackness came ever nearer with every verbal and physical assault. I was now pummelling my face and shouting the same vile insults at myself; except that it wasn't me shouting these insults; it was them, my mother and father, my brothers and sisters, my so-called friends, the teachers, the nuns, the Christian brothers, my so-called workmates. It was all of them together.

As I punched my face with both fists I shouted the same obscenities over and over:

'You stupid fucking bastard!'

'You fucking retard!'

"Fucking antichrist!"

'You are nothing but a spa head!'

'You're stupid!'

'You're an antichrist!'

'You're nothing but a fucking nuisance!'

'You're nothing but a mistake and you shouldn't be here!'

And so it went on, abusing myself verbally and physically; it was awful; so awful, in fact, that my mind started to go; literally. Not only did I feel powerless to resist, I allowed myself to be drawn into it. And as I was drawn into this black void, I began to lose consciousness. I was entering the mental abyss and there was nothing to stop me. Until that is, Maria came home and heard my screaming from downstairs. She rushed up to see what was wrong. The sight must have been terrifying for her, not knowing how to deal with the situation. Here was a woman of six feet tall, standing on her bed, beating herself to a pulp and in terrible convulsion; and this other woman of just four feet something, not knowing what to do, except to reach out her hand and call out to me.

I barely remember her touching my hand and ever so gently getting me to step down from the bed and sit down. She called my name over and over, Sara, Sara, Sara. What is the matter? What's wrong with you, Sara? What's happened? Tell me what's happened!' But I couldn't. I was unable to answer. Her voice seemed to be coming from a distance and I was unable to respond. I really don't know how long this went on for, but I do remember her getting me to say my name over and over again. 'What is your name? Sara, tell me your name. Please say your name.'

More time passed and as it did I gushed floods of tears as my body began to shake violently. But Maria kept calling me and, as she did, she held my hands more tightly and refused to let me go. It was as if she, too, could see the engulfing darkness and was determined to stop me from being swallowed up by it. Had she failed then, that would have been the end of me.

The darkness began to recede as her voice became clearer, and, as it did, I began to respond by saying my name. Slowly but surely, the convulsions stopped. I was left with the tears flowing freely down my face as I choked from the build-up of mucus in my nose and throat. Maria gave me some tissues and began stroking my hair in order to soothe and comfort me, something I had not experienced in all my life. I was in a mental and emotional twilight zone. She managed to get me into bed and left me to rest; coming in at regular intervals to check on me. I can't remember anything else until I woke up the next morning. Maria insisted that I stay in bed and rest while she brought me up some food, but I was barely able to eat it.

Later that day Maria came to my room and told me she had arranged for me to go on a three-day break to Lahinch, after which I was to be taken to a psychiatrist for a consultation. The consultant was Dr Jack O'Regan at Barrington's private clinic in Limerick city. I was completely gobsmacked by her generosity. It was quite beyond me that someone would be so kind, so much so that I simply did not know how to cope with it or how to respond.

We arrived in Lahinch on a Tuesday. That same evening, Maria was on the phone speaking to someone – it turned out to be my mother. Concerned for my welfare, Maria had made the decision to contact her. I told Maria that I did not wish to speak to my mother, but she insisted, and so with great reluctance I did. What my mother really wanted to know was, why I was going to see a counsellor and what I was going to discuss with him. I told her it was absolutely none of her business and that I did not wish to speak to her any longer. She then threatened me that something would happen if I dared to reveal anything about what my father had done to me or to my sisters. I was trembling and could not wait to hang up the phone, which I eventually did, and with great relief.

Shortly afterwards I received another call. This time from my brother Fred. He too sought to find out what I intended to say to the psychiatrist. And as with my mother, I told him it was none of his business, that it was between me and the psychiatrist. Then, as with my mother earlier, he threatened to sort me out, and that he would knock my lights out; a typical threat of violence designed to intimidate me into silence. I hung up the phone, then tore into Maria for making contact with them without my knowledge or permission. Only after doing so, did she realise her mistake and how terrible my family were to me. She was shocked and could not comprehend how they could be so completely unloving towards me and so violent. It made no sense to her. But the damage was well and truly done. I was terrified of what would happen next. I reached a point where I felt I must do the only thing that was left open to me if I was ever to get away from them or have any peace. I decided to end it all there and then.

I told Maria that I was going for a walk, that I needed to be alone. I left the hotel and walked down to the beach. It was midnight and there was no-one around. I went straight into the sea until the water was up to my waist. I stood there for awhile, and as I did I could feel the water rising and my legs getting heavier and sinking beneath me. I just stood there thinking about what I really wanted to do, but also thinking of Maria in the hotel on her own and what would happen to her if I let myself drown. I felt it was wrong to do that to her and so returned to the hotel.

When Maria saw me, she freaked out. She screamed at me that she was terrified of anything happening to me. I was barely responsive. She got me to get out of my clothes and into my pyjamas. Somehow, we got through the next three days and returned to Limerick on the Friday. We went straight to my appointment with Dr O'Regan in Barrington's. He asked me how I had come to be in Limerick. I told him the whole sorry story, about the years of abuse, and the abuse of my sisters and how that was affecting me. I told him about the phone calls and the threats and about my breakdown a few days earlier. I also told him of my 'cross-dressing' — as I thought it to be at the time. He could not have been blunter with me: 'If you stay in Dublin, you will die. And I cannot treat you from there, so you will have to decide if you want me to treat you. If you do, then you will have to decide to move to Limerick.' I told him I was prepared to do whatever it took to get the help I needed. He then told me that the hardest decision I had to make was whether or not to leave, and harder still would be carrying out that decision. He certainly wasn't wrong about that. I left him and re-joined Maria who had been waiting outside by the stream. I told her what had happened, of my decision to leave Dublin as soon as I could find somewhere to live in Limerick. She immediately offered me the same room I was staying in and offered to do everything she could to help me. She kept apologising for going against my wishes regarding her contacting my family and promised never to do it again. But alas, if only she had kept to it!

I returned to Dublin on the following Saturday, sort out my affairs and pack my things for the move. Barbara was pleasant enough when I arrived home. She said she had missed my company. I was careful not to misinterpret her meaning. I told her about all that had transpired, but she responded with her usual indifference. I then proceeded to tell her of my decision to leave Dublin in order to receive treatment from Dr O'Regan and of his advice to me about leaving. She told me that it was the right thing for me to do. She then said that she would miss me, which I found surprising. The next day I put my plans into motion and began sorting out my affairs. I made sure to bring all outstanding bills up to date and managed to change the mortgage repayments, so they would be easier for Barbara to manage.

On the Friday before I was due to leave, I called into Tesco to say goodbye to one of my sisters, Rachel. I told her that I could not tell her all the reasons for my leaving but that I would miss her. We used to be close, but not since the incident with the garda detectives calling to her at work looking for a statement. Rachel used to confide in me quite a bit over the years and I never once broke her confidences. I used to sit on her bed and listen to her as she confided in me about her boyfriend troubles and other problems. Now, she was very hostile and tried to ignore me. It was a very difficult moment and I left, knowing that I might never see her again and that the situation between us would never be resolved. But at least it wasn't for the want of trying on my part. And I found peace in the knowledge that I was not responsible for what happened to her when the gardaí arrived at the shop.

Friday arrived, and I began packing my car (a brown mini metro) with my clothes, computer and a few books and some other bits and pieces. The few days prior to this were completely awful: as bad as the situation was between us, it was extremely upsetting to be leaving. What made it worse was the fact that she never actually believed I would do it. She tried to wish me well, but it was obvious that even she was upset, which made me feel even worse. As I was leaving, she began to cry, but it was far too late for tears I had to remind myself of all that she had done and of the affairs, the leaving me for other men, the beatings and verbal abuse and her indifference to my feelings and sufferings. And then there was Charlie and Dino, our two dogs. It tore at me so much to have to say goodbye to them. There is no denying that they knew something was wrong and they kept a very close eye on me. As I left the house, I gave Barbara a hug and wished her well. I was determined that there was going to be no acrimony, at least not on my side. I thought there was none on hers either but was to be woefully disappointed.

Chapter Twelve

New Beginnings

Voilà le commencement de la fin
This is the beginning of the end.
[Charles-Maurice de Talleyrand]

I had a mental and emotional breakdown. I didn't ask for it, plan it, welcome it, or enjoy it - who would - and it very nearly cost me my life. There now, I've said it and the world has not come to an end, my true friends have not deserted me, and I am not alone in the world. But it really could have been so awfully different – especially had it not been for Maria's several interventions. It seems incredible but in so many ways I'm grateful for that breakdown, because not only did it save my life at that crucial period, it also made me wake up and do something about my situation with Barbara and my family. It had little to do with my gender identity at that time as I was still repressing that part of my *self*. But there is no doubting that the breakdown and all that subsequently emanated from it started me on a journey that has brought me to where I am now. It is so sublimely wonderful to be where I am today because of Maria's intervention, and, as I'm now learning, the spirits who have been looking after and protecting me all this time. I should be dead so many times over, but I'm not; in fact, I could not be more alive! But that is not how it was when I left Dublin, it was quite the contrary.

I drove away from my home on Ballyfermot Road in my brown mini metro. I did so with feelings of deepest sadness and distress, which as I drove on gave way to feelings of elation then back again to feelings of sadness and then despair. I didn't realise it at the time, but I was in a state of shock and grief. It was truly awful. I really had no idea what I was letting myself in for, but I did know that I had reached the point of no return. What I needed to do was to get through this long journey as safely as possible and in whatever way I could, make a new start. As I was leaving Adare, on the last stage of my journey, I seriously considered driving the car into a wall or a ditch and ending it all. At another time, I came ever so close to steering headlong into an articulated lorry which had been coming towards me. But something, I cannot say what exactly, kept me from doing it and kept me going to my journey's end. It was Friday 31st August 1995.

When I arrived at Maria's house, she showed me to my room and prepared a meal for me. While I was unpacking my clothes, I kept breaking down emotionally and felt completely overwhelmed by the enormity of my situation. I found it impossible to believe it was ever going to get any better. And for awhile, I was right. The whole situation was just too much to cope with and so I resolved to put an end to it for once and for all. There was no question of me ending my life violently; that was for men to do, not me. There would be no hanging, shooting or driving my car into a wall or off a pier. On the contrary, it would be done gently and with dignity, there was to be no mess, just a quiet departure. I thought of how much better off everyone else would be when I was gone. I had absolutely no doubt that my family would have been relieved by my departure from this life. Their consciences would be silenced with my silence. I went to bed around seven o'clock. I took my Rivitril tablets, which I had been prescribed for panic attacks, and nearly all of my supply of Aspirin with some alcohol. Slowly but surely, I became unconscious and my body became cold and turned blue.

It was at this stage that Maria had come to my room to check on me and to see if I had settled in. she knew immediately that something was seriously wrong. She could see that I was unconscious and that my body was changing colour. She saw the empty tablet bottles and knew that I had overdosed on my medication. I can only imagine what went through her mind on discovering me in this condition, but she felt strongly that there was not enough time to get an ambulance, and get me to hospital, so she and her husband Doney took very drastic action to bring me round.

In order to revive me, Maria and Doney dragged me from my bed and took me downstairs. They put me into a very, very cold bath in order to shock me back into consciousness. I started to come in and out of consciousness and as I did Maria poured cider vinegar down my throat. This was to get me to vomit up any tablets that may have been in my stomach. I vomited for quite some time and eventually was taken back to my bed. Maria sat and watched over me that whole night and used a hairdryer to keep my body temperature right. It worked, and I managed to sleep safely and soundly for the rest of the night.

Some people will say that Maria took very serious and dangerous risks in handling the situation as she did, and some might argue that she could have cost me my life. But I am convinced that she did exactly what needed to be done in order to not only save my life but also to prevent me from having to enter a psychiatric ward, which would most certainly have been a blight upon my life to this day; it wasn't for me, and Maria saved me from it. For that I am eternally grateful.

As extraordinary as it seems, Maria made sure that I was able to get up the next morning, in order to make sure that I was able to start a new job which I had secured in the Coach House. She felt it was essential for me to get on with living a normal life and making sure I could earn a living. Was I thankful to her for all she had done, at that time? No, I have to say that I wasn't in the least thankful. On the contrary, I resented having to cope with getting to work as I felt anything but fit for it: all I wanted was to curl up and sleep, forever. But I did start the next day. It is hard to say how I was able to get through my first day and the days thereafter. It is as if I was operating on automatic pilot. But get through it I did and, it did get that bit easier with each passing day. And, even though it was clearly not the job for me, I managed to stick at it as best I could. I was there about three months when my employer came into the office where I was working on his computer. He was really impressed by my computer skills. He said that I should set up a computer training business and train him and others in how to use their computers. I put the idea to Maria and, true to form, she and Doney agreed that it was a really good idea, but more than that, they set up a training room for me at the back of their home and allowed me to use their side entrance for the students to come and go. The room was fabulous and within no time at all I was getting clients. It was very exciting, especially when the FÁS CES Supervisors started to send their employees to me. This was the beginning of a new life for me in my own business.

Maria had the most wonderful garden at the back of the cottage. You could go out the back door and up a narrow path onto the lawn. There were trees which provided shade against the hot summer sun and added a balmy air in the warm afternoons. It was a real little haven and she and Doney took great care of it. It was wonderful to sit and relax, to read a book or just chat to each other, or better yet, just sit and reflect. However, not even this tranquil environment could compensate for the problems that were to arise over the following months; events that could so easily have pushed me completely over the edge again and lead me to attempt suicide again.

I wasn't in Newcastle West long before I started to see the psychiatric consultant. I rarely spent more than ten to fifteen minutes with him after the initial interview. I had told him about my suicide attempt and he told me that he would have to sign me into the psychiatric ward (the infamous 5B) for a minimum of three months, during which time I would be heavily sedated. I told him that this was not an option I was prepared to consider. He replied that I must at least give him a firm undertaking that I would not make another attempt to commit suicide and that I must agree to have my medication supervised. I told him honestly that I could not give him the undertaking as I still very suicidal. He made it clear that without such an undertaking and my unwillingness to consider sedation, that he was not prepared to prescribe me any more medication. I was left to battle my depression, anxiety attacks and suicidal tendencies alone. It was to be like climbing the tallest mountain naked and on my knees. It was truly awful, but I was determined to do it, and I did. I had attended a number of GROW meetings, but very quickly realised they were becoming a crutch that I could not depend on too much. I wasn't happy about repeating the same thing over and over and listening to others doing the same but never actually making any progress or improvement.

After several visits to the consultant I was passed over to a clinical psychologist, whose name escapes me. It was he who urged me to write my story down and then if I wanted, burn it. I thought this to be a waste of time as I would only ever write my story if were to serve a better purpose than just getting everything off my chest.

It was a few weeks after arriving in Newcastle West that I was lying in bed suffering from a nasty bout of gastroenteritis. Maria brought me a letter. It was from my pastor at Grosvenor road Baptist Church. He accused me of leaving Barbara to move in with a doctor. It went on to tell me that should I attend church in the future, I was not welcome to attend the Lord's Table. This was devastating to me. In the fragile state I was in, this very nearly pushed me over the edge; as did a letter from a member of the same church, in which she also accused me of abandoning Barbara. Another Christian from my former church also accused me of the same thing. But rather than go under again I decided to speak up for myself. I wrote a letter to Barbara, in which I confronted her about spreading lies and false accusations for why I left Dublin.

It was to my utter astonishment that, shortly after my autobiography was published that I received a letter from one of these church members. In the letter she apologised to me for believing Barbara, and for writing as she had previously. She also apologised for leaving it so long to write. She told me that she had been visiting Barbara on a regular basis, and how during one of her visits she was shown the letter I'd sent refuting all the false allegations and reminding Barbara about our long unhappy history, her conduct throughout and why I really left Dublin. She told me that she had confronted Barbara about this and asked her directly if what I had written was true. She (Barbara) confirmed that everything in my letter was the truth. Her response was one of utter disgust and deep regret for the hurt she had caused me.

We got to meet a few weeks after receiving her letter. We met in the Swan Shopping Centre in Rathmines. During our meeting, she told me she was deeply saddened at having read my book and discovering the many years of unhappiness and distress I'd been experiencing, especially the fact that I had protected Barbara all that time while she was behaving so badly towards me. She was especially upset at learning of my years of suffering from living in the wrong gender, and the fact that I'd been so badly treated by other Christians. It was probably because of this that she felt able to open her heart to me and share her deepest feelings about how badly she and especially her husband had been treated so badly by these same Christians. She expressed her astonishment at my willingness to forgive my family and others for what they had done. She then told me that she could not forgive those who had treated her husband so badly. Most remarkable of all for me was her comments on how she felt about meeting me in my true gender. She told me I looked beautiful and that she preferred me this way; that I looked far more natural and at ease with myself. We parted on the best of terms. Sadly, I never got to meet her again. I am immensely grateful that we did get to meet and that we were able to be open with each other in ways that would have been impossible before. This was in stark contrast to the other church member, who although she had also seen the same letter chose to continue her animosity towards me.

I moved into a shared house in Portland Drive, where I was able to concentrate on building up my business. I then moved my business into an office on Church Street. The business was doing so well I had to employ several people, so we moved to a much bigger premises across the road, which meant I was able to expand the range of services I could provide, and that we would have our own training rooms. The business was looking good and so was my future. It was a very positive time in my life and I was getting on very well with just about everyone. I was getting an increasing amount of business from FÁS and our presentation of certificate evenings were very well attended and well received. It was around this period that I'd commissioned a competition amongst the students on the Post-Leaving Cert course to design a new sign for my business that would be in keeping with the local Desmond Castle. It was a huge success. I was also involved in organising the Knights of Desmond Festival in 1997. It was one the most successful ever, despite significant doubts on the part of the community and the media, after the previous festival was a disaster. I was proud to be the chairman that year and for making it the great success it was widely acknowledged to have been.

It is fair to say that my hard work and perseverance was finally paying off, and who knows what might have happened had I kept it that way and stayed living on my own. But fate was lurking in the background and was about to lead me to decisions that were to have the most astonishing impacts on my life forevermore.

Chapter Thirteen

Second Chances – The Great Folly

Consuetude est altera natura
Habit is Second Nature
[Auctoritates Aristotelis]

It was in September 1996 when Barbara called me and asked if I would travel to Dublin to meet her as there was something she wanted to ask me. I refused and insisted that if she wanted to see me then she should travel to Limerick instead. She agreed and arrived a few days later. I really wish she hadn't; of course, I had no prescience of how this one decision would create a link of multiple decisions that would ultimately take me to the life I have today.

Barbara arrived on a Wednesday and stayed with me for a few days. The reason she came to see me was to say that she had made the most awful mistake and pleaded with me to give her a second chance. To my eternal regret, I gave her that second chance and paid dearly for doing so. We discussed the possibility of reconciliation by phone over the next few months, as a result of these conversations I agreed to spend Christmas with her in Dublin. She seemed like someone who really had changed and who was anxious to make a go of things; and if truth be told, I really felt sorry for her.

Our Christmas together was pleasant enough and she certainly seemed to be on her best behaviour, so that, slowly but surely, my resistance to giving her a second chance began to wane and it was increasingly difficult to say no. Before returning to Limerick, I had made the decision to say 'yes' and to give her a second chance. In March 1997 she and our two dogs moved to Limerick, where we tried to rebuild our relationship.

We put our house in Dublin up for sale. I did not want to have any attachments to Dublin. Throughout the period of the house being on sale I asked Barbara if she was sure this is what she wanted. She said she was certain and so we continued with the sale. During the months of our separation I'd offered to sign the house over to Barbara as part of an agreement that included my applying to the courts for an annulment. On the day of completion of the sale, I made it absolutely clear to Barbara that if she changed her mind and didn't want to sell the house, to tell me, as I did not want her making a mistake. She assured me that she was happy to go ahead and so we signed the contracts and completed the sale. After we paid off the balance of the mortgage, we divided what remained between us and we were free to spend the money as we chose. I opted to invest it in the business. Barbara invested some of her money in the business, but unfortunately, she squandered a substantial part of it on drinking and smoking. All of this was to come back and haunt me later.

To help us get off to a positive start I booked a weekend in the Silver Springs Guest House in Killarney, where we'd spent the first week of our honeymoon. I distinctly remember driving towards Castleisland with John Denver playing on the car cassette player. I had such terrible feelings of regret: I knew I'd made the most awful blunder in agreeing to give Barbara a second chance; but as I'd made it, I was determined to see it through. I hated it then and I hate it now, not being able to keep my word.

During our time at the Silver Springs, the lovely Mrs O'Rourke reminded me of some things that had occurred while we were there previously. She reminded me of how I had walked all the way into Killarney town just to get cigarettes for Barbara, and she reminded me of how I joined with the family in searching for their dog, and how much they always appreciated me for doing that while on my honeymoon. But then she said something that was quite sad; she told me that they had been observing us and couldn't help noticing how Barbara had behaved towards me and that it was obvious to them that she didn't want to be with me. They were very sad for my situation and felt I deserved better, especially as they witnessed how devoted I'd been to her, and how many times I excused her behaviour.

After about three months of Barbara coming to Newcastle West, we moved to a farmhouse in Rathfredagh. I would like to say that this was our choice to move, but it wasn't. My landlady, with whom I had an extremely good relationship, asked us to leave as a result of Barbara's behaviour, especially the way she allowed the dogs to mess up the house. For the first time in many years I came into contact with rats. The rats appeared shortly after we moved in. Barbara frequently left the doors open for the dogs to come in and out at will, which, of course, was an open invitation to the rats; and they certainly took full advantage of the opportunity. I would come home from work late at night only to see the rats running into the house. While we sat watching television, we would hear the rats in the kitchen. Their droppings would be all over the kitchen table and worktops and in the drawers; everywhere really. No surprise then that I became increasingly ill and frequented my doctor with stomach and bowel problems, not to mention the ever-increasing stress and depression. I was reaping the whirlwind for having given her a second chance. And Barbara's response? Utter indifference. The rats were nothing when it came to the dogs being free to come and go at will.

The rats aside, things really did look like they were going to work out, but after the summer of 1997, Barbara was beginning to show all the signs of reverting to type. She became less interested in me and began talking about how much she fancied one of my brothers! The brother she was interested in was my arch nemesis Fred; the one against whom the gardaí told me to hold my powder dry! She later revealed that she had an interest in our postman and that she regretted us getting back together. I had already figured out that there was something going on with her and the postman, given his behaviour when he saw my car was at the house and when it wasn't.

He would drop the mail at the front door after coming to the back of the house and seeing my car was there, but he would park at the back of the house when my car wasn't there. I saw this happening several times when I would arrive home. It was so obvious what was going on. I eventually confronted Barbara about it but received the expected response.

It was around October when I overheard Barbara on the phone to her sister Mary. She told Mary that she had made a terrible mistake and that she should never have come to Limerick. A few weeks later she showed me a birthday card she was sending to her former lover Ryan, whom she kept in touch with despite trying to save her marriage. The card was completely inappropriate, but as my worst fears were now being realised I did not give much of a reaction.

On a more positive note, the contrast between what was happening in my marriage and what was happening to my public reputation could not have been more different. While Barbara was back to her old ways, the people of Newcastle West were taking me to their hearts, especially after the hugely successful Knights of Desmond Festival. More and more people were recognising my worth, and I felt genuinely respected by the community as a whole. It was only after I'd left that I was to discover just how much I was respected, despite the gossip that followed my leaving and moving to Cork

Christmas 1997 was one of the stormiest for years and it knocked out the electricity around West Limerick. We were without power for five days. My then office manager Geraldine phoned to see if we needed any help with Christmas dinner. I accepted Geraldine and her mother's very kind offer to share their Christmas dinner with us. Because of this we had a pleasant Christmas Day, for which I was very grateful. We passed away the time playing games like Frustration and listening to the radio. Barbara and I talked a lot about the future, it was obvious she regretted coming to Limerick. I already knew this for several months after overhearing her telling her sister Mary about her regrets. And of course, her carries on with the postman!

It was in early February that the whole situation came to a head. Barbara had been in contact with the home help supervisor, who informed her that she would receive all her benefits again if she was living alone. She told me this in a way that left no doubt as to what she wanted me to do. So just to be sure I asked her straight out: 'Are you telling me that you want me to leave so you can get your benefits back?' Her reply was short and very much to the point: 'Well, if you want to, you can, and it would mean I'd get my benefits back. This is not going to work.' This felt really awkward but not anywhere near as bad as when I left Dublin, but in saying that, I was at a loss as to what to do in the situation. What is the point in trying to save a marriage where one person is so intent on ending it? I went around for days with my head in a spin. What was it going to take for me to cop myself on?

I eventually pulled myself together and decided to look for somewhere else to live. Whilst I was coming to terms with things and looking to build a new future away from Barbara, I still felt conflicted about it. It was quite ridiculous really, given that I was not remotely responsible for what had transpired in our wholly dysfunctional relationship; and at this stage I was not a practicing Christian, so that at least no longer informed my decisions and actions. Where I definitely was at fault was my not having the courage and self-worth to do something about it much sooner. But I was in a new state of mind and as a result, things were about to take a dramatic turn, which would eventually lead to another series of decisions that eventually led me to making the most unimaginable and positive changes I could ever have thought possible.

I met the lovely Kathy O'Sullivan in April 1998. Kathy is the mother of one of my former employees. I met her after dropping him off after a day's training in Ennis County Clare. When I first met her, I was immediately struck with her beauty and by her aura, which is truly amazing and very affecting. She was a true mother and homemaker and had all the qualities that were missing in my own mother, and so I was very drawn to her. She was also by far the most feminine woman I'd ever met in my life, bar none. She very quickly found a place in my heart, which she still holds to this day.

When I met Kathy, I had no idea that she was going to have the most profound effect upon my life. It is no exaggeration to say that Kathy did more to help me develop a better sense of myself than any other person I'd ever met, again, bar none. I would visit her often and enjoyed her company immensely; we had many things in common and I felt we could be very good friends and companions, which I am proud to say is what we became.

When Barbara was introduced to Kathy and her family, she saw how well we got on and did everything she could to encourage it, for motives she was soon to reveal. I genuinely resented her attempts at encouraging me to have an affair with Kathy, as that is not at all what I was interested in, or, how I felt. When I challenged her on it she unashamedly told me that she was seeing our postman! I can't say I was surprised, but I was taken aback by her delight at telling me. As I got to know more about Kath's life I learned about her unhappiness and the many terrible things that had been done to her and the more I learned, the more convinced I became that we were in the same boat, especially with our being trapped in unhappy marriages.

As the situation with Barbara was deteriorating and I was struggling to keep my business going, I was unaware of my being in a state of depression. It was so bad that I felt I needed to get away altogether, and so decided not just to leave Barbara but to also leave West Limerick altogether and start over somewhere else. This decision was to result in some later difficulties but moving away from West Limerick and from Barbara was to mark the end of my days as Thomas Duffy and open the way for me to finally emerge as the woman I was always meant to be.

I told Kathy of my decision to leave West Limerick altogether. To my amazement, she replied that she, too, wanted to get away and have some time to herself to think about what she wanted to do with her life. So, I started to look for a suitable place to live and to set up another business. While I was reading the Irish Examiner, I came across a business opportunity in Midleton. I asked Kathy if she would be interested in coming with me to look into it, and so we travelled to Midleton on a Saturday in August to meet the man who had placed the ad. When we got to Midleton we took to it immediately. I had a meeting with the man who had the IT training room. It was above a jeweller shop on the main street. We also viewed offices at the Rosehill Business Centre in Ballinacurra. I wasn't convinced that either property was suitable, but I was undeterred and went to see an estate agent on the main street. And, low and behold, I found an apartment in Coolbawn Court. I decided to go for it. I was on a high with the possibilities and felt very optimistic about my future. No matter what might happen with the business opportunities, I was determined to make a fresh start and move to Midleton. I told Kathy of my decision and told her she was welcome to come with me if she wished.

Over the next several weeks I did everything I could to get the deposit and first month's rent. It was really tough, but I managed to do it. However, I had a mere £800 in total to bring with me when we moved to Midleton, on the 18th September 1998. Kathy's decision to move to Midleton was entirely her own. There was no question of us living together. It was entirely about Kathy having somewhere to stay and clear her head before deciding her next step, which was most likely to go to England and stay with one of her sisters.

In moving into the same apartment, Kathy and I would lay ourselves open to rumour and accusation, but the truth of the matter is, we were two unhappy people whose friendship would sustain us through difficult times. And we remain friends to this day. It is entirely understandable that her family were deeply upset when she left Newcastle West. It is even understandable that they and her so-called friends misunderstood the true nature of our situation as it was then. It was Kathy's own decision to try and find a new life for herself; that was entirely her right and it should have been respected. I had heard of the vulgar comments and accusations being made about me, but I comforted myself with the truth and held steadfast to the fact that I knew how things really were.

Chapter Fourteen

Starting Over

Home, home, sweet, sweet home!
There's no place like home! There's no place like home!
The Maid of Milan [J.H. Payne]

When we moved to Midleton, my only income was £160, which I received as a wage from my business in Newcastle West. The reason it was so low was to make sure that all my staff's wages were paid. The £160 per week had to keep us both in food and rent until I completed the sale of my business in Newcastle West, to one of my own employees. I sold it at a ridiculous price, but it was the best I could do at the time, and I didn't want it dragging on. I used the proceeds from the sale to start up a new business, MetaCom Consultancy Services. I moved into the premises at Coolbawn in November 1998, a couple of months after we moved to Midleton, where I was doing ECDL computer training, Health and Safety and the Personal Development courses for FAS, just as I had been in Newcastle West. In fact, I was the first person to bring ECDL training to Midleton along with the first accredited test centre.

I had been told by the owner of the training centre on the main street how difficult it would be to do business in a town like Midleton. And I would have to agree that it did prove tough at times. I won't lie and say that I never experienced difficulties, however, for the most part I was very well received in Midleton; so much so that I made some wonderful friends there.

It was only several weeks after moving to Midleton that I came face to face with the extent of my depression. I had been struggling with my growing debts, and the situation with Kathy was becoming increasingly tense, due in no small part to her not coping with the new situation and being very unsure of me and my intentions, and vice-versa. It was of course an extremely stressful time for both of us. No amount of getting on with things could ultimately hide the fact that we were really struggling with what was in every sense of the word, a very strange time. It was during this period when I made the first of four attempts to commit suicide. I went into the river beside our apartment to drown myself. We had gone out for a drink with Kathy's son and his girlfriend. Something was said that upset me and so I left the restaurant in a very agitated state and went for a walk. I really had no idea until then just how depressed and fragile I had become. Something snapped that night which left me feeling in a state of utter despair. And the feeling of aloneness was simply beyond description. I just wanted it all to stop and so went down into the river. But as in the case of going into the sea at Lahinch, I realised how awful it would be for Kathy, so I left the river and went back to the apartment; only to be greeted by two gardaí. Kathy had reported me missing. she must have sensed how bad I was and was worried enough to contact the gardaí.

The pressure I'd been under from work, our financial difficulties and Kathy's constantly moving back and forth to Newcastle West continued taking its toll on me. The reason why her going back home mattered so much and why it was so distressing was, I had fallen madly in love with her and desperately wanted to have a permanent future with her. And I thought the feeling was mutual. So, when she started returning home to Limerick it was more than I could bear. I was distraught, and not at all able to cope. On several occasions, while she was in Limerick, I took an overdose of tablets and alcohol, and three times I was found in time to be taken to hospital.

I must say something about my experiences while in all three hospitals, CUH, The Mercy and The Royal Victoria. The treatment I received from the staff in all three was not very nice and only added to my distress. In fact, it is fair to say that some (not all) of the doctors and nurses were quite unsympathetic and abrupt, and made it very clear that they disapproved of my being there. They were not in any way supportive; quite the contrary, they made me feel disapproved of and humiliated.

It was also around this time that the issue of my real gender identity resurfaced once again. It came completely out of the blue one day after a disclosure from Kathy. She told me that during one of her visits to see Barbara, she was shown my women's clothes and undies. But she was never told by Barbara why they were there. This understandably left Kathy feeling very confused, however she said nothing to me until a few months after we'd moved to Midleton. She came home from Newcastle West one day and noticed that her dresses were hanging differently in the wardrobe but wasn't exactly sure why. Then there was an occasion when we were out shopping in Roches Stores in Cork. Kathy saw me looking at some lingerie on one of the mannequins and becoming very agitated. She got the strange idea that I was going to attack the thing, which, of course, was absurd. However, she was right about me being uncomfortable in the situation; how could I have been otherwise, given everything I was feeling inside. She was also right in observing that I showed little or no interest in men's clothes; it was entirely functional when I did. I absolutely loved shopping with Kathy, but the downside was the frustration I felt every time I could not buy the clothes I really wanted.

One of my greatest difficulties, and something that really hurt me at the time was being accused of eyeing up other women while we were out together. She noticed how I'd be looking at them while driving or walking about. She interpreted this as my "fancying anything in a skirt." I found this very upsetting because nothing could have been further from the truth. What I was doing was looking at what women were wearing and picking up ideas on what and what not to wear for my height and shape etc.

A few days after the incident with the mannequin, Kathy questioned me about my reaction and her clothes being rearranged. It was as clear as day that the subject could no longer be avoided and that the time had come to confide in her about the problem I'd been having with my gender conflict – or cross-dressing as I understood it at the time. Why did I leave it so long to tell her? Because I wasn't sure if she was going to be staying around or if she was going to England to her sister; and because my situation was far too sensitive to be telling people about it, only to find myself alone after telling them and seeing them walk away. This after all is one of the most terrifying things to deal with for those who disclose their struggles with their gender identity. It is an extraordinarily lonely place for a person to be in, not to forget humiliating. It should come as no surprise then to learn that the number of gender dysphoric (transgender) people attempting suicide is four times the national average. But hardly a word is ever said about it! I hope my story helps to address the subject in a way that takes this aspect of gender identity out of the darkness and into the light, where it is safe for people with gender dysphoria to live safe and happy lives.

I finally plucked up the courage to tell Kathy of the lifetime I'd spent living with the stress of feeling like a woman in a man's body and my need to dress accordingly. In doing this, I was about to do one of the most frightening things I've ever done in my life. What made it so terrifying was that I really enjoyed having Kathy in my life and so what I was about to do could literally destroy our friendship forever, especially as I couldn't give a precise reason for why I felt this overwhelming sense of being in the wrong body. Like so many others, I didn't know the exact reason for feeling as I did, but I was certain that I'd been living in the wrong body. What was happening now though was about to change all that. And it all started with one simple (or not so simple) suggestion. However, before I say what that suggestion was, I want to point out that this was undoubtedly the single-most turning point in my life. Everything that has happened from here on can be attributed to this one suggestion and the words spoken after I did as Kathy suggested.

Kathy said she wanted to see what the dressing was about and suggested that I try on one of her dresses and use her makeup. She waited downstairs while I nervously dressed and put on the makeup. I didn't have a wig to wear and felt really weird and stressed. I had a sense of this being the moment of truth and a point of no return, regardless of how she reacted.

I came down the stairs, watching her reaction as I came into view. Her face said it all and it was evident that she was immediately upset by what she saw, but not for the reasons I'd imagined. I thought I looked like a freak to her, but what she saw was summed up in her own words: 'you're definitely a woman and you need to do something about this. You'll have to go and see someone about this.' She also told me that she was very distressed at seeing a completely different person in front of her and that even my voice had changed and that she was scared. And she looked every bit of it, so I immediately went and changed back into my own clothes.

It really is hard to say that the experience was in any way enjoyable, but it certainly marked the beginning of the end of my having to live in the wrong body. Kathy overcame her initial distress and, from that moment on, whenever we went shopping she would encourage me to buy my own women's clothes, and she helped me choose what would suit me most. I had some very funny, and frightening moments, when shopping with her. She would forget who she was talking to and spoke to me just like any other woman, even though I wasn't dressed that way. We would be looking at something and she would turn and say, 'You should get that, it would look really good on you.' The only problem was that other women would be standing close-by and would look over at us, wondering why she was talking to me like that. I would go red and nudge Kathy. She would say that she just felt natural about it, and that it was none of their business. Wow!

The more we shopped, the more clothes I bought, and I began to dress more frequently. Whenever Kathy was away, and we spoke by phone, she would ask me if I was dressed. I would ask her how she knew:

'Because your voice always changes.' I honestly hadn't realised that it had and it made me think about what would happen if I lived every day of my life as the woman I felt inside. I didn't dress everyday as that would have been impractical, but I did every chance I got, and it felt more comfortable every time.

I was doing some personal development courses for FÁS Community Employment Schemes. It was while doing these courses that people noticed certain telling female traits coming through. As I discussed various issues regarding relationships, it was very obvious as to where I stood. The women on the course were at a loss to understand how I knew so much about being a woman and this struck them as extremely odd. Never once during these courses did I ever let on about my gender struggles, but that didn't stop them from noticing and questioning my motives.

I remember two instances in particular. One was a course I taught in Ennis, Co Clare. As the course progressed, the women began to question how I knew so much about being a woman. I couldn't explain it to them other than to say it came from experience, which was partly true, but how could I explain the rest of it when I didn't fully understand it myself; it was just second nature to me. At the end of the course, I received a cake and a massive-sized Thank You card which everyone signed. One of the ladies wrote: *'keep something for yourself'*. As it turns out, she was a counsellor and so would have known if I was merely bullshitting everyone. She came to me on the day we finished and told me she was hugely impressed and thought I would do well as a trainer. I was so encouraged by this, especially at a time when I had made myself open to being misunderstood and humiliated.

The second instance was a Health and Safety course I taught in Mitchelstown for the staff of a well-known local paper. One of the course modules was manual handling. As part of the demonstration, I had to show the women the incorrect way to lift loads. Women have a very different method of lifting to men: the locked-knees' method and the side-and-twist method. They are distinctly feminine and completely different from the way which men lift. There is simply no mistaking the difference, and you really have to be a woman to lift a certain way. When I was demonstrating the incorrect method to the ladies, one of them literally said: 'Is there something you want to tell us?'I immediately replied with a very red face, 'Yes, but not right now.' Ultimately, when my disclosure was made, I understand that there was a lot of delight amongst some of these women, because they had known that something was different about me that now finally made sense. And who could blame them?

Before I got to this point, however, I would have to go lower than I ever had before. As mentioned previously, there were other occasions when I attempted to commit suicide. On three occasions, I took an overdose of tablets and downed a lot of alcohol. My last attempt was in 2001. I couldn't cope with the strain my situation was putting on my friendship with Kathy and the constant stress from trying to earn a living. Then there was the problem of Barbara's resisting my application for an annulment of our marriage, despite her having agreed to it previously.

I felt extremely fortunate to have someone as strong as Kathy with me, or so I thought. I was mistaken, and soon came to realise that she was not as strong as I'd assumed. She too was clearly very distressed and very angry at what was happening with my gender identity and my suicide attempts; the whole situation really. But she clearly did not understand the depth of my anxieties and the seriousness of my depression. And I regret to say, neither had I realised how she was also suffering from stress. One of the truly awful aspects of being depressed is how it makes us so self-consumed, which can be to the detriment of those around us; this was certainly the case with myself and Kathy.

As a man I was expected to be the strong one all the time, but that really was impossible; not least because I was really a woman, and a very sensitive one at that, who was finding it increasingly intolerable trying to behave like the man I was expected to be. What mattered was that I get on with trying to run my business, so I could keep a roof over our heads and food on the table, and deal with Barbara's legal team giving me a most awful time.

The whole situation was getting to Kathy and brought her to breaking point. Her husband had died, and she was feeling very torn between wanting a new life and missing her children. She was also struggling with the horrible things people had been saying about her and the fact that her so-called friends had abandoned her. Not one of them ever tried to make contact with her after she left Limerick, nor did they ever try to find out why she left. She was extremely hurt by this, and rightly so. She also felt extremely guilty about having left her children, even though they were all adults at the time. So, she really didn't need to be coping with all my shit when she had her own problems to deal with. I certainly did try as much as possible to help, but I didn't have the answers or the resources she needed. Something had to give, and it did. Kathy returned to Limerick and her family. I was certain this was for the final time, and so once again I was on my own. I honestly could not see any way through the seemingly endless difficulties, which once again brought me to thoughts of suicide as being the only way out. Of course, it was not, but when you reach such a low point and all around you seems utterly dark and hopeless, you see suicide as a final relief for yourself and those you leave behind. It is of course a distorted way of thinking, but it seems so logical and reasonable at a time when no other solutions are on offer. And, so it was, that I once again decided to end my life, believing as I did that I would not be missed by anyone, especially not by my family.

It was on a Sunday afternoon when I made myself ready. Before I went ahead I did try to contact Kathy in the hope of telling her how I was feeling and that she might be able to offer me some hope and comfort, but she was not answering her phone. In my hyper-sensitive state of mind, I thought it was because she didn't want to talk to me. I got the message and was determined to succeed this time. However, what I didn't know as I downed the tablets and the whiskey was, that

Kathy was already on her way back to Midleton with her daughter and her daughter's boyfriend. They arrived at the apartment only to find me in a semi-conscious state. I was taken by ambulance to the Mercy Hospital. Even in my semi-conscious state I was able to see how angry Kathy was and how she'd had enough of my persistent efforts to kill myself. Those with her wanted her to leave me there and have nothing more to do with me, even the nurse and doctor attending me in the hospital said it to her, but to her great credit and my eternal gratitude, she chose to stick by me and reassure me that everything would be okay.

I was kept in overnight for observation and Kathy was to collect me around lunchtime the next day. I slept right through to the morning. I spent the entire morning reflecting on what I'd done. This was to be my sixth and final attempt. I remember thinking that I wasn't very competent at ending my life, or, I was clearly not meant to die, and there must therefore be some purpose to my life. I thought of all the reasons why I felt so depressed and came to the conclusion that I had to stop seeking approval from everyone around me, which was partly responsible for my living a false life. Most importantly though, I also finally accepted that I could not go on living as a man and that I was going to have to find the courage and determination to do something about it. I didn't have a clue where to start but start I must. It was with this new resolve that I went home to Midleton determined to turn all the horribleness that had gone before into something positive

Another thing which helped me at the time was a radio interview I did with the lovely Ger McLoughlin at the RTÉ studios in Cork. That was in 2001. Describing me as a very gentle and kind man, the interview was about how I was struggling to deal with my depression without the help of medication or psychiatric intervention, as I was absolutely certain that my depression was not clinically related. This decision helped me to realise that, even in my depression, I was on a journey of discovery. The interview had a very positive effect on me, so much so that it changed my perception from one of fear and dread to one of purpose and determination.

It was in this much more positive state of mind that I resolved to look for the help I needed to deal with my gender problem and to remain steadfast in my belief that my marriage should be annulled; nothing else was going to do me now. I resolved to use my suicide attempts for the good of myself and for others. I used them as a barometer of the true nature and extent of my own difficulties: nothing could bring me as low again as when I was sitting on that hospital bed alone. It worked then and continues to work now.

The defining moment came when I went onto the internet and typed in words like, 'transgendered', 'transsexual', 'cross-dressing' and 'Ireland'. The result was a number of e-groups that offered support for people with gender problems. Diane Hughes was among the contact names I found. It was Diane who gave me the name of Dr James Kelly, a clinical psychologist specialising in gender identity. She also gave me his phone number and encouraged me to make an appointment with him. She bemoaned the fact, rightly, that Dr. Kelly was only one of three specialists in Ireland helping people struggling with gender issues. I promised her that I would make an appointment, but I didn't, at least not at that time. In fact, it was to be another two years before I would contact him; this was for several reasons, one was a lack of courage, the second was I simply wasn't ready, and third was my fear of losing Kathy if I went ahead and did something definite about resolving my gender issues.

I spent the intervening period building my business and dealing with my depression. I did not seek a medical intervention however, as I did not believe I had clinical depression. Once I made my decision never to attempt suicide again, I found an inner determination and strength to see it through. I decided to put a plan in place to build a new life for myself and started by giving Kathy all the reassurances I could that I would never put her through that kind of distress again. Another of my plans was to develop a much more positive state of being, both in mind and body, and to rebuild my health and wellbeing. This involved making contact with my parents in order to give them one last chance to reconcile with me and if they didn't, then it was going to be fine. I was determined not to keep carrying the weight of hurt, which they had caused, on my shoulders any longer.

I started to dress more frequently but still hadn't made an appointment with Dr Kelly, partly due to my business keeping me very busy and the whole situation with the annulment of my marriage to Barbara. The Legal Aid Board had finally assigned me a solicitor to deal with my application for nullity. I was busy preparing discoveries and affidavits for the courts. In the meantime, we also had to move house a couple of times during this period, from Midleton to Castlemartyr and back to Midleton. It was while in Midleton that I secured a two-year contract as Associate Faculty Lecturer with the National College of Ireland. This came completely out of the blue. It followed my stepping in at very short notice for a lecturer at the Crescent College in Limerick. The lecture was a great success; and in spite of having very little time to prepare, all of my students got through their assignments successfully. I received excellent feedback from the college, which pleased me greatly. They contacted me afterwards to offer me a contract. I did not have to do an interview as they were sufficiently impressed with the job I'd done after stepping in for their lecturer. The next year I was given another contract. Things were definitely looking up.

When I received news that I was to get a contract, Kathy and I decided to go to the Midleton Park Hotel to celebrate. We discussed so many things that night, but one subject really stands out and that was the name I should go by if I decided to go ahead and live as a woman. I preferred the name Jenny, but Kathy felt that the name did not suit me, that Sara-Jane suited me a lot better. I agreed and felt that she had given me a very precious gift. Her support had meant the world to me and so it was a terrible loss to me when she finally returned to live in Limerick, following some really bad advice from her GP, who knew sod all about me and even less about gender dysphoria. But at least she was with me when I first went to see Dr Kelly and later when I stepped out for the first time as Sara-Jane. This is probably a good time to mention that her GP was not alone in suggesting she leave me. There were plenty of others doing the same thing, but in their case, it was about my age and how I was supposedly only with her for money, while for others, the men, they were interested in her for themselves, so they did what they could to undermine me. The fact is, I was never interested in her money. Money has never been and never will be a motivation for me to be in a relationship with anyone. Regardless, the weight of these people's, especially the GPs advice were to finally work against me, and so it was that Kathy finally moved back to Limerick permanently. She did visit me from time to time, but of course nothing was the same afterwards. The fact is I was utterly devastated to find myself abandoned at the most vulnerable of times in my life, by the person who meant more to me than any other, bar none. I was knocked back and knocked down by Kathy's departure. But as has so often been the case before, I was not going to stay down. I was going to get back up and go forward, and that is precisely what I did.

Chapter Fifteen

Being Myself – The Beginning

And above all these things to thine own self be true
Hamlet [Shakespeare]

It was August 2003 and I was driving to Dublin full of apprehension and excitement. I was finally going to get to the heart of why I felt so much like and needed to dress as a woman. I had often thought that all of this was due to some maladjustment during puberty and adolescence and that it had something to do with my sexuality and my inability to determine whether I was heterosexual, gay or bi-sexual. I was completely open to whatever Dr Kelly had to tell me and was very happy to resolve the situation for once and for all, especially if it meant finally coming to terms with my need to be and dress as a woman. This was a really big deal and I had a sense that all those years of praying and fasting might finally be answered for once and for all.

Dr Kelly took me by surprise with his rather conservative views on the issues we discussed, which actually gave me a lot of reassurance. I felt secure in whatever he had to say, and I was genuinely prepared to be told that my problem was nothing more than a compulsion to cross-dress. Now that I was here I wanted to put this all behind me and move on with my life. But in order for that to happen I had to be absolutely honest with him. I told him that I was cross-dressing and that I felt it could be because of a maladjusted adolescence. I was open to find out the reason and getting whatever help I could to resolve the matter. Then I said, 'But if you were to ask me how I really feel, then I would have to say that I feel like a woman inside.'

Dr Kelly suggested we start at the beginning and asked about my family background. As the interview went on, my body language changed completely as did my voice. I was so relaxed that my female personality came out, despite all my efforts to hold it back. Why? Because I didn't want to contrive a situation where I would get the diagnosis I wanted. I had a very good idea of what was at stake and so wanted there to be no doubt whatsoever about his conclusions.

Dr Kelly told me that he would have to carry out a second assessment before he could give me a diagnosis. I had to return in a couple of weeks, and it was some wait I can tell you. I spent the whole time imagining what Dr Kelly was going to say to me and how my life was going to be affected once he did. I tried to imagine him telling me that I was a woman in a man's body, and where that news would take me, not the least being any decisions I might have to make about gender reassignment and what it would entail.

I returned to see Dr Kelly, but this time I wasn't alone. Kathy accompanied me for moral support, which was probably just as well, given the enormity of the news I was about to receive. Dr Kelly diagnosed me as having Gender Identity Disorder, later to be known as Gender Dysphoria. He also made it clear that from the moment I arrived for my first assessment that he had no doubt in his mind that I had a female gender identity, but that he was not able to state it definitively until he had completed his assessments. So, I'm not a freak or a mental case, I had a real congenital, Gender Dysphoria. It is about how my brain developed as female while my body was male. Thankfully something could be done about it, but that something was anything but easy or straightforward.

No sooner did I get my diagnosis than I was discussing being referred to Dr Donal O'Shea, the Endocrinologist at St Colmcille's Hospital in Loughlinstown, to commence hormone treatment and the gender reassignment process. I was also to undergo a second psychiatric evaluation to confirm Dr Kelly's diagnosis. But there was one other very important matter: I was required to come as Sara-Jane on my next visit to Dr Kelly. Oh, my god! I thought. It is one thing to know myself to be a woman trapped in the wrong body and having the longing to be set free to live my life as I was meant to live it; but it is quite another to actually dress fully as that woman and go out in public, something I hadn't done all my life! But everything I'd been through over my lifetime was pointing to taking this one great step; to step into the world as my true self, as Sara-Jane, and despite all the difficulties I anticipated along the way, I was completely determined to do it. I asked Kathy if she would come with me on my next appointment. To my absolute delight she agreed. I was so happy and appreciative of her being with me that it gave me the courage I needed to go through with it.

My next appointment to Dr Kelly took place on a clammy November day. I could hardly sleep the night before between the excitement and the terror. I got up about 5.30a.m. and got myself ready. I had breakfast but could hardly eat on account of being so nervous. I wore a white blouse with jeans and boots, a long grey coat with a fabulous fur (false fur of course!) hat. As I took one last look in the mirror before leaving, I was rooted to the spot; there was a momentary panic. All the times I'd dressed and put on my make-up was behind closed doors; they were never like this; how could they be? This was it. This was me going out into the world as Sara-Jane for the very first time. I had to do everything I could not to burst into tears. I had no idea where this was going to take me; I just knew it was now or never. We left for Dublin about 7.30 a.m. but not until after I'd made numerous trips to the bathroom. The only good thing about the journey was being in my car. I was warm and sweaty. I would normally make one stop on the way to Dublin, but this time I had to stop about five times!

We eventually reached Dublin and headed towards Capel Street Bridge. My nerves were getting the better of me, but as I was bursting to go to the toilet again I didn't have time to worry about them. We went to the toilets in the Jervis Street Shopping Centre. I was so nervous imagining what would happen to me when I got there that I hadn't thought about my first culture shock as a woman, which as it turned out was waiting in a queue to use the women's toilets! I was the most self-conscious I had ever been in my life while standing in that queue. My entire body was stiff with terror and I was in full flight mode as I stood in line. But I needn't have worried as just one young teenager looked at me. I thought this was very strange, as I had expected more people to stare and ridicule me. I know that this is going to sound strange, but, while I sat in that cubicle, I felt like I really belonged, and oh my, did it feel good, and amazingly peaceful. But as I was leaving the toilets I was overcome with panic. I kept my head down and rushed out of the shopping centre and back to the car.

Poor Kathy was taken aback as she could see nothing wrong, and no one looking at me. She suggested we go for a walk as this would give me the chance to calm down and relax before going into Dr Kelly. We walked along the boardwalk on the Liffey. As we headed back towards Capel Street Bridge a man was walking towards us. He was looking towards me and seemed to be saying something. Of course, I thought he had sussed me and was saying something rude, but as he got nearer he looked straight at me and said: 'I was just saying to myself, that you're a very lovely looking lady.' 'Oh my gosh! Oh my gosh!' is all I could say in response, while Kathy said: 'There you are now, and there was you wondering what people would think.'

It was five minutes past two and we headed for Dr Kelly's office. I went in ahead of Kathy and when I entered Dr Kelly's office, he just kept looking at me as if I was a total stranger. 'Hi there, sorry I'm late,' I said. He just kept looking at me and said, 'I'm sorry but I'm expecting someone else, but their appointment isn't until half-two.' It was at this point that Kathy came through the door and then the penny dropped for Dr Kelly. 'Is that you Sara-Jane?' I confirmed that it was in fact me and thanked him for not recognising me. He told me that I looked very impressive and very passable, especially as this was my first time ever out in public. He said I was already 80% of the way there, even at what was essentially my very first step in living my life as a woman. He then proceeded to take me through the various stages of my reassignment. One of the stages involved a tracheal shave, that is, having my Adam's apple shaved in order to give me a female shape to my neck. 'But I don't have an Adam's apple.' He was very surprised about this. He said it was going to be a significant advantage going forward.

He then asked Kathy how she felt about it all, to which she replied that it was my life, but that she couldn't understand why as a woman I would still be looking at other women. Dr Kelly explained that it is perfectly normal for women to look at other women, especially as women always compare themselves to each other — what they wear, their hair, their figures etc — and that it was entirely natural for me as a woman, even trapped inside a man's body, to be making the same comparisons and trying to imagine what it would be like to look like those women. He also tried to explain that my gender identity had nothing to do with my sexuality. I was delighted to let him say all this as I'd been trying to explain it to her but was getting nowhere. She had been listening to all kinds of opinions from her friends and acquaintances in Cork and Limerick; who, though they knew nothing about my situation nor gender dysphoria, were telling her that I was just doing this for sex; that I was gay and that I wasn't prepared to admit it. She also had to listen to other vulgar and disgusting remarks which can't have been nice and which are unrepeatable here.

I got to see Donal O'Shea, the endocrinologist, in February 2004. He did his assessment for hormone treatment, but before he could proceed he needed to get a second diagnosis, so he referred me to Dr James Lucey at St Patrick's Hospital in Inchicore. I met Dr Lucey's colleague, she was very warm and pleasant and, though the assessment was very difficult emotionally, she made it less stressful than it could otherwise have been. The longer the assessment went on, the more emotional I became and cried quite a bit. The whole situation was overwhelming for me. The doctor was amazed at the transformation taking place in front of her eyes as once again my body language and voice changed, which is what usually happened once I didn't have to hide my true gender from people. She was in no doubt as to the soundness of my diagnosis and so went in to speak to Dr Lucey. She was gone a while so I used the time to contemplate the various stages of the process still in front of me and whether I would have the courage to see the whole thing through, especially when I imagined the reactions I was likely to receive from my family, friends, my clients and strangers.

Dr Lucey eventually arrived in with the doctor who had assessed me. He told me that, based on the information I had given, he would have no problem confirming Dr Kelly's diagnosis. Then he asked me a strange question: 'Would you not think of staying as you are and not going ahead with having the reassignment surgery?' I immediately responded by saying that this was not a sexual thing for me, that it wasn't a fetish, that I hadn't come all this way not to complete my reassignment. He then asked me how I felt at the prospect of losing my genitals. Again, my response was immediate. I told him I couldn't wait to have the body I knew I should have had since I was a child and that nothing would be allowed to dissuade me from that. He seemed pleased. He then said, 'I wish you the very best, Sara-Jane, you have a very interesting journey ahead of you.'

The meeting with Dr Lucey and his colleague was extremely difficult and I was emotionally and mentally exhausted from it, but I also felt that I had achieved something monumental in demonstrating my determination to see all this through. I was prepared to put myself through these gruelling evaluations, even if it meant constantly retelling my history and having to recount the long years of abuse. It was really hard, but it was so worth it to get to this stage of my journey. Every single stage of this process was proving to be slow and difficult and a constant test of my resolve. There were, over time, so many reasons I could have given for deciding not to go ahead, but giving up would have been a fate worse than death.

In making their diagnoses, Dr Kelly and Dr Lucey had to consider the possibility of what are called <u>contra-indications</u>. These are other possible explanations for my persistent sense of being a woman in a man's body. For example, they had to look at the possibility of a maladjusted adolescence, a failure to come to terms with my sexuality or over-exposure to female company and influences. Then there was the need to consider the possibility of fetish tendencies, such as cross-dressing and transvestism. In the case of Dr Lucey, he had to look at the possibility of psychiatric disorders that could lead me mistakenly to believe myself to be a female born into the wrong body. Once they had satisfied themselves that these had been safely eliminated they were able to make their diagnosis of Gender Dysphoria.

It is extremely important to remember that a person presenting for a diagnosis of Gender Dysphoria must have at least two years of persistent discomfort living in the role of the opposite gender and demonstrate that this is the only possible explanation. This was a no-brainer in my case as I have had this throughout my life.

On Thursday 20 June 2004 I returned to Dr Donal O'Shea. He was satisfied that everything was in order and gave me my first prescription for hormones. Dr O'Shea advised me that I would become very emotional and experience mood swings as a result of taking the hormones. I told him that I was already very emotional in a female kind of way. We had a good laugh about it. I was started on Premarin (oestrogen) and aspirin; the aspirin was to stop my blood from clotting. I started on the lowest dosage of Premarin for a number of months in order to allow my body to get used to it. A few months later I was prescribed twice the dose, which I remained on for about a year. It was a surprise to find I'd reached normal female hormone levels over such a short time. I did notice, though, after I started the Premarin, that my palpitations returned for the first time in many years. This made me wonder about the connection between the palpitations I'd suffered during my adolescence and my monthly breakouts of female acne, and if this was a result of having higher-than-normal levels of female hormones back then.

I was later prescribed Zoladex, to kill off any remaining testosterone in my body. It was a monthly injection, into my tummy, just below my navel. The needle is about two inches in length. I opted to inject myself, this was to avoid long waits in my doctor's surgery and it also helped to keep my costs down. Gender reassignment was hugely expensive and many people, myself included, could ill afford it. One of the major effects of Zoladex is that it significantly reduced my libido, which, quite frankly, was a great blessing. This is extremely important to me as it shows that going through gender reassignment is not a sexual matter. Another benefit of Zoladex was that it softens the skin and facial features. These changes have been noticed by many people which gave me great confidence in how I look.

Of course, one of the biggest benefits was seeing my breasts grow. Thirty-three years I'd waited for this; thirty-three years before my body could feel in some way normal. It was one of the most joyful things in the world for me and made me long for the final stage of my transition even more, my gender realignment surgery. I had seen the surgery being performed and what happens afterwards for those who have gone through it. It is hard to express the sheer joy and ecstasy that I felt at the thought that that will be me one day. Little did I know how long it would take to get to the final stage of my journey and the many obstacles I would still have to overcome.

In thinking about the final step in my transition, I have had to consider where to go to have my realignment surgery carried out. As things stood, I had three options, being referred to Charing Cross in London, to Leicester General or go to Thailand. Going to Thailand meant going private, and though it was not as expensive as going to the UK, it was still quite expensive. Also, there were very serious risks in travelling so far away for such major surgery, especially if there were to be any post-surgical complications. There were no post-surgical supports here in Ireland for people who go to Thailand for their surgeries. I've seen first-hand what can happen when someone goes that far away, especially when they have not thought it through. Going to the UK was much slower and involved having to go through a whole lot more evaluation and re-evaluation, which could be very frustrating and discouraging for those who had already gone through the evaluation process here in Ireland. However, I found it very reassuring that they were so thorough and meticulous about it, ensuring that people were certain about what they were doing. For me, there was absolutely no doubt, and I recognised that the process had to be thorough, despite the frustrations. Given my public role in raising awareness and wanting to encourage people to act responsibly in getting the best care possible, it was important for me to set a good example throughout my own transition, which I hoped would be of benefit to others.

It was extremely difficult going out in public and going to work every day. Meeting my clients and explaining my situation to them was especially challenging as was shopping and meeting my friends. all that potential for stress, panic attacks and freaking out. There were plenty of reasons to give up and to revert to living as a male, but what a horrible thought; it's enough to make me keep going. The thought of going back was too god awful to think about.

One of the key pain barriers to cross in gender reassignment is removal of facial hair by laser treatment. It is so painful and not for the faint-hearted. I had my whole face done each session. The results were worth all the pain; even looking like a Martian with all the green Aloe Vera gel spread over my face. I looked quite the sight stopping at traffic lights, with other drivers looking in at my green face. I just hummed away to myself, delighted that I had withstood yet another torture session. Everything was a milestone.

Buying clothes was tricky so it was great having Kathy come along and advise me on what did and didn't look right on me. Most of my shopping was done in Evans and Marks & Spencer's, as they sell to the larger-sized lady. They are also friendly towards people with gender dysphoria. I was size 24-26 when I started out and was determined to get my weight down, which I've managed to do; so much so that I'm able to buy my clothes from high-street boutiques. I've come down to size 14-16, and am not far of a size 14, which is ideal for my 6.1 height.

I know I have mentioned this elsewhere, but it is worth pointing out here that for people who are genuinely gender dysphoric and who have gone through the required clinical assessment and diagnostic process, that going through the transitioning process, including hormone treatment and gender realignment surgery, is the *prescribed* pathway for realigning the bodies with their internal gender identity. This is why I believe gender dysphoria should never be included under trans terms.

Chapter Sixteen

Blood is Thicker than Water, My Arse!

Against stupidity, the very gods fight un-victorious
Letters and speeches of Oliver Cromwell [Thomas Carlyle]

Another huge milestone for those of us with Gender Dysphoria is telling our families and friends about it and then having to cope with their reactions. It can be hard for them to understand that our gender identity is congenital and neurobiological and not a lifestyle choice or a fetish, and not just a phase we will get over at some point in the future.

But as difficult as it might be for them, it is infinitely more difficult for those who have to tell them. I first told my family about my condition in April 2003. It was the culmination of a very difficult family meeting and numerous phone conversations with my parents and siblings. After many years of having little or no contact with my parents, I had begun a series of phone conversations with them, the purpose being to try to achieve some form of reconciliation between us. I regarded these phone conversations as make-or-break and made this clear to my parents, so they would be in no doubt where the fault lay if we failed. I was delighted with their response, especially when they both apologised for what they had done to me even up to the time in which I was discussing it with them. I really thought, that they had changed; I genuinely did. This is very important to understand for what was to transpire later on.

Christmas 2003 was to prove one of the most momentous events in our family's troubled history. I received several phone calls from my brothers and sisters telling me that there had been some angry scenes in my parents' home over the Christmas and consequently a family meeting was being held in Bunclody, where they now lived. They told me I was welcome to come down and express my feelings about what our parents had done to us. I made it clear that I had already started the process of reconciliation with them and that I was making progress (as I thought) and that my reason for going to the meeting would be to confront the rest of my family over the way they too had treated me over the years. They agreed that I should be able to do that and encouraged me to attend.

The meeting was held early in January and was attended by most of the family. Two of our siblings stayed away. I was determined to use this opportunity to get closure on the various issues I had with my brothers and sisters.

Our eldest brother, James opened the meeting, explaining recent events and the need for the family to confront our parents over their behaviour towards us. My mother tried to make out that we were ganging up on them and that this was wrong. Her tone and body language betrayed her attempts to put us on a guilt-trip from the off. It didn't work, and so one by one we expressed how we felt about how we'd been treated over the years. It truly was a momentous event and even my eyes were opened by some of the revelations that came from my brothers and sisters. I was the second-last to speak and in doing so made it clear how I felt about their treatment of me. This followed an acknowledgement from all bar one brother, that their behaviour towards me had been wrong and inexcusable, and that they would make sure never to repeat it again. I really thought I had finally received reconciliation and closure with them; so much so that it influenced my next major decision, to disclose my gender dysphoria.

It was in April, several months after the family meeting, that I phoned my mother and asked if I could come down to visit, as there was something, I needed to tell her and Dad. It was arranged for me to travel down with Kathy. The visit was on a Sunday. I brought some photographs I'd had taken while Kathy and I were on holiday in Salou in 2000, my first holiday with Kathy as Sara-Jane. I was extremely nervous driving to Wexford that Sunday morning, so it was a great comfort to have Kathy with me. We had a lovely lunch with my parents and the atmosphere was convivial and conducive to sharing my news with them. I started by telling them about how I'd always found it difficult to live as a boy growing up and that I had been dressing as a woman for a number of years, and the reason for it, that that was how I really felt myself to be inside. I then showed them the photographs of me as Sara-Jane, as I was calling myself when in female mode. They were shocked at the news and even more so when they saw the pictures. They said I looked like my younger sisters, which was a huge compliment given how beautiful I knew them to be. My father poured wine into our glasses then stood up and toasted my courage and wished me every happiness for the future. My mother then thanked me for my courage and trusting them with my disclosure, she promised that I would never regret doing it!

I was deliriously happy and felt absolutely that I had done the right thing in telling them. They even thanked me for trusting and confiding in them. My father and Kathy went onto the patio and left me and my mother to talk in the dining room. We had a very open and frank discussion about whether she should tell my brothers and sisters. She said that she would keep my secret, but I told her I had nothing to hide and that I'd prefer it if she told them. So, it was agreed that they would be told over the coming days.

Initially, there was a mixed reaction to my disclosure by my brothers and sisters, but it was positive for the most part. In fact, most of them promised to come and visit me in Cork and even suggested having a party to celebrate having a new daughter and sister. I was on such a high during those few months. By the end of 2003 at least four of my siblings had met me and had been really impressed with, and supportive of, my transformation. Three of them openly declaring their support and one invited me to her wedding, as Sara-Jane! I had travelled from Cork to Portlaoise and to Cavan to visit my sisters and a brother in order to introduce them to Sara-Jane. They were undoubtedly nerve-wrecking experiences, but they were so worthwhile.

The last family function I attended before my sister's wedding was my mother's 70th birthday party. I was still living between the two genders and just getting used to my new situation. The party was a nice occasion, and everyone seemed happy to meet me. Some of my brothers told me they were going to be the same towards me as Sara-Jane as they were before I started my transitioning, which included being vulgar. I told them I didn't mind so long as it was based on acceptance. Surely now, for the first time I could truly feel like I belonged to this family.

It was eighteen months since they had been told of my gender dysphoria, and numerous expressions of support had been expressed along with numerous promises to come to see me, and the invitation to my sister's wedding. It would not be hard to imagine, therefore, the utter devastation when I discovered that they meant none of it and that despite being well advanced into my transition, I would be asked by my sister to attend her wedding as a man! How did all this come about? Two words: *my mother*.

All the time my mother was letting on to be supportive of me she was making it abundantly clear to my brothers and sisters that she had no intention of ever accepting me as Sara-Jane. She had me as a son and that was that; never mind the fact that she told me in the most shameless manner that she never wanted me, always resented having me and resented my being so different as a child. Her initial support when I had visited with Kathy had really been just for show — she didn't want to be embarrassed in front of my friend. Of course, my brothers and sisters would do anything rather than go against her so, in spite of all their outward professions of support, some of them began to refer to me as a clown and a freak while others would try to persuade me to change my mind and not go ahead with my gender reassignment. All this from those who never met me as their sister.

I learned about all this from my brother James, who made it abundantly clear that I was not welcome at my sister's wedding as Sara-Jane, and that if I did attend it would be as a man, regardless of the fact that my breasts had grown, my voice was female, and I was a woman from head to toe, bar one. They said I would look like a freak! Even at size 26 (XXXL), and in the very early stages of my transitioning, I looked nothing like a freak. What made this beyond grotesque was their utter hypocrisy. They had no problem with my sister's fiancé's gay brother coming with his gay partner, and they had no problem with an openly gay bishop presiding over their wedding, but not the sister they had pretended to accept. No, she was either to remain out in the cold or humiliate herself for the sake of the cowardly prejudice and intolerance of her own family. This came as close as it gets to being unforgiveable. But I have always been and always will be better than that.

It was in December 2003 that I was invited up to my sister's house in Sallins, County Kildare. I was told that my closest brother Peter was coming down from Dublin to see me, primarily to meet me and for me to explain my gender dysphoria to him, in order to give him a better understanding of it; that it was going to be a friendly and supportive experience. But that is not how it turned out, far from it. I had been in Martina's house a while when Peter phoned to say that he was on his way and he wanted to know if I was dressed in women's clothes, because if I was, then he wasn't going to come down. Martina assured him that I wasn't dressed in women's clothes and so he agreed to travel down. He eventually arrived at the house, but before he came in he looked through the window to check that I wasn't dressed.

Immediately on arriving, Peter slagged off my car, without so much as a proper hello. He then made some very provocative and disgustingly offensive comments about immigrants and how they were nothing but a load of scroungers and thieves. The more I resisted his ridiculous attempts to incite me, with my rhetorical questions, the more agitated he became, until I thought his head would explode. So, I stopped the argument by asking him why, after not seeing each other for so long, he would choose to behave in such a manner. He shocked me with his response: 'To prove that there's no fucking' way that yer a fucking' woman!'

I was completely gobsmacked. 'Are you for real?' I asked him.

'Yes,' he said, and he was indeed deadly serious.

'And how do you make that out?' I asked.

'Because there's no fucking way that a woman could be as fucking logical as you are.'

I burst into laughter at such a ridiculous assertion, then turned to my sister to see her reaction. She was clearly shocked by what she'd heard.

'So, let me see if I've got this right. You're saying that I can't possibly be a woman because I'm too intelligent?'

His answer was immediate and as clear as could be. 'Yes, that's exactly what I'm saying and, if you don't like it, then tough fucking shit.' The penny was finally dropping for me. I asked Peter if he was trying to prove that I wasn't a woman and if this was the real reason for his coming to meet me in Martina's house; to try and talk me out of going ahead with my gender reassignment. He said that this was correct. I then asked him if he was aware of just how offensive this was to me and how terribly hurtful. Again, he was as clear as could be: 'I don't give a fucking bollocks if you're offended, just get fucking over it.' The only thing more frightening right then than Peter's hostility was the realisation that I had been set up by these two, and quite possibly, by the rest of my family and that these were the two who had volunteered to carry out the plan to get me to change my mind. They had *chosen* to see my condition as nothing more than a state of mind, i.e. just another one of my attention seeking phases. It was their old worn out mantra.

I needed to get away from them and clear my head before deciding what I should do next. I told them I was going for a walk. I left the house and walked around the estate in the early hours of the morning and in freezing cold weather. The questions going around and around in my head were: how many more of them are involved in this setup? Are my parents involved? If they are, that means they are not really accepting me despite leading me to think that they were. So how many of my brothers and sisters have also been lying to me? I determined to return to the house and put these questions to them. But as soon as I returned Peter apologised profusely for his outburst, justifying it on the grounds that he was nervous and wasn't sure how to handle it. I accepted his apology, only because it was necessary to get me through this most god awful situation.

Martina opened a rare bottle of Spanish liqueur, saying it was a special night. She had the pictures of me as Sara-Jane that had been sent to her earlier and she showed these to Peter. This was the first time he had seen them and could see right away that this had nothing to do with my being a transvestite or cross-dresser. He was also shown pictures of the different hypothalamuses. He said that seeing them helped him to make sense of what I was talking about. We spent the rest of the night and the early hours reminiscing about the past. Martina told me how proud she felt whenever we talked on the phone and how she used to tell her husband of how eloquent I was. My hope returned, for a little while at least.

Despite all their promises to come and see me, only one actually bothered and that was my sister Sophie. I was at the stage with them that if I was to have any contact then I would not mention anything to do with my gender reassignment. Eventually, I decided to write to each of them so as to bring them up to date with where I was in my transitioning. I enclosed an up-to-date photograph that had been taken during a photo shoot for a feature in the *Irish Examiner* and a leaflet that explained GID. I expressed my disappointment that none of them had come to see me as they had promised and hoped that they would do so soon. I also requested that they call me Sara-Jane from that moment on. A couple of weeks later, I received a number of phone calls in which I was accused of putting the family under pressure! I couldn't believe my ears. This was around August and September 2004, a full eighteen months since they had been first told. I mean, seriously?

Matters became irretrievably worse after I'd received a most disgusting letter from one brother in which he made it clear that, not only was he not prepared to accept or to respect my request to be called Sara-Jane, but that he would call me 'shithead, dickhead, and any other name he liked, except Sara-Jane, until I'm ready.' I was doubly hurt because this brother, of all my brothers, had more reason to treat me better, after the many times I'd stood by him, including the time I helped him get back on his feet after he went through some major difficulties (he spent time in prison for manslaughter). I helped him to set up a business, while getting myself into debt in the process. He also tried to invade my privacy by demanding that I give him the name of my consultant, so he could question him about my condition. He demanded this as a condition of accepting my diagnosis. His arrogance was simply breath-taking.

But the biggest test of my determination still lay in front of me. The last time I had spoken to my mother was during the whole wedding debacle. I was very honest with her in telling her how I felt about the way she and my family had treated me, and that I found the whole thing an act of betrayal by all concerned. I challenged her to give me one good reason why she was not prepared to meet me; she had none. I really was hurt and decided not to have any further contact for the foreseeable future. As it turned out, we never spoke again.

It was ten o'clock on Friday 23rd September 2005 and I was sitting at my office desk working. The phone rang, and when I answered it was my father sounding very distressed. I'm afraid I've some bad news. Your mam died this morning at half-eight.' He went on to tell me that she had had a major asthma attack and that she had not responded to her ventilator. He told me how he tried unsuccessfully to apply CPR. She died in his arms. It is hard to describe the effect this news had on me. I had been grieving for the loss of my mother for over twenty years and now she was finally gone for good. She died without accepting me as her daughter, just as she had failed to do throughout my entire life. I felt the most incredibly sublime peace and knew immediately that I would not be going to the wake or to the funeral. I wanted to be left alone and come to terms with the overwhelming realisation that she could never hurt me again, never.

At about 11.30 a.m. I received a phone call from my sister Sophie who wanted to know if I'd heard the news and to know how I was. She then asked if I was going down to Wexford, to which I replied that I would not.

'Well, she was still your mother, Sara-Jane.' I told her I did not wish to discuss it further and wished her well. But she insisted that I should go down. I replied by telling her that I was not going to be a hypocrite and pretend to grieve for someone who had treated me so badly right up to her death. 'Well, I think you're wrong.' She handed the phone over to my brother Graham, who also tried to convince me to go down, but again I refused. He said: 'We know you had your differences, but she did love you. I know she loved you.' I told him I disagreed with him, and as with Sophie, made it clear that I had no wish to discuss it any further.

The next call I received was from my brother James. Had he heard right? That I wasn't going to Wexford to say goodbye to my mother. I repeated that I wouldn't be going, to which he replied: 'You mean you're not going to your own mother's funeral?' I simply replied that I had my reasons for not going and that I really did not want to talk about it. He just said, 'Good luck so,' and hung up. He called me again about 3pm, at which time I was walking around Douglas Court Shopping Centre. He started on at me again about my not going to Bunclody for the wake. And I repeated to him that I was not going and that that was the end of it. He could hear I was fully resolved and hung up.

When I got up on the Saturday morning, I noticed a missed call on my phone. It was from another sister, Brenda, saying they were concerned for me, that they loved me and that she would call back later on that day. She never did. Indeed, that was to be the last time I spoke to any of them; until Friday 3rd November 2006, when my sister

Martina called me as I was driving onto the M50 heading to Dublin. I could barely hear her, so didn't recognise her voice at first. She eventually came through clearer and told me why she was contacting me. It was to tell me that she was calling out of respect to let me know that the gardaí in Ballyfermot would be contacting me, to come and see me in order to take another statement about what I knew of my sisters being abused by our father. 'Sweet Jesus' was my reply, followed by a long pause. I really struggled to come up with a response. On the one hand, I really didn't want to be talking to any of my family, and I was shocked to be hearing that the case against their father had been re-opened. I say *their* father because just like *their* mother, he was certainly no father to me. But I did make a statement when the gardaí arrived in December. The case went forward for trial in April 2010.

I have been in two minds on whether to include this next section again after what transpired when the book was first published in 2008. But I've decided to include it if only to demonstrate the futility of putting our trust and hopes in those who are inconstant, lacking in courage, and utterly unwilling to do the right thing when it matters most.

Since first writing this chapter, I was contacted by two of my sisters and a brother, who wanted to re-establish their relationship with me. In fact, I'd already met my two sisters, and understand that a third also wanted to contact me.

When I met my sisters Sophie and Claire it was a wonderful and loving experience and demonstrated the utter futility of the divisions and distance between us. We had very open and honest conversations about the various issues that divided us and the fact that I'd been so shamefully treated by my entire family. The girls accepted this fully and apologised to me not once but several times over. I have to admit to having been suspicious about why they wanted to meet me after all this time, but they have since demonstrated how genuine they were, especially with Sophie and her husband travelling all the way from Cavan to see me. And I even got to have a life-long dream come true:

to have a real girly time with my sister as we hung out together on her sofa in our pyjamas watching movies and drinking wine. It was every bit as wonderful as I'd always imagined it would be.

My brother Peter (the one who said I was too intelligent to be a woman!) heard about my appearance on TV3's Ireland AM programme, and that I'd looked very well, so he decided to contact me. He said he wanted to meet me. He had spoken to my sisters and had been shocked to learn the extent of the lies that had been told about me over the years. He seemed to want to put matters right between us. He concluded one conversation over the phone by telling me: 'Sara-Jane, you don't have an evil bone in your body and you never did anything to any of us.' He then offered to help me get some photos together for the book, and we even arranged a meeting to see if we could establish some sort of a relationship in the future. It felt wonderful to have a family again. This was the way it should have always been, and how I hoped it would from that time on.

Sadly, there is a postscript to this. The first is the difference in my sister's behaviour on the day my book went on sale and my appearance on the Late Late Show that same evening. She was supposed to be with my sister Sophie in the audience but decided not to go and tried to discourage Sophie from going. To Sophie's eternal credit, she did go and had a great time. The second part of the postscript is my brother's failure to meet me as we'd arranged and from that day to this has never explained why or apologised for standing me up, knowing that I had travelled from Cork to Dublin especially to see him, and had even texted him from the hotel to let him know I had arrived. Shameful!

One of the most frequent questions I've been asked since my story was first published is: how I could be so forgiving of my parents and siblings given their god-awful behaviour towards me? It is due in part to the understanding I've had of their craven need for their mother's love, both in life and death. For them, this love has been and always will be more imagined that real, at least not to the extent they would have desired or believed. For my own part, I reconciled myself to the fact that I was never loved by my mother (despite the claims to the contrary from my siblings), and so, I have never succumbed to their delusion. For them, all roads lead back to the source of their insatiable need to be loved by their mother. Mary Wollstonecraft stated it thus: '*mankind(s)…wish to be loved and respected by something, and the common herd will always take the nearest road to the completion of their wishes.*' To this I would add, people will pursue this need even at the price of their own and other's destruction. This is certainly the case with the broken relationships within the entire family.

So, despite how cruel they have been, they are more to be pitied than blamed. I have discovered that the source of love comes from being my true *self* and the power of knowing I am *enough* within my own being; something I truly wish they could also discover. It is a heavenly freedom to have true and unawkward love for oneself and others. It is the source of good mental and emotional wellbeing, happiness and contentment, which transcends all the hurt ever visited upon me by my family.

PART FOUR
Endings and Beginnings

'The extraordinary always starts with the ordinary. It's simply a matter of what we choose to do with the ordinary.'

Sara-Jane Cromwell – 1960 – Inspirational Speaker and Author

Chapter Seventeen

Going Public – Trusting My Country

Truth demands a response.
[Gail Peters]

There was never a single doubt in my heart and mind about making a public disclosure of my gender dysphoria. Was I afraid? Absolutely; actually, afraid doesn't begin to cover it; I was genuinely terrified. Such a disclosure could easily blow up in my face. There was a lot to lose if it went wrong, but there was so much more to lose if I didn't tell the truth. Hiding away was never going to be a long-term option for me. Yes, I stayed confined to my home and afraid to go out, but I used those occasions to work through my fears and then step out once and for all. It occurred to me that some real good might come of all this. A great difficulty at this time was that there was no other Irish person in mainstream society who was doing what I was about to do, and there was no one taking the approach I was about to take. There were some who were trying to raise awareness, but they were very much on the fringes, mainly within the LGB community, and through organisations like GLEN and LINC, where ironically many within that community were against what they saw as people living a certain sexual lifestyle. They were having little or no effect within the LGB community, and even less so within mainstream society. Then there was the very problematic issue of the language being used, e.g. using terms like *transsexualism* and *transgenderism*. These terms were being used to lump gender identity in with all manner of sexual fetishist lifestyles and inter-sex conditions such as Androgen Insensitivity Syndrome. Their use then and now are for the most part problematic. This is especially so with public perception.

There were others who felt as I did, that we have absolutely no wish to have our gender identity confused with sexuality, and certainly not to be associated with sexual fetishist lifestyles. This had long been a cause of misunderstanding and confusion, and it has to be said, not without justification. This is extremely important, because this confusion has led to a great many problems being experienced by people with gender dysphoria. So, in order to get our clinical condition properly understood and to stop feeling obliged to apologise for it, it was important to take a radically different approach. The question at the time was: who is going to do it? The fact was, there was no one I knew who was even thinking along these lines, let alone demonstrating the ability to take on the responsibility of speaking about and representing gender dysphoria in an accurate and effective manner. Given everything I'd known about societies attitudes towards people like me, it would have been so easy not to get involved. But rather than ask the usual question: *why me?* I chose to ask another question: *why not me?* And *why should I leave it to someone else to speak up for me?* It really was that simple for me to decide on what to do, and so I did it.

Even before I had received my diagnosis, I was fully aware of society's ignorance of Gender Dysphoria (GD) and the negative treatment of those struggling to live according to their true gender identity. I was aware too of sensationalist TV shows, such as the Ricky Lake Show, Jerry Springer and Montel; and tabloid newspapers, portraying such people as a bunch of freaks. This only served to reinforce the confusion and prejudice that surrounds this clinical condition.

I knew all this before I was diagnosed and before I chose to proceed with my gender reassignment. I was aware too of the limitless accusations of deceit and selfishness endured by those of us who tried to live as we were meant to live, normal lives within our families, places of work, communities and within society as a whole, in the gender identity acquired before birth. I was also aware of how most families could be more concerned about their own embarrassment and what their neighbours might think, rather than about doing the right thing by their own loved ones. It is understandable that they might find it difficult to understand and accept that gender dysphoria is congenital in nature, but that was no excuse for the cruelties perpetrated against their own flesh and blood.

So, it is fair to say that I was fully aware of what I was getting myself into, and despite the many sacrifices, frustrations and outright bullying and discrimination, I have no regrets, especially given the many achievements that have resulted since my own diagnosis fifteen years ago. It is against this background and the fact that there was no support organisation of any kind to help people with GD that I felt I had to go public with my condition, in the hope that speaking openly and publicly of my situation would help me through my own transition and would also help those coming after me. There are large numbers of people with gender dysphoria who, like me, suffer deep distress and depression and many have either seriously considered or tried to commit suicide. This was utterly intolerable, especially as at this time there was no one speaking or advocating for us and no practical support. This was another reason why it was important to speak out and to work towards making a real and lasting difference for people with gender dysphoria.

My first attempts at disclosing my situation publicly was in March 2004, when I moved to Rockgrove in Midleton. I can still remember the overwhelming sense of dread I felt. Kathy was happy to live in this area of the town, whereas I would be facing into my transition in a neighbourhood in which I knew no one and where there were lots of children and teenagers. Moving outside of town was my preferred option because of the highly sensitive, and to be brutally honest about it, terrifying prospect of transitioning towards my new social gender role. I wanted to live somewhere that would allow me to come and go quietly without attracting attention, ridicule and judgment that others in my situation were experiencing at that time. It seemed an entirely reasonable strategy to adopt. But, no sooner had I committed to the move to Midleton than I had my first panic episode: *Jesus, what am I going to do now about my transition?* I found myself in a serious dilemma, and I needed to resolve it fairly quickly.

One of the options I considered was to defer my transition indefinitely, which would have been intolerable and heartbreaking in equal measure, while the other was to try to keep my head down as best I could and let on that there were two tall people living in the house, one male and one female! Another mad idea we came up with was for us to go to Spain to complete my full gender reassignment then come back as Sara-Jane. The only problem with this rather silly idea was that Kathy would then have to explain what happened to Tom and, who was the woman that came back with her? I know; I know, it was really silly, but this is what can happen when going through something as drastic and nerve wrecking as gender reassignment!

However, I need not have worried. I decided upon a different course altogether and that was to allow a certain time to pass in which I would try to get to know my neighbours and give them the opportunity to get to know me, as a normal person like themselves; as a responsible member of the community and as someone who just wanted to live in peace and get on with her life. Thankfully, I got to know my immediate neighbours in a very short period of time. This gave me the confidence to approach them individually and to explain my gender dysphoria in an open and frank way. I put together an information pack which I used to explain it to them, and what was going to transpire over the following months. They admitted that they were shocked and did not understand it, but they expressed their appreciation to me for telling them and wished me well. Others told me to tell them if I ever needed anything. Carmel Shortiss and her family were especially wonderful in this regard. I had spoken with her husband Ger, who asked me if I was going to stay in Rockgrove. I received a note the next day from Carmel. In the note, Carmel thanked me for trusting them with my situation and told me I was to let them know if I ever needed anything from them in the way of help. I spoke to four of my neighbours in total and gave them permission to tell my other neighbours, as they were then likely to get more accurate information about what was happening. I was dumbfounded by their kindness and acceptance, which made all the difference to me, and undoubtedly helped me to overcome some of my worst fears. I can honestly say that I have never felt as safe anywhere in my entire life as I did in Rockgrove. They all exemplified the best of what good neighbours should be.

Shortly after I told my next-door neighbour Gail, she invited me to a girls-only night in her home. She invited me because she immediately identified with me as Sara-Jane. She had seen me transform in front of her eyes as I shared my situation with her. I did not dress on that occasion as I had not yet met one or two of the neighbours and I didn't want them to feel awkward. It proved to be the right decision. The girls made me feel completely relaxed and never once did they say or do anything to make me feel awkward or embarrassed. One of the girls was fascinated with the whole thing and would come to my defence whenever she heard her friends and schoolmates saying anything nasty about me. We share the same shoe size and it has been a running joke that Victoria has larger feet than me!

On hearing about what was happening, one of my neighbours told me that her family thought I was one of a couple who just happened to be tall and who were working shift work. She said how they felt sorry for us as it must have been difficult for us to be coming and going at different times. I was chuffed to hear that and couldn't help laughing, just as I do every time people call to the door and want to know if my husband is home! There have been times when a few of the men going door to door selling carpets and looking for work, asked if I had a husband and when I said I hadn't, wanted to give me their phone numbers!

Perhaps one of the most wondrous experiences I had over this period, and indeed beyond, was the number of invitations I received from my neighbours in Rockgrove and Castlemartyr, were I lived before moving back to Midleton. I received invitations for numerous occasions, such as Christmas Eve and Christmas Day, Easter, Anniversaries celebrations and Birthday parties. Whilst I had every belief in the goodness of people and their ability to respond to the information given to them, I can safely say I never expected a fraction of the many kindnesses I received then and continue to experience to the present time.

Of course, there were the adverse experiences too, whether to my face or behind my back. But I was adamant that these people were not going to rob me of the joy of being myself. It wasn't easy dealing with such situations and I was constantly self-conscious about my appearance, as we called it back then, my *passability*. There are several examples I could give of these negative experiences, but two will suffice. The first was one of my clients going into his restaurant after having read about me in the Irish Examiner. He shouted in front of his customers that his safety consultant had become a woman. I lost my contract with him after that. The second incident was my solicitor's secretaries. He had been informed of my situation. I told him that my next appointment would be as Sara-Jane. I went into the reception to wait, and as I did both girls burst into laughter. As awful as this felt, I decided to make light of it by joking about it. That was certainly one of the more difficult experiences at the early stage of my transition. There were others through the early years, but in all truth, they were remarkably few and far between; certainly, compared to the experiences of others going through the same process.

What took me completely by surprise throughout this time was the resentment I experienced from others in the same situation, because I was considered far more *passable* than they were. They really didn't like that. I never saw that one coming. But rather than keep it to myself –understandable given their behaviour–what I tried to do instead, and many times since, was to explain why it might be, and tried to give them the benefit of my experience. It was with the sole intention of trying to make their transitioning that bit easier. To the best of my knowledge, not one of them took me up on the offer. But some people are not for learning anything and can't be helped.

It was around June when I called in to see my client Conny Ovesen, to discuss a business matter. Conny had just become a new client and we clicked immediately, so much so that I felt I could tell her about my situation. Conny introduced me to Alice de la Cour of the *Irish Examiner*. She encouraged me to tell Alice about my situation. Conny had found the whole situation fascinating and thought I was very courageous to have told her and others about it. She actually felt proud to know me and so encouraged me to tell Alice. Alice asked me if I would be interested in doing an interview for the Irish Examiner. I said I would if it was handled sensitively and in good taste, being extremely mindful of my friends, neighbours, clients etc. Alice promised that the article would be entirely respectful and sensitive to my story.

Alice was as good as her word and I was contacted some days later by a journalist, Helen O'Callaghan. We agreed to do the interview on 29th July. Helen arrived as arranged. I was very nervous at the beginning, but once we got started I relaxed, which helped the interview go very smoothly. Towards the end Helen asked if she could confess something to me. I said 'sure' and so she told me that when she was thinking about meeting me she wasn't sure if she'd remember to call me Sara-Jane and whether she would be comfortable. But she said that when she'd arrived at the house all she saw was a tall, elegant lady. I was chuffed and went red in the face with embarrassment.

On Wednesday 4th August, the photographer came to take photographs for the article. I was feeling very awkward at having to pose for the camera, but it had to be done, so I just got on with it, and as I so often do, I made it into a fun experience. I received a phone call from Alice on the Friday following the photoshoot. *'Sara-Jane, if you don't mind my saying, I've seen the photographs and, to be honest they don't do you justice.'* I was taken aback but before I got a chance to reply Alice said, *'Sara-Jane would you mind if I spoke to my editor and arranged for you to have a makeover? I can't help feeling there is a beautiful woman in there bursting to get out and I want to help her to do that. Would you mind if I look around and get you some outfits that I think will suit you better than the one you're wearing in those photos?'* I was absolutely thrilled and not a little red-faced. I agreed to her suggestion and we both finished the call very happy and excited about doing the makeover. Me getting a makeover? I was euphoric, like the cat that got the cream.

On the following Monday, Alice arrived at my house with three outfits, fashion jewellery and make-up, all of which were given on loan from Andrew Thomas Jewellers on North Main Street, Unicare Pharmacy and Evans boutique on Patrick Street. Gail was with me during the makeover and she was completely amazed at my transformation. Alice made me over from head to toe. It was exhilarating. I remember when she was putting on my eye shadow and suddenly jerked backwards and said, *'Jesus girl, I'm starting to fancy you meself. Your competition for me now, so you better stay away from my patch.'* That did wonders for my confidence. We were just finishing the makeover when Conny arrived with a bouquet of flowers, a bottle of champagne and a fabulous cake, which was for after the photo-shoot.

Alice asked me if there was somewhere we could go to do the photoshoot, as the front of the house was not suitable. I suggested Water Rock House. She thought it was a great idea, so I contacted the owner, Tom Cleere. Tom very kindly agreed to let us use the grounds for the shoot. There was no one around when we arrived, so I had to go looking for someone to let me into the side room to get dressed for the shoot. I had no idea that my friend Tricia was on duty. As I came out of the kitchen she came out from the bar and stared straight at me and asked if she could help me. She didn't recognise me for a few moments until I indicated that it was me. She was completely shocked and delighted at the same time, and after the photo shoot was finished

I got her and Conny to get into some photos with me. It was a truly wonderful experience. We returned home and had a girlie night in devouring the cake and the champagne!

I also did interviews that year with the Sunday Observer, BBC Radio Scotland and Cork 103FM.

One aspect of disclosing my gender dysphoria that made me very unhappy has been the way people automatically assumed they could ask me questions about my sex life and my sexuality. Some have been quite crude, especially those men who would say things like, 'Jaysus girl, you have great balls to do what you're doing. I know I certainly couldn't do it in a million years.' To which I would immediately respond: 'Not any more I don't.' People would ask me if I'm heterosexual, lesbian or bi-sexual. My reply then was that I'm sexually ambiguous to asexual and have very little interest in that particular aspect of my life. That there were far more important things for me to think about. It was a simple matter of fact that my sex drive was virtually non-existent at this point and throughout my transitioning. I knew this could happen once I started my hormone treatment, and quite possibly continue after my surgery. And this is how it transpired. In all truthfulness, it has been quite a liberating experience, as it freed me to focus on more important issues, like raising awareness of gender dysphoria and other forms of gender identity; and the sorry state of things for those of us unfortunate enough to be born into the wrong body, which it is worth remembering, is through no fault of our own.

I've also had my fair share of smirking, ridicule, speaking behind hands, nudges, name-calling, filthy remarks about me behind my back, people trying to avoid me and so on, *but all they've done is afford me the opportunity to demonstrate that I am the better and stronger person, more resolute in my determination to remain true to myself no matter what comes against me. I refuse to be put down by these people or allow them to frighten me into giving up.* I have been blessed with more than enough friends and supporters, who made sure that I would never go back to those dark days.

Life went on throughout all these events and some lives were coming to an end. In May of 2004 Kathy's sister Nell died from cancer. This was a life-changing experience for me as I was present when Nell passed away. Nell and her husband Tony had returned to Ireland to retire, having lived in England for many years. Nell had been taken into the Mercy Hospital for some tests and her husband Tony came to stay with us for a few days. Nell's daughters followed on, and rather than have them separated in a strange city, we offered to put them up. They stayed with us for two weeks, during which, they were told that Nell's cancer had become terminal. It was arranged to have Nell return to England, where she would receive palliative care. There was a sense of relief that she would be amongst her loved ones during the last few weeks of her life, but regrettably that is not how things worked out.

On Sunday morning at around a quarter to five we received a phone call from the hospital asking us to go up as Nell had taken a turn for the worse and was not responding to treatment. We arrived around half five and found numerous doctors and nurses trying to bring Nell's blood pressure back up, and for a while it looked as if they had succeeded. Unfortunately, though, there were other complications and her situation continued to deteriorate to the point where they gave up trying. To relieve her pain, Nell was allowed to control her own morphine drip.

Nell clearly knew that she was reaching the end of her time and so began to prepare herself to say goodbye to her family. Her deterioration was more noticeable by the minute and it could be seen in her demeanour that she was fully accepting the inevitable. She took the rings off her fingers and placed them in a mahogany box, along with some other personal items, she then handed them to her husband who sat by her bed. He was trembling at the prospects of what was to come. The doctors came back to the ward and called Tony senior and junior to one side in order to explain what was happening. Rather than leave Nell on her own I went over to her bedside and held her hand and stroked her hair. When the daughters who had returned to England were informed that the end was near, they got to speak to Nell by phone. The expressions of love and the sounds of goodbye through the phone were absolutely heart-wrenching. Nell was dying during these calls while another daughter was talking to Nell's daughter-in-law in an adjoining room. Within moments Nell began her slow graceful descent into her eternal sleep and as she did so I went to tell her daughter-in-law: 'it's time,' as she sat full of tears, trying to tell her sister-in-law that her mother was in the process of dying even as they were speaking. We returned to the ward and sat and watched as Nell slowly, effortlessly and peacefully slipped away.

It is an extraordinary thing to think that I had only ever met Nell twice before. It was in her home in Listowel that Kathy had told Nell about my situation and Nell replying that she worked with people who were in the same situation and how she found them to be very nice people to work with. She then asked Kathy what she should call me the next time she met me. Her acceptance has always meant a great deal, and so I was delighted to offer hospitality to her husband and children during their time of great distress and be there with her and be a comfort to her in those final moments of her life. It was an immense privilege. I am still affected by this experience.

A few weeks after Nell's passing, I was to learn that one of my favourite aunts had also passed away. My aunt Carmel, whom I dearly loved, and who was only ever loving and kind to me, was gone. The funeral Mass took place in the Church of the Assumption in Ballyfermot and she was buried afterwards in Palmerstown Cemetery. There was a reception afterwards in the CIE Social Club. I was asked to sing in her honour and so I sang two of her favourite songs, 'The First of May' and the 'Fields of Athenry', after which I asked everyone to raise their glasses in her honour. My uncle Tommy and cousin Anthony were very touched by this.

2004 was proving to be a remarkable year for me and I find it surprising after so many years of difficulty, just how much I achieved in that one year. Not only had I gone public through the newspapers and radio, but there were still more momentous events waiting to occur. It seemed as if destiny had well and truly intervened in my life and taken me to places and events that I simply would never have imagined.

Chapter Eighteen

Finally Free – My Annulment

The court doth make an order declaring:
That the purported marriage between the Applicant and Respondent…was and is
null and void and of no legal effect.

Monday 26th June 2006, was a red-letter day by anyone's standards. It was my birthday and I could easily think of other places I would rather have been, but here I was again, hoping that it would be the last time I would appear in court on this issue; my application for an annulment to my marriage. It was like something you'd see in a movie. For years Barbara and her solicitors had pursued me for maintenance, and thus, an admission of sorts that a valid marriage had existed, but I was resolute that that was not the case and for several very good reasons.

For years Barbara and her representatives delayed a hearing for my nullity application and put me through several discoveries and affidavits, which were not granted by the courts. They were originally granted a discovery order for three years accounts, but I gave them seven years in total, from which it was obvious I had no means to pay maintenance. That did not stop them from abusing the discovery order and harassing me with long lists of questions. This caused me untold stress. They were relentless in their efforts to pursue a judicial separation, but I was equally adamant that I wanted an annulment. It was heart-breaking to think that after all that she had put me through that she could get away with this too. However, I was determined to see this out, even if I had to do it myself. Thankfully, I didn't. Such was my determination to see this through that after I received the second list of discovery questions, I decided I'd had enough. I decided to take charge of the situation, so I called my solicitor and instructed him in no uncertain terms to go into court and inform the judge that I had exceeded the requirements of the original discovery order and that the other side had abused the order. My solicitor was taken aback by this but assured me that he would. He did, and the discovery order was finally struck out. This cleared the way for my own hearing to go ahead.

In February 2005 I had written to my solicitor to inform him of my diagnosis and my decision to go ahead with gender reassignment. He told me that this would affect my application for nullity and that I would need confirmation from Dr Lucey by way of a report for the court. So, I returned to see Dr Lucey for the report, only to be told they had lost my original assessment records and would therefore have to go through another one. During the meeting he made it clear how impressed he was with my transformation since the last time he had met me.

This was my third court hearing but my first as Sara-Jane. I was as nervous as could be and just wanted the case to be heard and get out of there as quickly as possible. I felt extremely self-conscious and vulnerable as this was the first time my legal team were meeting me, as would Barbara and her legal guardian and legal team, not to mention the judge and everyone else in the courtroom. I sat in one of the consultation rooms with the court-appointed psychiatrist, Dr Draper. We were left hanging around waiting for Barbara to arrive, only to be told that she wasn't coming and that the hearing would not now go ahead. I was livid, but there was nothing I could about it. I was plunged into more despair as I was convinced that this was going to go on forever. I was so dejected returning to Cork, but I had to pick myself up and keep going; not an easy thing to do, but do it I must, and I did.

However, there was one positive thing to come out of these events and that was receiving the court reports from Dr Lucey and Dr Draper. Bearing in mind everything I'd been through and all the stigma, bullying and abuse I had been exposed to over my lifetime having been branded a mental retard and a freak, their reports would have a profound impact upon me. Dr Draper wrote:

Findings:
(S)he presented as a well-dressed attractive female. (S)he had laser treatment to remove facial hair and a very female complexion and soft skin. (S)he feels that (her)his health is improved and (her)his depression and stress is lessened, (S)he has no suicidal thoughts and now has a strong sense of self. The transition has been very positive for (her) him. (S)he made a lot of friends. (S)he is writing a book on gender dysphoria. (S)he plans to change (her)his name by Deed Poll after (her)his case has been heard, (S)he appeared to be very relaxed in (her)his role as Sara-Jane and displayed predominantly female traits...(S)he did not want to be a cross dresser as it is not a pleasure thing...

Opinion:
It is my opinion that because of (her) his life-long female gender identification it would have been impossible for (her) him to enter into and sustain a normal heterosexual marriage...

Dr Lucey wrote:
On mental state examination she was a tall, pleasant woman wearing an auburn wig and purple eye shadow. Her speech was fluent, coherent with NO RETARDATION and no psycho-motor alteration. Her symptoms were confined to issues in relation to her gender identification. There was no evidence of psychosis, no panic, anxiety, no phobia, NO COGNITIVE IMPAIRMENT. Her mood was normothymic.

In summary, Sara-Jane (Thomas) Duffy is a 45-year-old woman with Gender Dysphoria. Born as a male, Thomas Duffy, she has been attending a personal psychotherapist since 2003 in relation to Gender Dysphoria and has been on long-term steroid hormone replacement therapy for that condition. She has multiple life stresses and a disturbed personal background. She acknowledges that she did not reveal these details to the court-appointed psychiatrist in the past. These factors do need to be taken into account when considering the validity of her marriage contract.

In a nutshell, I am a perfectly normal woman who happens to be tall and attractive and, I did not have a valid marriage contract. But most importantly of all for me, I am not, nor ever have been a <u>mental retard.</u> I had to wait forty years to see this in writing and I've cried many tears over those words. It would have been nice had my mother just said 'Sara-Jane, I'm sorry for letting on that you were mentally retarded.' She never did and she never will, but my psychiatrists did and put it in writing for the court and the world to see.

And so it was on the 26th June 2006, that twenty-five years of unmitigated marital misery were to end after just twenty minutes in court. After all the efforts made by Barbara and her legal team to frustrate my application, I was told on the Friday before the court hearing that they were prepared to withdraw their objections to my application for nullity. And the reason for this sudden change of heart? They wanted me to agree not to use Barbara's psychiatric court report as evidence. I was perfectly entitled to use it, but as it was not going to be necessary I agreed. It was obvious from the little I'd seen in the report that it was extremely unfavourable towards her. To have used it would mean causing her humiliation, that was not what I wanted.

And so, it was that my case finally got underway, but just before it did the judge questioned why I'd changed my name to Cromwell. My barrister responded that it was my right to choose whatever name I liked and that the court was bound to accept it. The judge was quick to assure my barrister that he was not commenting one way or the other, that he was just curious about the name. The hearing then proceeded, and Dr Draper was called as a witness. I was genuinely shocked and impressed to learn of his credentials and to realise that I had such an esteemed witness giving evidence in my case.

The judge asked him if I could simply say I was gender dysphoric for the purposes of getting an annulment, then revert to being male afterwards? Dr Draper could not have been more emphatic in his response: he made it absolutely clear that my condition was medical, that it was a prenatal condition and that it could not be cured. The judge was completely satisfied and said that he was prepared to grant my application, providing there was no objection from Barbara's legal counsel. She stood up and said that there was no objection and that there were no other applications before the court, with that the judge declared that the marriage was annulled. It is very difficult to describe how I felt at that moment. Here I was, Sara-Jane Cromwell, whose name had just been changed by Deed Poll, who had only been living six months permanently as a woman, experiencing serious financial difficulties and trying to cope with the daily trials of starting a whole new life, and struggling with being on my own. It was simply amazing. I could only wonder at what kind of life awaited me when I left that courtroom for the last time.

Chapter Nineteen

Stepping Out

Often the struggler has given up,
When she might have lifted the victor's cup,
And learnt too late when the night came down,
How close she was to the golden crown!
Success is failure turned inside out,
So stick to the fight when you're hardest hit,
It's when things seem worst when you must not quit!
[Don't Quit]

Once I'd made the final decision to go forward and complete my gender reassignment, I gave the go-ahead to my solicitors to take care of my deed poll. That was in March 2006. It should only have taken about two weeks to complete and have it sworn in the High Court, but it took three months before I could finally and legally call myself Sara-Jane Cromwell. I finally managed to collect it a week before I was due in court for my nullity hearing. My deed poll was the greatest legal commitment I could make towards completing my transition.

The undisputed highlight in changing my accreditations was when I contacted the National College of Ireland (NCI) to request them to change my Diploma, and to be allowed to have my graduation photographs retaken as Sara-Jane-Jane Cromwell. I received the loveliest letter from a girl named Fiona, the letter invited me to visit the college in October when the conferrals were due to be held. They very kindly gave me my cap and gown (which I didn't have at my first graduation!) at no cost, and made the photographer available to retake my photographs, also at no charge. This is not untypical of the kinds of responses I've received. It has been the same when dealing with the Revenue Commissioners Motor Tax Office and the Passport Office. Through all these interactions, I found the people I've been dealing with to be very professional courteous and willing to assist me in any way they could.

One of the rights of passage towards transitioning was to get rid of all my male clothes; all of them. This was more of a challenge than I had anticipated, but there could be no holding on to them in case I changed my mind, because having them would have been a crutch I could fall back on and that would have been disastrous for me. Getting my weight down was another major challenge. I was size 26 in a woman's size, (XXXL). So, it was for health reasons and in order to be as passable as possible that I committed to losing as much weight as I possibly could. I am currently at size 14ish, which is quite an achievement. The joy of losing so much weight is that I am much healthier and of course it also means that I can now go and buy my clothes in the same high street boutiques as everyone else. The day before I finally dumped my old cloths, and just out of curiosity, I tried on some of my male clothes and not a single one of them fit me anymore. They were huge on me. I had such a laugh over it and decided then and there to finally get rid of them. It was an incredibly scary but at the same time liberating experience. So before heading to work on the Friday morning, I packed them all into black sacks and left them at the front door, to be collected by the vans that picked up clothes for the various charities. When I arrived home at lunch they were gone. And that was that!

Whilst going public has undoubtedly helped me enormously to stay the course there were still other major challenges I had to face and two in particular: going to work and travelling abroad. From the earliest period of my diagnosis I had told a small number of my clients about my situation, while others read about me through the different articles that had been published in the newspapers. In particular, I want to acknowledge all the folks at MHC Shop fitters who were absolutely fantastic and made it so much easier to cope with going to work as Sara-Jane for the first time. Shortly after I told Karen and Ivan Nixon about my situation, I had to go into their workshop to carry out a safety audit inspection and a few weeks later I had to do a health and safety course for their employees. It was a Friday and I was a total bag of nerves; that's putting it mildly. I was trying to decide what outfit to wear. I felt very self-conscious in a skirt, but then thought better of it. I thought, 'Sod this, if I'm going to do this then I'm going to look as feminine and professional as I possibly can,' so I wore my black-and-blueberry pin striped pencil skirt suit and a blueberry coloured blouse. I also wore tights and court shoes.

I arrived at the Water Rock training centre feeling very nervous. As I was heading towards the stairs who should appear but Tom Cleere. He was completely gobsmacked at what he saw and was highly complimentary. That was a good omen for what was to be one of the biggest of the challenges I was having to face. Kathy very kindly agreed to come along for the day as moral support. She told me during the first coffee break that I looked and sounded completely natural and that there wasn't even a hint of maleness. She said she could not get over how natural and professional I was considering the immense pressure and stress I must have been under but given how well things were going she wondered how I could possibly have been nervous to begin with. She wasn't wrong about the pressure and stress as there were definite moments when I really wanted to run out of the place, but I never once let on about how I was really feeling. I had to get past my nervousness if I was to have any hope of making a successful transition with my clients. The training was an absolute triumph.

A few weeks later I was at a meeting with the production manager and during, which he told me that he and his colleagues were hugely impressed with what I achieved on the Friday and some of them wanted to stand up and give me a round of applause but were afraid to do so lest I would be embarrassed or upset. This was remarkable by any standard and far exceeded my expectations.

The next major challenge with my work was to actually visit the construction sites I'd been working on. MHC had the 'fit-out' contracts for some of the Harvey Norman stores around the country and, as their safety consultant, I was given the job of taking care of health and safety on each of the sites. This was going to be a major challenge for me, to go onto male-dominated sites, but I can honestly say that from the start to the finish of each one of these projects I have never had a single problem with the men. On the contrary, some of them paid me the ultimate compliment by referring to me as the *safety bitch*, whenever they saw me on site or heard that I was due to arrive. Others referred to me as a tough woman. No prizes for guessing how thrilled I was. But the best experience had to be when I was asked out for a drink and invited to dinner by some of the guys, while another asked for my phone number!

It is fair to say that of all the clients I notified, the response was overwhelmingly positive, which undoubtedly helped during this crucial period of my transition. It also served as a wonderful validation and affirmation of who I am and who I am meant to be. There is however, no getting away from the fact that my transition and all my work on behalf people with gender dysphoria has caused a lot of disruption to my business and my income. It has been extremely difficult to pay my bills and sustain a decent standard of living but I've never run away from these difficulties and have stayed the course. I have also kept in touch with my creditors to keep them up to date and let them know I am still here. They have been absolutely fantastic and have been inordinately patient with me. For this I am immensely grateful.

There could really only be one person I would consider travelling with for the first time on my new passport and that was Kathy. We travelled to Spain in February and stayed for a month. I normally take only one holiday in the year, so I try to make the most of it. This holiday was going to be like no other holiday before. My first hurdle was coping with the check-in at the airport, then going through security, then hanging about waiting to board the plane, then being in such close proximity to people for such a long journey and all the while thinking of the many opportunities for being spotted and potential public humiliation. Then there was the security at Malaga airport and the possibility of being body searched! Can you imagine it? Then there was checking into the hotel, being surrounded by so many guests and the general coming and going for a month, only to go through it all again on my return to Cork; and all this for the first time as Sara-Jane.

The first good omen I received was from Kathy's granddaughter Tracy. That child was as cute and could spot things that most adults would be hard pressed to notice. Kathy's daughter Maureen brought us to the airport. I sat in the back seat with Tracy. We had the best time playing and all the while she was calling me Sara. When we got to the airport Tracy wanted to stay with me, so we held hands walking around the airport. At one stage Maureen and Kathy took Tracy with them to the toilets, while I was eating my lunch. The next thing I heard was, 'Sara, Sara, where's Sara gone?' You can't imagine how much that gave me a lift and how much confidence it gave me, at least until we reached security. I was certain they would spot me and embarrass me by doing a body search just to be smart. But they didn't stop me, and they treated me just like any other passenger going through. They did stop and search Kathy though! That was the funniest thing to happen under the circumstances. I was thrilled. It was plain sailing, or should I say, plain flying from then on. When we got off the plane in Malaga and were walking down the ramp, I heard one of the passengers making reference to recognising me from one of the newspaper articles, that was the only time bar a brief incident in an optician in Marbella that I had anything like a negative experience; except that is for the first day I went out with full make-up on, forgetting that you don't do that in Spain.

On our first full day we travelled up to one of our favourite places, Mijas, to look around and take in some lunch. And I swear I really do think the angels were sent to Spain ahead of me given the various experiences I had that continually reaffirmed my acceptance as a woman; and that day in Mijas was unquestionably one of the best. We went into one the restaurants where all the while I was waiting to be spotted, but nothing happened. I was trying to take pictures of Kathy when the waitress came over and asked if I'd like her to take a picture of us together. I was delighted; and still nothing happened. Something did happen though when we were leaving, but nothing at all as I would have expected in the circumstances. Kathy went to the bathroom and I made my way outside to wait for her. As I was leaving, I was approached by the waiter who had invited us in. 'Hello, you are very nice woman. Where do you stay?' I replied that we were staying in Benalmadena at the Sunset Beach Club.

'May I take you for a drink while you stay?' I told him I'd ask my friend if that's okay as I did not want to be leaving her on her own. 'Thank you and my name is Gerard, what is your name?'

'Sara-Jane.' 'It is nice to meet you Sara-Jane.' He took my hand and kissed it then kissed me on the cheeks. Wow! And wow again, and again and again. I was on the greatest high. What Gerard did for me that day he will never know; it gave me so much confidence to get through the next day and the day after that.

Every day just got better than the day before and everywhere I went I was treated as just another Senora! We went to the Corte de Inglés in Malaga and spent a great deal of time trying on coats. Kathy found a coat that she particularly liked and spent a great deal of time trying it on. The store assistant came over to see if we needed any help and stayed with us for quite some time during which I was chatting away to her and trying on some coats myself. Again, it was a totally natural and exhilarating experience. I made some purchases of my own and when I went to pay for my items the lady looked at the name on my credit card and said that my name is *bonito*. This was yet another positive affirmation of my being a woman.

While we were in Malaga we went to look for a wig shop we had been to on our last trip. Kathy wanted to try out a different colour for her hair and take a break from using hair colours. She saw this beautiful honey blond bob style and bought it. She looked fabulous in it. When we got back to the hotel I asked if could try it on, she said I could and when I did the reaction was instant. Kathy looked positively shocked at the transformation and so did I when I looked in the mirror. It completely transformed my face making it look more feminine than ever before. It was decided then and there that I would buy it from her. I wore it for the rest of the holiday and the effects were only fantastic. So much so that men everywhere were taking notice, with a few wanting to know where I was staying so they could meet me for a drink.

One of the funniest incidents was at the Friday market in the Arroyo de Miel. I was paying for some scarves when the man giving me my change kept rubbing his hands against mine and telling me I'm *bonito*. Kathy started to make mischief by telling him that I was single and freely available. He was delighted to hear and said *in Espana, you are called wappa! You are wappa lady!* I was mortified and went beetroot red. But I also felt as happy as I could possibly feel, though at the same time I couldn't help wondering what he meant when using the word wappa? I didn't have to wait too long to find out. The next time we were in the Corte de Inglés, where I came across a glossy magazine with the name WAPPA on the cover. Also on the cover was a picture of a beautiful woman so there was no need to keep guessing what he meant by *wappa!*

It really didn't matter where we went in Spain over the month, everywhere we went we were treated as two female companions on holiday together and it was simply the best possible first holiday for Sara-Jane to be on. However, it was a hugely emotional time and I can't fully describe the amount of emotional and mental energy I used up over that four weeks, except to say that I was absolutely drained and exhausted when I got home. It took me weeks before I was able to get back to work properly.

Doctor James Kelly's diagnosis of Gender Dysphoria in 2003 has proven to be my salvation. Despite the many difficulties, hurts and losses I have had to endure prior to and following my diagnosis, it has set me free from a lifetime of internal and external conflict and abject misery. It has also opened up a whole new life for me; a life I once only imagined but never believed I would have; the joy of experiencing my own womanhood, for which I am immensely proud. I have seen the best and worst of people through this experience. I thought I had experienced prejudice until I made my disclosure and started to live as Sara-Jane, but the prejudice I have experienced since has taught me that even in this third millennium, with all our access to information and education, people are as wilfully ignorant, judgmental and intolerant as they have always been, and are determined to remain so.

But one of the key lessons I've also learnt, and it is an important one, given where I've come from in life, is this: *that it is not about me, or who and what I am.* It is about them, their character, their ignorance, their poor values and their choices. This has been extremely liberating for me in the years since completing my journey. And there is a third lesson and it is this. There are far more decent people than there are those I've just described above. These are the kind of people who accept others for who and what they are. They are the kind of people I have in my life in great abundance and for whom I am forever grateful.

Chapter Twenty

Making a Difference

All of us [are] driven by a simple belief that the world as it is just won't do-that, we have an obligation to fight for the world as it should be.
[Michelle Obama]

Space does not permit me to go into detail on all the major achievements at this time and since, but it is important to mention some, in order to demonstrate the many positive developments that have occurred since I was first diagnosed in 2003 at a time when there was an absolute dearth of resources available in Ireland for those struggling with their gender identity. Few of these developments were in flashing lights, and they weren't, to use the modern marketing term, *sexy enough*, especially when it came to receiving any sort of funding or, being able to fundraise in public. The stereotypes around gender identity and the various terms being used, were just too strong at the time. So, we were fighting an endless battle to make any sort of progress.

We did not help matters though; we were too predisposed towards the negative and by a conviction that nothing would ever really change in Ireland. Having a recognised Diagnostic and Treatment Pathway and Legislation allowing us to change our Birth Certificates was the stuff of Neverland! It is true to say that I was a lone voice in stating the opposite view, and in developing objectives, goals and strategies that would see my beliefs become reality. Of course, there will be those who will choose to state it differently in light of all that has happened since, but this is most definitely how it was at the time. There are of course those who now jump on the positivity bandwagon but this is not how it was in 2008.

One of the most momentous events of 2004 was the founding of the first support organisation in Ireland for people with Gender Dysphoria. I invited a number of people to my home at Rockgrove, with a view to setting up an organisation, to be known as Transgender Equality Network Ireland. The name was originally created by Diane Hughes and Dr Nicholas Krivenko, who came up with the name during their submissions for the Nexus Report, which had been commissioned by the Equality Authority. However, the original name they went under was *Transsexual Equality Network Ireland*. The purpose of the Nexus Report was to examine the then situation regarding access to healthcare services for people with gender conflict and those who had been diagnosed with GID. The meeting was held on Saturday 7th August 2004 during which the first committee was established. The original and founding members of TENI were myself, Diane Hughes, Lynda Sheridan, Nicholas Krivenko, Kyra and her friend from Waterford, and another lady from Cork whose name escapes me; seven in total. I was appointed as PRO and later on as Co-Chair with Nick Krivenko; whom I eventually succeeded as sole Chair. My vision for this organisation was that it should be an all-inclusive organisation for people with GID and their families. Our primary aims were to be a voice for those suffering in isolation and raising awareness about the true nature of the condition and the urgent need for an adequate healthcare service, along with the need to give legal recognition for those who were going through Gender Realignment Surgery (GRS). However, I had one great concern, which was the use of the word *transsexual*. It was a wholly inappropriate term and it was doing far more harm than good; so, although I really had to fight for it, thankfully the committee eventually agreed to remove the term *transsexual* and use *transgender* instead. And this is how TENI came to be. I cannot go into all the details here but suffice it to say there was nothing like this before in Ireland. This was a landmark achievement.

Part of my job as PRO was to seek opportunities for raising awareness about GID. With that in mind I made contact by email with the <u>Big Bite</u> show. I wrote to them asking if they would consider doing a segment on GID and the plight of people with the condition living in Ireland. I received a very quick response from Zoe Liston, who said they would love to do a segment and asked if I could forward more details. My original thinking was that there were enough people to go and do the interview and that I would not need to go myself, but I would still have been doing my job by setting it up. I sent Zoe details of the people she could contact and invite onto the programme. But to my surprise, Zoe came back to me and said they really wanted to do my story as I was the one who contacted them in the first instance. She also asked me if I could get others to go along and be interviewed. I asked Lynda Sheridan, a colleague in TENI, who in turn asked her daughter Aisling, and I asked Nick Krivenko as he was a female to male. They all agreed as did Dr Kelly.

When I arrived at the studio I was greeted by Zoe and brought up to the hospitality suite. I was the last to arrive and when I did I found Nick and Dr Kelly discussing how they thought the issues should be addressed and who should answer what questions and in what order. But when they tried to share their ideas with Zoe she stated that the format of the questions was already decided and that I was to be asked the first few questions as I was the one who contacted the show. I felt strange about this as I was more than happy to defer to my colleagues. In fact, when we were brought into the studio I deliberately walked behind everyone in order to allow them to pick their seats, knowing that some would want to sit alongside David McWilliams, the presenter. But as we approached the seating area we were placed in our pre-assigned seats; mine was beside David on his right, while Lynda was placed on his left side. The interview lasted about half an hour. It was a great success and I couldn't have been happier, not so much at my own contribution, but because it was the first time our issue was being discussed on the biggest broadcasting channel in the country, and in a way that could not have been further removed from those salacious American shows that were so popular at the time. This marked a real change in the way mainstream media saw and dealt with gender identity issues. There were still those sensationalist elements in the media, but there was no doubting that the early PR work I did helped to bring about real and lasting change, and I am proud to have made my own contribution towards bringing that about.

When the show ended, I was approached by a number of the production staff who shook my hand and told me they really enjoyed the show and felt it was one of the best they had ever done. As I was leaving the studio I was approached by the producer, who thanked me for contacting the show. She said they felt honoured and privileged that I had trusted them with my story and that she hoped they'd done it justice. I assured them that they had. David McWilliams must have said goodbye to me about five times that day. Just as I was leaving Zoe approached me to tell me the whole team were delighted with us and that I should contact them if there were any further developments. I mentioned in passing that I was thinking of writing my autobiography and a book on the subject of GID. She was very interested and asked if I had anyone to publish it. I told I hadn't and wouldn't know where to start. She gave me the name of a publicist and told me that I was to mention her name when speaking to him.

I cannot commend the production team at the Big Bite enough for the courtesy and consideration with which they treated us and the encouragement this gave me to keep going. I started this year and our new organisation without the slightest idea as to where it would take me. Nothing could have prepared me for the journey; even now I look back in wonder at what I've achieved. It is these achievements and the loving support of my friends that have made me realise that I was reaching the point of no return.

A more personal momentous event in 2004 was an interview for the British *Observer on Sunday*, It was Friday 15 October when Nicholas Krivenko, a fellow member of TENI, and I met the journalists and photographer for the Observer, in the Front Lounge on Parliament Street in Dublin. It was only my second time out in public and I was a complete bag of nerves. They were amazed to hear this and told me I looked fabulous; every compliment gratefully received! We had lunch and as I was not driving decided to have a couple of glasses of wine, which was just what I needed to relax. And believe me it was needed!

While we were being interviewed the photographer came along and said she needed to take the photographs quickly as she needed to be somewhere else, so we got up to go with her, thinking that she would be taking the photographs on the premises. But as luck would have it, she wanted to the take the photos down by the Millennium Bridge, on the River Liffey. 'For fuck's sake,' I muttered under my breath. I was mad as could be but had to hold it in, because I was so uncomfortable with the idea of having to walk down to the bridge then stand there posing, knowing that hundreds of people would be passing by and in their curiosity stare at us. As already mentioned, this was only my second time out in public, the first being my travelling to meet Dr. Kelly, so it was easy to see why I would have felt so exposed in a public place. But as I had done so many times before, I decided to just grin and bear it as best I could, hopefully the photographer would get it over and done with as quickly as possible and let me get back for a much-needed glass of wine, or two, or maybe even three, bloody heck.

The photographer had us pose in different positions on the bridge, and as expected, we were being stared at by lots of passers-by. To make matters worse, there was a strong wind blowing down the Liffey and I was terrified that my hair would fly off into the water below; so, I had to hold onto it, but in such a way that it looked like I was giving a girlie curl with my fingers. Honestly, the things a girl will do to get the job done. We eventually finished taking the photos on the bridge, but much to my chagrin she wanted to take more, only this time along the streets in Temple Bar. She had us walk up and down the street and engage in conversation as if we were oblivious to the camera and the people looking on; fat chance of that. But rather than waste my time feeling sorry for myself, I decided that if we're going to be doing this in front of all these onlookers then we might as well have some fun, so I started telling Nick some funny stories which led to us having a good laugh; and this was the picture that ended up in the paper that Sunday! We finally got back to the Front Lounge where I had that much needed glass of wine.

Later that same evening Nick took me to a sushi bar. It was my first time to go to one and I have to say that the food was only delicious. When we left and made our way to get a taxi, I was approached by a man who asked me I'd like to go for a drink with him. I declined of course, but I was chuffed silly.

The next day we attended a conference of the Law Society, to mark the first year of the enactment of the Human Rights Act. It was a who's who of the legal profession from Ireland, Northern Ireland and England. Nick wanted us to go up the auditorium and sit somewhere in the middle, but I was having none of it as I would need to go to the toilet quite a bit and didn't want to be constantly get up and drawing attention to myself. He very graciously acceded to my request and so we sat at the back of the auditorium. There were several hundred people there that day and I surprised myself with how easily I settled into the occasion. I felt I was amongst friends. Some of the speakers included the Lord Chief Justice of Northern Ireland, Baroness Kennedy from the UK and our own William Binchy amongst others; some of whom had been sitting alongside me during the course of the day and with whom I shared some humorous exchanges.

When we returned to our seats after lunch who should we run into but David Norris. Nick introduced us to each other. It was a very nice moment. I would meet David again some time later, at the launch in Outhouse of the confidential Garda advice service for the gay and lesbian community. David was one of the special guests and I was sitting in the audience. I went up to him to say hello and said, 'You might not remember me as it's about two years ago now…' With that, he said, 'Of course I remember you my dear and isn't it very pretty you are looking too. That man really does now how to charm a lady! I met David a third time in 2011 after our meeting in Leinster House with Minister, Eamonn O'Cuiv TD.

I returned to Cork on the Sunday evening, elated with my sense of achievement. To sit amongst that many people was just incredible, and it emboldened me to do something else that I had been dreading; go down the town and buy myself a bottle of wine. I went down to O'Donovan's off-licence and as I went to pay for the wine, who should be serving me but Warren, the son of my friend, Roisín. He asked me how I was and what I'd done for the weekend, so I told him about the conference and the newspaper interview. As the conversation went on I was wondering if he recognised me, so I came out and asked him, 'Do you know who I am?' He responded: 'Yes, of course, you're Sara-Jane. Can I say something, and I hope you won't be offended?' I told him to go ahead and say what he wanted to say, and he did: 'I was just thinking that you make a very pretty woman and you look a lot better now than when you were a man.' I was so delighted with what he said and went red with embarrassment. I then went home, put my feet up and reflected over my glass of wine about all the momentous events that had taken place over that weekend. It was immensely satisfying.

It was around 2006 too that I requested a meeting with the CEO of the Equality Authority. The purpose of this meeting was to deal with the Nexus Report, which I felt was wholly inadequate for addressing the many, varied and complex issues which people with gender dysphoria had to deal with on a daily basis. It was during this first meeting that I proposed the first ever medical symposium on gender dysphoria. This was immediately agreed to, as was the idea of setting up a steering group for this purpose. It was considered essential to invite the HSE to a meeting to see what healthcare provision if any, they were currently providing to people with gender dysphoria. The answer was as stark as it was brief: not very much at all. In fact, they didn't even know what we meant by gender dysphoria (or Gender

Identity Disorder, as it was known at the time). This was the ideal opportunity to educate them, and so it fell to me to do it. Sad as it may seem, I was the only one of the TENI group who had gone into the issue with any real depth, and the only one who insisted on us focusing on the clinical issues first and foremost. I felt certain that this was necessary to progress all the other issues around it. It also has to be said that this was neither welcomed nor supported by the vast majority of my colleagues, whether they were the first or second committee. But it was the right strategy, which ultimately worked to great success.

The Steering Group held a number of meetings over a period of about two years, during which we enjoyed a very cordial, professional and productive relationship. It should also be said, that without the work of all those on the steering group, the developments and achievements we see now in relation to diagnosis and treatment, would not have happened. It was towards the end of our work that we saw more definitive progress in the area of sponsorship of the symposium and seeking the Minister for Health's endorsement. And, it was also towards the end that we agreed a Diagnostic and Treatment Pathway which we would unanimously agree to put forward to the HSE for implementation.

These and other projects I initiated and with which I shared the credit with my colleagues should have been reasons to be proud, but alas that is not how it turned out. Without going into it too much, I resigned as Chairperson of TENI, under extremely distressing circumstances. What I will say though is that I was not prepared to do anything that would besmirch my own character or the reputation of the organisation I had helped found. Also, I was not prepared to continue working with people who were so utterly disrespectful and who tried on numerous occasions to undermine my position, which really amounted to bullying; even if it meant putting all *our* good work at risk. So rather than see this continue, I felt it best to step down and allow the others continue on with the invaluable work that was being done. This was an extremely difficult decision to make, especially as it meant that I may not be around to finish the work I'd started. But as it was never about me it was important to do the right thing.

After I announced the decision to my committee, I informed my colleagues from the Equality Authority, the HSE, Department of Health and Children and the Revenue Commissioners of my decision and the reasons for it. Needless to say, they were shocked; although some not so much. Apparently, some had felt it would happen having witnessed some of the disrespectful behaviour first hand. But what was most gratifying for me was the acknowledgement of my contribution and the request that I consider setting up another organisation that would enable me to continue my work. The way it was put to me was, that if I walked away – and it was understandable if I did– that the issues we'd all been working on would *be set back at least twelve years!* And I was assured that this wasn't being said just to be nice, hence the reason for asking me to set up another organisation. As much as I hated the idea of others taking the credit for what I was certain would be a great success, I simply could not remain as Chair or play any further role with TENI, as to do so would mean compromising my character and integrity beyond breaking point, and I'd felt broken enough as it was. They were also aware of this and it was one of the reasons they urged me to think about what I wanted to do. It was just before Christmas, so they suggested I think about it over the Christmas and New Year period and come back to them with my answer. They made it clear that they really liked working with me and thanked me for everything I'd done up to this point. I thanked them in return for acknowledging my efforts and promised to give serious thought to their suggestions. And so it was that my next big decision was to prove fateful in ways I simply could not have imagined. But this is often the case with decisions such as these. Before I continue to discuss that decision I first need to provide a postscript to what has just been outlined above.

Following the publication of Becoming Myself, a letter was published in the Irish Times on 18th February 2008, in which the representative from TENI sought to refute my assertion about the differences between myself and them on the use of terminology and the inclusion of as she put it,' *all manner of fetish lifestyles, which had nothing to do with GID.'* Whilst this is now a moot point, I stand over what I know to have been true at that time, and there was nothing misleading about what I asserted then. The dogs in the street knew this was a running sore at the time between myself and my former colleagues. I was entirely open and consistent on this issue throughout my time with TENI and subsequently with GIDI; and the only time I know of this being challenged at that time was this letter.

All this aside, the actual reason for my resigning from TENI was far worse than was previously indicated; but I decided to leave it out, which remains the case here, because my intention is not to open old wounds or bear grudges. But it is nonetheless important that I be able to express how I was so badly affected by the behaviour of my colleagues at that time, and how despite my own feelings of wanting to have nothing more to do with GID related activities, as mentioned earlier, I was requested by several key people at the time to continue with the work I'd started. For my own part, I am proud of all I've achieved working on the various issues and challenges relating to gender dysphoria. And I am delighted to acknowledge all those, TENI, my former colleagues in GIDI, various government officials, officials at the HSE, CAMHS the Equality Authority etc., who worked with me and who also contributed towards getting us to where we are today. There is of course a lot of work still to be done, and I sincerely wish all the organisations involved in serving the needs of people with gender dysphoria and other gender identities every success in their worthy endeavours.

All the hard work of the Steering Group on the symposium came to fruition in February 2008 when the first medical symposium on Gender Identity Disorder in Ireland was held at the Mansion House in Dublin. The symposium had a full attendance. It was officially opened by the then Minister of Health and Children, Mary Harney. Ms

Harney showed a very genuine interest in the symposium and asked to hear the first two speeches before giving her own official opening address. The symposium was reported in the national media including the evening news. I was the second speaker. I gave what was probably the shortest speech of them all. The reason for that was my desire to be as positive as possible rather that recount the many negative issues that could be raised, the previous speaker had already spoken at length about them, so all I had to do was pick up from where she left off. I did of course address them, but it was in the context of the breakthroughs I was convinced were on the horizon. My speech went down like a lead balloon amongst the nay sayers who preferred to believe that nothing would ever change; and as for there ever being a diagnostic and treatment pathway or, a law granting legal recognition and making provision for people to acquire their Birth Certificates, well that was the stuff of fantasy. I am proud of the fact that I was undeterred and openly stated my conviction that these would come to pass and that we would be a better country for it. I found out later on that my speech made a hugely positive effect on Mary Harney and others present. I was told by two of the guys from GLEN that she had been asking for me at a couple of events where I was not in attendance. There is no getting away from the fact that it was a real breakthrough moment in the fight for access to proper healthcare and legal recognition for people with gender dysphoria. Everyone involved had reason to be proud.

Back in 2008 there was an appeal pending from the Irish Government to the Supreme Court against the High Court judgment in the Lydia Foy case. The High Court made a Declaration of Incompatibility against the Irish State due to there being no legal recognition for people with Gender Identity Disorder/Gender Dysphoria, and their being denied the right to alter their birth certificates. However, in 2011 the Government withdrew its appeal and established the Gender Recognition Advisory Group (GRAG) instead. The purpose of setting up this inter-departmental group was to consult with a variety of bodies and experts on how best to introduce legislation on Gender Recognition. GID Ireland was invited not only to make a written submission to the Advisory Group but also to meet with them. During our meeting we made our concerns known about the need for strict criteria for those applying to have their Birth Certificates changed and the need for clinically appropriate terms to be used and a total avoidance of all *"trans"* terms, regardless of how unpopular this might be in some quarters. There was a clear understanding between us and we were delighted to see our submission included in the Group's final report and recommendations to the government.

We also had meetings with government ministers before and after our meeting with the Gender Recognition Advisory Group. We met ministers at the Department of Social and Family Protection and the Department of Health and Children. We were able to express our views and concerns on the importance of using appropriate terminology and criteria in the forthcoming legislation on Gender Recognition. I was also invited by one of the principal officers at the Department of Social and Family Protection to assist her and her colleagues in preparing the first draft of the Heads of Bill. We provided her with plenty of research data and a DVD containing a documentary on the lives of children with gender dysphoria. It was during this meeting we were informed that the Minister for Social and Family Protection and the Attorney General's Office instructed the officers responsible for preparing the first draft, that they were to confine themselves to the criteria included in the GRAG Report and that they were *not* to use any ambiguous terms. This is exactly what we sought in our written submission to the Advisory Group and from the ministers and government officials we had been meeting up to this point. Needless to say we were delighted with the outcome and felt vindicated for all our hard work.

The Gender Recognition Bill was published in December 2014. I was very happy with it overall, with the exception of how it would affect those already married; and there were of course others who had their concerns, which they made known and which led to a number of key amendments. The Bill was enacted into law in 2015 and became known as the Gender Recognition Act, 2015. What a truly blessed day that was. It was quickly followed by the launch of the application form for the Gender Recognition Certificate. This all happened within a few short months after I had my Gender Reassignment Surgery in the Imperial College Hospital, London.

In 2010, my second book entitled "Wrong Body, Wrong Life: Living with Gender Identity Disorder in Ireland" was launched in City Hall by the then Lord Mayor of Cork Darragh Murphy. This was a very successful launch. The book was donated to GIDI for free distribution as part of our National Awareness Programme. It has been broadly welcomed by professionals, people with gender dysphoria and parents. We have been distributing the book to public libraries throughout the country and to those participating in our National Awareness Programme. We have also distributed the book to universities and colleges.

In the course of my work and the publication of both books, I have done over one hundred media appearances to date, raising awareness about Gender Dysphoria. Over forty of these interviews were for Becoming Myself. Some were for Wrong Body Wrong Life, while others still were to do with various issues arising in the media, including the Lydia Foy case. It is evident over the past number of years that this work has also produced positive results. Yes, we still have a long way to go in this regard, but it is important to take a moment's pause and acknowledge any positive developments that have occurred and use them to motivate others to do better. So yes, we are seeing a very definite and more responsible approach in the way the media in this country reports on issues relating to gender dysphoria and gender identity more generally. And we are beginning to see a real difference in the way people are responding to those coming forward for help (I will share more about this later). Ireland is not an easy place to succeed at anything, especially when it comes to something as little known and widely misunderstood as Gender

Dysphoria. But we are definitely heading in the right direction and there is a lot of genuine goodwill from those I have been dealing with on this issue, as evidenced by the successes we have had to date.

I am not complaining when I say that the personal cost for all this work has been truly enormous. As with so many others, debt is a constant stress in my life these past few years. But the alternative to not doing what was necessary, as I've been reminded so many times by others, is that we would be at least twelve years behind where we are now. And when I think of the increase in the numbers of younger children being diagnosed with gender dysphoria, and parents who are better able to understand and deal with what is happening with their children, and better able to make the right decisions and provide appropriate support for them, then my work has been worth the sacrifice and the many risks taken to get here. I know that the work of the last fifteen or so years, has helped to save a number of lives too due to it being made easier for people struggling with gender identity issues to get the help they need. The work is essential in ensuring a better future for our children. It is truly wonderful to know that these efforts are helping others, especially children, who will never have to experience the awfulness that results from living in the wrong body and wrong gender role.

While Lydia Foy's case was before the courts did help raise awareness of the legal issues faced by people with gender dysphoria, especially the right for us to change our Birth Certificates, most people were none the wiser regarding the nature of gender dysphoria. They were, and for many still are unaware of the neurobiological and congenital nature of gender dysphoria, and that this has nothing to do with a choice made by the children affected, nor for that matter for teens and adults. Our gender identity is utterly unchangeable, regardless of what some would have us believe. Conditioning can of course affect our self-perceptions, behaviours etc., but not our gender identity. To continue living in the wrong gender is one of the cruellest things a person can ever experience, it is quite simply intolerable that we should be expected to. This is extremely important for people to understand, especially when it comes to the more controversial issue of Gender Reassignment Surgery and why it is a vital part of the gender reassignment process, and whether or not the person affected will have a successful outcome. I am extremely proud of the fact that my article in the Irish Medical Times (March 2009) helped in shaping the discussion around placing the clinical diagnosis and treatment of gender dysphoria within mainstream medicine.

This is precisely why it was essential to have gender dysphoria included in *mainstream healthcare* and why it is essential to have an appropriate and safe diagnostic and treatment pathway in place for all those seeking help, regardless of their age and circumstances. And as of January 2016, that is precisely what happened when the HSE finally signed off on it. Whilst they have been slow in coming, it is important to acknowledge that they are now in place. There is however a very serious issue regarding the lack of resources being made available to deliver this much needed healthcare to transgender people and especially to gender dysphoric people. Also worthy of acknowledgement are the many people who helped to bring this about. Particular mention should be made of, Niall Crowley (pronounced Neil), then CEO of the Equality Authority, TENI, and my colleagues in GIDI. However, I must single out Dr. James Kelly, Clinical Psychologist, Prof. Donal O'Shea, Endocrinologist, St. Colmcille's Hospital and Prof. James Lucey, Director of Mental Health Services, St. Patrick's Hospital. I know of no three clinicians who have done so much in helping people with gender dysphoria and other gender identity issues. And I can say without fear of contradiction that between them they have saved many lives, including mine.

I would like to close this chapter with a quote from Marie Curie:

'Life is not easy for any of us. But what of that? We must have perseverance and above all confidence in ourselves. We must believe that we are gifted for something, and that this thing, at whatever cost, must be obtained.'

This remains the purpose of my life.

Chapter Twenty-One

Publish and be Free

Then you shall know the truth and the truth shall set you free
[The Bible, John 8:32]

The original book's journey started on the day I appeared on RTE' Big Bite Show, hosted by David McWilliams. After the show Zoe Liston came to thank me for trusting them with my story and wanted to know if I had any projects going on. I told her I was thinking of writing my autobiography and that I had made a bit of a start but nothing more. She encouraged to me to go ahead with it and gave me the name Cormac Kinsella, who worked in publishing and suggested I contact him. Shortly after this I contacted Cormac and we agreed to meet in the Front Lounge on Parliament Street, Dublin. I showed Cormac what I had written up to that point, which was some of this book, with the other on Gender Dysphoria. He suggested that I combine them both into one book, but when I told him they were serving a different purpose to each other, he agreed that might be the way to go. He said he would read both manuscripts and get back to me. He did after several weeks. He told me that he had spoken with Rachel Pierce and that she was very interested in hearing more about the project. A few weeks later Rachel contacted me saying that Cormac had sent her on the manuscript and that she was delighted to receive it. She said that her first words to herself were, "wow, this girl can write," and "this is a gift on my lap." Needless to say; I was thrilled to hear this, especially when she told me she would help me look for a publisher. I was struck by her genuine enthusiasm for helping me.

In hardly any time at all she managed to find three publishers who expressed an interest in the book: Hodder & Stoughton, Penguin and Gill & Macmillan. It was Gill & Macmillan who asked Rachel to hold off sending the manuscript and proposal to the other publishers and to give them a chance to look at it first. Having read the manuscript, the publishing director Fergal Tobin contacted me asking for a meeting to discuss the book. We met at the Morrison Hotel in the city centre. Fergal was talking about the book for quite some time when I interjected with a question: "does this mean you want to publish my book?"

"Of course, he said, I thought that was obvious."

"Not so much," I replied. He was obviously very enthusiastic about it but hadn't said specifically that he would like to publish it. So, we agreed to take it to the next stage which was to prepare a publishing contract. This was February 2007, just a couple of days before I was due to go on my holiday to Spain. It was a completely surreal experience sitting on the plane thinking about what was ahead of me over the coming months, not least the fact that I had to turn a ten-thousand-word manuscript into a full-sized book, which I did, all 120,000 plus, words of it! The working title of the book was Wrong Body, Wrong Life, but after my meeting with the publishing team it was agreed to change it to Becoming Myself. I was given until July 2007 to submit the final manuscript which I managed to do, and once done it with was handed over to the publishers. It was a rollercoaster of emotions for the next seven months as the manuscript went through the publishing process.

There was one day I will never forget; it was my meeting with the publishing editor Alison Walsh. We met at Bewley's Hotel, Newlands Cross. Alison had the printed version of my manuscript, which was full of yellow sticky tabs. She looked at my crest fallen expression and astutely realised that I was dejected at the thought of there being so many grammatical errors to be fixed. That was indeed my assumption but as it happens I was completely wrong. This was an unanticipated defining moment in my life. It was the first time apart from college that my English was to be scrutinised in a way it never had been since I first started to teach myself to read and write at fourteen years of age. In saying this, I was not marked for my English in college, just my assignments and my exams. I suddenly felt exposed and inadequate. Those sticky tabs represented a day of reckoning I had not anticipated when submitting my writing for publication. The feelings were only momentary though, as Alison explained to me that the tabs were for sorting and arranging the text into fewer words and chapters. She told me that I wrote in beautifully simple English. She told me how affected she was at the simple way I described things, especially what happened to my mother in the bedroom next to ours. She was full of praise for my writing ability, which genuinely came to me as a complete shock.

One of the most memorable things about our meeting was her description of me as being quite decorous in my writing. I asked her what she meant, to which she replied that I was very restrained in how I described events, including my marriage, i.e. that there was nothing salacious or sexual in the story. I asked her if that was another way of saying I was a bit of a prude because I did not include anything sexual. She said yes. She was right, and it was quite deliberate on my part; it needed to be if I was to achieve my ultimate goals in having the book published. My purpose was twofold, to assert my right to be myself as the person I was born to be and would have been had I been born with the right body. The second was to explain to people what life was like being forced to live the wrong life in the wrong body, and to distinguish it from the fetishist lifestyles of transvestites and cross dressers. Thankfully I have been successful in achieving both.

The publishing process continued over the following few months with the manuscript going backwards and forwards. Then there was the collection of images for inclusion, some of which made me grimace a bit, for fairly obvious reasons. It was necessary to have pictures taken for the cover and inside, so a photo shoot was organised. It was held at a studio in the Liberties in Dublin. When I arrived at the studio, the photographer said to Anita Ruane from Gill & Macmillan, 'you're right, she doesn't stop smiling.' I went up to the studio and was greeted by a makeup artist who got me ready for the photo shoot. We tried all sorts of shots without any real success until I suggested we take a brief break and try some music in the background. It did the trick. I just relaxed and did my own thing which included telling them some funny stories. This made me laugh to the point where the photographer instantly saw the pictures he was trying to capture, and without saying anything he kept taking shots while I just got on with being my smiley self. They were delighted with the results, which ended up in the book.

During lunch in a local pub, Anita asked me about my name change, why I chose it and whether I ever missed the other name. I told her that I have never missed it, not even for a moment. She was surprised by this and expressed her amazement at how relaxed and happy I seemed to be. I told her that despite all the difficulties I was experiencing up to that point and was bound to experience thereafter, that I was absolutely delighted to be finally living as I was meant to and that I was seizing every day as a blessing. I still do this, only more so.

The months between signing off on the final draft of the manuscript and the publication date was busy enough. I was focusing on my work with GIDI and the ongoing difficulties with trying to earn a living. Added to this was a preoccupation about whether the book would actually go ahead, especially after I informed some of my siblings that the book was being published. I fully expected them to interfere and try to have it stopped so I was on tender hooks much of the time, until the day I was given my first copies of the book. Then I was given the publication date for the book, it was Friday the 15th February 2008. This was to be one of two amazing days that February, and both were equally momentous, though for quite different reasons. The other date was Wednesday 20th February. This was a momentous day for people with Gender Dysphoria and the fulfilment of my vision of having the first ever medical symposium in Ireland. They were both very different experiences, and both had their share of negative minded people, but frankly I was with Red Butler, I frankly didn't give a damn! These were two life changing days, not just for me but for many others and I was not going to let the small minded begrudgers ruin them for me.

Becoming Myself was published by Gill & Macmillan and went on sale on Friday 15th February 2008. In the lead up to the book going on sale I was given an interview schedule, the first of which was Books Ireland. In the week of the book's release I did a number of interviews in the Westbury Hotel, Dublin. Amongst some of the journalists who interviewed me were Sarah McInerney, Sunday Tribune; Sue Leonard, Irish Independent; and Kathy Sheridan, The Irish Times, to name just a few. The articles were a mixed bag which was to be expected and for the most part they were in good taste. I remember doing five in all in the Westbury Hotel over two days, and I can safely say they were exhausting. There were over forty interviews for the book, with some taking place as late as April and May. It was a whirlwind of activity and it was overall a positive experience, with just two exceptions. The first unpleasant experience was with Q102, the second was the Tallaght and Ballyfermot Echo newspapers, for reasons that will soon become all too apparent. One of the most gratifying things about the live interviews were the expressions on the journalists and presenters faces when they met me for the first time. It was very obvious they were not expecting to see a *natural* feminine looking woman. There was simply no escaping their surprised expressions, try as they might to deny it, so I had a bit of light-hearted mischief with them when I said, "it's okay, I know you were expecting to see Lily Savage, the drag artist/TV presenter." To which they all replied with a denial, but then acknowledging that that was the case. It served as a great icebreaker and set a good tone for all the interviews that followed. One journalist in particular came right up to my face. She suddenly realised what she was doing and apologised profusely for the rudeness of invading my space. She said she was looking to see if there was any hint of my being a male and was shocked to see nothing at all, especially not an Adams apple! As with so many other things I had to deal with during these interviews, I made the choice to be light about people's sometimes inappropriate questions and comments, as to do otherwise would have made things unnecessarily stressful and there was already enough of that as it was.

On the day my book went on sale, I was due to appear on the Late Late Show, which is Ireland's and the world's longest running talk show. They put me up in the Westbury Hotel for the night on account that I had to travel from Cork to make my appearance. But it is amazing that I ever got to appear on the show and do the interview the following morning on Newstalk. I had called to see a friend the previous Wednesday at the local bookshop. When I called to the back of the shop I was hit by what can only be described as a wall of mouldy dust which went straight up my nose and to the back of my throat. By the end of the day I had the most awful throat infection which worsened over the next couple of days and left my appearance on the Late Late Show in the balance. But I was determined not to lose the opportunity, so I travelled to Dublin on the Thursday as planned.

I stayed in the Plaza Hotel in Tallaght on the Thursday night as I was due to meet Richard Sterne, a producer from TV3 on Friday morning. He met with me to discuss the possibility of appearing on Ireland AM the following week. Richard was very complimentary of my book and predicted great things for it and for me. I did the interview the following week as agreed, and it went extremely well. What should have been a day of visiting bookshops to see my book on the shelves and celebrating all day-long, I was instead doing a site safety inspection for one of my clients. They were doing a shop fit-out for Harvey Normans at Nutgrove in Rathfarnham. I deeply regret doing this and not celebrating anywhere near as much as I should have done for such a momentous event in my life. But that was all too typical of my attitude towards my own achievements. That will not happen the next time!

I went straight to the Westbury Hotel from the Harvey Norman site. I was exhausted and tried to rest for a couple of hours before getting ready to travel to RTE. I have to say that I felt very unwell and extremely lonely on my own in the hotel, but I was determined not to let myself or my publisher down, as these opportunities are extremely rare and it would be a very, very long time before it would come my way again. I also had my family on my mind and the inevitable showdown that would occur once I had made my appearance, but I remained undaunted and never let on to anyone how I was really feeling; they really were none the wiser, which makes me think I should have become an actress! My friend Maria Broderick came to meet me at the hotel and we were chauffeured from the hotel to RTE. We were taken to the Green Room where we stayed throughout the show. I had my sister Sophie and brother-in-law Peter in the audience.

The interview with Pat Kenny went extremely well. One of the highlights of the interview was a humorous story about the first time I had to stand on a queue in the ladies' toilets and how much I felt at home sitting in the cubicle.

After the interview ended, Maria came down from the Green room to meet me on my way out of the studio and gave me the biggest hug, which was something I really needed. The reaction from the viewers was overwhelmingly positive, with barely a handful of negative comments. I was applauded by the show's Executive Producer on my return from the studio and from other guests in the Green Room. Some of the programme producers and researchers came to meet me when the show had ended to thank me for allowing them to do the interview and to say how very impressed they were and how they believed the book would do extremely well and possibly become a film. I was of course delighted at these comments, but something inside told me that I wasn't destined at that time for the book to be a great success, that it would be in the future; and only after I had a final showdown with my family. And as it happened, I was proven right, as just a few months after it was published the economic crash came, and my business was utterly decimated as a result.

I was joined after the show by my sister Sophie and her husband, Peter. Pat Kenny also joined me for a glass of wine and a chat. We spoke for about fifteen minutes. I found him to be a gentleman and I thanked him for conducting such a sensitive interview, and like his colleagues he too expressed his appreciation for being allowed to do the interview with me.

I did not have long to wait for my family's reaction, it took a mere fifteen minutes for the first nasty text messages to come through. I received a couple of vile texts from one of my sisters. She was calling me disgusting names and mocking my account of looking after her and my younger siblings, even though she knew full-well this was entirely true. And if this wasn't enough, she then accused me of lying about experiences I had before she was even born, but which she and other siblings had mocked me over many years; taking every opportunity to remind me of how much of a *sensitive sissy* I was! These were followed by a series of text messages from another sister and a brother. I showed them to Sophie, my brother-in-law and my friend Maria. They were of course disgusted and advised me to ignore them; that was easier said than done. I told Pat Kenny about the text messages and he advised me about the kind of nuts I could expect to hear from, including members of my own family. The texting went on for several months, with warnings to *"watch this space."* I spoke to the gardaí about what was happening but all they did was tell me to just block them, which I eventually did.

Over the following days of publicity for the book I was informed by my publisher that someone from my family had contacted them trying to stop the book from going ahead. I also learned that other brothers had contacted the Irish Times and the Late Late Show, in an attempt to have my book discredited. But they failed dismally as all three were more than satisfied with the veracity of the book and of my integrity as an author. I was then, and am now, extremely grateful to them for their support and for withstanding the pressure they were put under from those who would deny me the right to tell the truth of what happened in my life. But these members of my family were not finished yet; they and I were yet to have our last stand. This last stand was to produce a very strange outcome that to this day leaves me feeling immensely proud of the stand I took on that occasion. In fact, there were to be three other events that were to be the last three nails in the coffin that was our very dysfunctional family relationship.

One of the nasty incidents was at my sister Clare's house. Someone tore the picture of us together from the book and placed it on her doorstep with a candle. It was so sinister and mafia-like. There was of course no way of proving who had done it. The second nail was being informed by my sister Sophie that two other sisters had taken my book, photocopied it and took it to their solicitor to see if there was anything in it that would damage their case against their father. This was extremely hurtful given that they had been told numerous times that there was nothing of the kind within the book, which was also verified by their own solicitor. These concerns were addressed before the book was published. The other thing that hurt me was that they went behind my back to do it.

The third nail was the final showdown, which came on the 5th of March to be precise. This is the date on which the Tallaght and Ballyfermot Echo newspapers published an article by six of my brothers and sisters, who sought to discredit my book. The article was entitled *"Sex op Sara-Jane's family dispute her book's claims."* The title of the article was itself utterly despicable, as are all other similar titles. The article proceeded to quote members of my family who were allowed to make all kinds of false allegations about me, which were the same ones they made since my childhood; and they were allowed to do this without my being afforded the right to reply. They had absolutely nothing else to say about me. It was patently obvious from their allegations that they had not even read the book properly, as some of them had claimed, because if they had they done so they would have known I did not say the things I was alleged to have said. What was most telling about their allegations was how, apart from slagging me off as usual, they were really intent on defending their mother's conduct while she was alive. Their personal attacks were petty in the extreme and were it not for the more serious libel contained in the article I wouldn't have bothered taking them and the newspaper on. The two main issues I had were (a) where they called me a *"fraud"* and (b) where they asserted that my account of my mother's abuse towards me was untrue. These libellous accusations could not be allowed to go unanswered, so answer them I did, most decisively and conclusively.

Something very telling about all this was that of the well over forty TV, radio, newspaper and magazines I was interviewed by, it was only the Echo who paid any attention to their allegations. What upset me most about this, apart from the obvious libel, was the behaviour of the journalist involved. He had requested an interview from me in the middle of an extremely full schedule of interviews. I really didn't need to do this interview but agreed to it on account of having lived in Ballyfermot and Tallaght and had absolutely nothing to hide from anyone. However, the journalist never bothered to inform me that he was intending to publish the article about my family's claims and he failed to afford me the opportunity to answer their allegations, which could then have given some balance to the article and thereby completely avoid the fiasco that followed.

I found out about the article through my sister Clare. She informed me that it was one of her friends who saw it and that it wasn't very nice. I immediately contacted the journalist concerned and requested a copy of the *published* article, but instead he sent me two incomplete versions of it. But I insisted that he send me a copy of the newspaper containing the article, and when I eventually received it I was shocked, appalled and deeply distressed. It was every bit as bad as had been described. But unbeknownst to me the word was already spreading amongst my family and former neighbours in Ballyfermot that the article had appeared in the newspaper. Their reactions were a source of very great encouragement, and they strengthened my resolve to take on the six people involved and the newspaper group.

One of the fantastic things that happened was that some of my other brothers and sisters approached the newspaper and told them in no uncertain terms that everything I had written in my book was not only *true*, but that it was only the tip of the iceberg in terms of what had actually happened within our family, our mother's role, and that there was a lot more to come out in due course. They were of course referring to their own cases which were then with the Director of Public Prosecutions awaiting a decision on whether to prosecute their father, and which subsequently led to his conviction and a six-year prison sentence. Another instance involved my brother Stephen, who called to thank me for *not* writing the whole dark story about him and what he had done, especially what he had done to me. He said I had every right to and was totally amazed that I didn't. But I reminded him that I was not out to get anyone, I just wanted my story to be told, and that it was up to each of them to tell their own stories, which I understood at the time at least one of them intended to do.

It was following these events that I contacted the journalist concerned and formally complained about what had happened. He asked me what I wanted to do about it, to which I replied that I wanted the opportunity to publish a reply to their false claims. It was during this conversation that I mentioned the copy of the letter still in my possession from these same individuals, which was sent to me after being first sent to my three sisters taking the case against their father and the two brothers who were supporting them. The letter *is* dated the 29th July 2007. The letter was sent a full eight months *before* my book was published! What is also strange about this letter was my original intention to return or destroy it, but my gut feeling told me to keep it!

What is astounding about this letter is the way in which it actually substantiates what I had written in my book, albeit that they were trying to dilute their parent's culpability. They even referred back to the famous meeting in Bunclody in 2003. This was the same meeting during which the abuse I received from *both* parents and siblings was not just openly discussed, but where I received numerous apologies from those present. And yet here they were in this article doing a complete *volte-face*. Thankfully though this blatant act was not ignored by members of my immediate and extended family, or for that matter, by *some* of our neighbours who were all too aware of what had been going on within our family. Others of course denied any knowledge but were shocked to learn about them. There was however no doubting how many people knew about our parent's behaviour towards me and how far back it went. The irony of this for me was that I hadn't a clue as to just how many people actually knew, given that I had kept so much of this to myself. It was some of my other siblings who were telling others about what had happened, whilst others were present during the events recounted here.

Having discussed these issues with the journalist concerned it was agreed that the Echo would publish my rebuttal. The rebuttal was published on March 26th 2008, it was titled *"I stand over everything I have said,"* but it was an abbreviated version of what I had actually submitted. There was also a line at the end from the editor saying, *"Correspondence on this subject is now closed."* I don't mind saying that I was livid about this, especially as some of the facts I had referred to in the original article had been omitted. It was this that prompted me to take the matter further, which I duly did by making a complaint to the Press Council.

The Press Council were quite diligent in contacting me after submitting my complaint. They told me that the Echo newspaper was not registered with them and that it was not really possible for them to proceed any further. They did however tell me that the newspaper group's Managing Director was very disturbed by what he had heard and was anxious to speak with me about the matter. I agreed to this and a few days later he contacted me. Our conversation took place on the 12th May 2008. It was during this conversation I made it clear to him that I was not interested in taking a libel action against his paper, but that I wanted an apology to be printed in the same paper in which the offending article had been published. I also told him I wanted a donation for my charity GID Ireland. He agreed to these terms and duly published the apology and sent on the cheque for €500 to GID Ireland. I was extremely happy with this outcome and the fact that because of all that had transpired I had support from far more people than I had previously imagined. This was a great and welcome vindication.

The final nail in the coffin of my relationship with my family was hammered in on the August bank holiday. I was dog-sitting for friends in county Clare. It was a very stressful day having to deal with my bank and problems with my finances, so I was already feeling stressed before I arrived at my friend's house. The atmosphere was extremely quiet and eerie, which made me feel very uncomfortable, so I was perfectly set up for what was about to happen. It was midnight when I received two text messages telling me to phone the person sending them. When I called I heard a male with a Northern Ireland accent saying *"you're dead!"* Needless to say I thought it was a joke and so I just asked who it was I was speaking to, but all I was told was that it didn't matter as I was *"dead anyway."* I persisted in asking who it was and became very frightened. I screamed at the man to tell me why he was doing this; at which point he realised that I was very scared and distressed and so apologised. I persisted again in getting him to tell me who he was. It was then he told me he was a friend of one of my family and he was asked by that family member to call and let on to threaten me. I tried to find out which of them it was, but he refused to tell me and hung-up. I reported the matter to the gardaí in Midleton when I returned the following Tuesday, but I was told they couldn't do anything about it and suggested I contact the detectives in Dublin who were dealing with my sister's case.

I thought about this for a few weeks, in the context of everything that had happened over the previous months and how my sisters had done the dirt on me again. It was then I decided I could not suffer them any longer and that there was only one way I would ever be entirely free and that was to cut off all contact with them, including Sophie and Clare. The simple fact was that to have contact with one was the same as having contact with them all and I was simply not prepared to tolerate that any longer. I also decided to withdraw my statement to the gardaí regarding my sister's case, because to continue with it would mean having continued contact with them and that was more than I could bear; and because ultimately it was not going to affect their case one way or the other. The one thing my statement would do is act as just another affirmation of the prolonged abuse that had occurred over many years.

My father was finally charged and appeared in court, in April 2010 on 13 counts of indecent assault and sexual assault of my three sisters. He was sentenced in May to six years imprisonment, to run consecutively. My sisters read out statements to the court that were both very moving and disturbing. Their statements to the courts, plus the evidence of other siblings finally gave the lie to those other siblings who sought to blacken my name as well as my three sisters, and therein lay my final vindication for everything written here about my upbringing in Ballyfermot. Their father was sentenced just two days before the launch of my second book in City Hall, Cork.

I know it is a taboo to say this, but, there is no escaping the fact that some families can have a pathological hatred for the truth. This is certainly true for some of my own brothers and sisters. This hatred for the truth was matched by an equally pathological determination to defend the indefensible and those who were culpable for their actions. The mind boggles at the lengths some people will go to in order to protect those known to be responsible for some of the worst kinds of wrongdoing and do this against those they know have been wronged. This is precisely what happened to me following the book going on sale in Ireland. The vitriol aimed towards me from my family after my appearance on the Late Late Show, and for a number of months thereafter was truly disturbing and deeply distressing. But in the end, it has proven to be their last stand against me and my ultimate liberation from their clutches and their ability to hurt me any further.

All of this was beautifully balanced out by a visit to my niece Niamh on St. Stephens Day 2011. I was visiting with my niece *Niamh* and my former sister-in-law Gráinne. We were in the kitchen. Gráinne and I were chatting about various things when she suddenly started talking about how she and my extended family admired me so much for all I'd been through. She then apologised for *not* standing up for me against my brother and my mother as they would abuse me in front of her and others. This sometimes included using violence and threats of violence against me. I assured her that she had nothing to apologise for as she was young herself and my mother would never have tolerated her saying anything. And then came another moment of veracity; she told me of the aunt I mentioned in my account of the time I was brought home from school after excreting into my pants while in school. She told me my aunt told her and other family members that it was her who was there that day and that she too witnessed my humiliation on the kitchen sink, and that like my sister-in-law, she too regretted not saying something. I was overcome with emotion to the point where I thought I would burst, for never in my wildest dreams could I have imagined ever hearing these things from anyone.

The amazing thing in all this was that it wouldn't have happened had my niece *Niamh* not contacted me a couple of years earlier to re-connect with me, after almost thirty years. She made contact through my Facebook page, having read my story and listened to her mother over many years talking about how I used to visit them regularly, even after my brother had deserted them. We met a short while later and had been getting on wonderfully ever since. Unfortunately, we lost contact since then.

Twenty-Two

The Journeys End – A New One Begins

Doing the extraordinary to become ordinary
[Sara-Jane Cromwell]

The economic crash came for me in August 2008, just six months after *'Becoming Myself'* was published. The first financial hit came when a restaurant owner refused to pay me for work I'd done, despite the fact that he was fulsome in his praise for what quality of the work. The rest of my clients fell away like dominos. I was barely getting by with the income I had, due to my involvement with GIDI and the many projects I'd been working on, including several family interventions of people with gender dysphoria, counselling families, travelling up and down the country raising awareness around gender identity issues etc. I regret to say that one of my greatest disappointments in doing this work on behalf of people with gender dysphoria, and families who availed of our services was, that all bar one of them failed to keep their promise to contribute towards the help they had received; the exception being a family up in County Meath, who at least paid the travelling expenses whenever I travelled up to meet them.

So, there was nothing to buffet me against the crash, which led to long years of serious financial difficulties, serious rent arrears, and unbeknown to all but several people, having no electricity for ten weeks in 2010; during the coldest winter in fifty years. I had to burn video cassettes and DVDs and other materials to keep warm. My neighbour from across the road loaned me a rechargeable fluorescent light, which I was able to charge up in my office in Kilbarry Business Park, and I was given the use of a small generator to light a single light bulb. They weren't adequate enough though for the long cold nights. Also, there was no running water for about two weeks due to the big freeze.

Those who visited me over the ten weeks were astonished at my good humour, but what they didn't see was the fear and distress I felt from not knowing were my food would come from and how I could possibly earn a living again; and whether I would keep the roof over my head. I did receive two payments from the community welfare officer, but that was it. I did try to sign on for job seekers allowance, but that was going to take weeks and I would have to give up my business; that simply wasn't an option in the long term, so I had to get by as best I could. There were times when I came close to a complete breakdown and literally had to pick myself up from the floor several times after collapsing in convulsions of tears from all out panic. It was without question the most prolonged period of stress in my life. It was a time when I could have been forgiven for giving up completely.

Given all this, it was difficult to conceive of any hope of completing my transition. It was so bad that I seriously thought of not going ahead with it. I even tried to comfort myself with the frequent comments from friends and others that I had the best of both worlds; whatever the hell that meant. I think it meant that I could be with both men and women sexually. The very idea was abhorrent to me, not the being with men or women, but living the rest of my life with the god-awful disfigurement, which would prevent me from being fully the woman I always knew myself to be. The very thought of this was too much to endure, and it was all I needed to bring me back to my centre and why I'd started this journey in the first place. So, I composed myself (I nearly said something else here that would have been an unfortunate pun), regained my focus and determination to complete my transition and went ahead with my application to the HSE for the funding for my surgery. If I was certain of one thing, it was that I had not come this far to stop now. I was also certain that my being in this situation had damn all to do with sex, and I was utterly fed up with people thinking it was and alluding to it in whatever way they could, including some journalists who covered mine and other's stories with wholly inappropriate headlines. It wasn't acceptable then and it is not acceptable now. We have the same right to our privacy as anyone else, whether we are still in or have completed our transitioning. It is surely time to give up the inappropriate hypersexual and salacious curiosity around this issue, and to respect people's privacy. Our lives are far more interesting than that. Great, glad I got that off my chest!

Something else that needs to be said before I go any further in sharing about applying for funding for gender reassignment surgery and speaking of going through the surgery, I need to answer those people who assert that the HSE and taxpayers should not be funding this surgery. Let me remind them that for the most part, they have not the slightest idea of why this surgery is necessary and why it should be funded through the HSE. The fact is that gender dysphoria is a recognised clinically diagnosable condition within mainstream healthcare, and surgery is prescribed as an essential part of the gender reassignment process. Nor do these people have a clue as to the devastating effects of the psychological and emotional distress experienced day in and day out by those living with a body that does not match their neurobiological, psychological, emotional and spiritual gender. This is difficult to explain in a way that people can easily understand, but it is very real and has resulted in countless numbers committing suicide, or, hiding themselves away from their families and from society; precisely because of the kind of wilfully ignorant, stupid, uninformed and nasty comments made by some people. I would challenge anyone who might find themselves born with such disfigurements to say that they would not do everything in their power to correct them and use any means available to do so. And finally, we are as much citizens and taxpayers as anyone else in the state and are therefore entitled to the same rights and recognition as those enjoyed by every other citizen, period! I would prefer not to be saying this in my personal story, but it needs to be said.

When I received funding approval it was all systems go to get my appointment at the gender identity clinic in London, however there was just one more glitch, I had to get assessed all over again (this was about my fifth and sixth assessments at this stage). I had to return to Prof. James Lucey to be assessed and then be referred to Dr Rosemary Shinkwin at Midleton Hospital. It would have been so easy to get discouraged by having to do this for the umpteenth time, but I was absolutely determined not to be put off this time. Once I had done these assessments I made my first appointment with the gender clinic in London. I was told it could take several more assessments before I would be finally considered for surgery.

I made my first appointment for the gender clinic but was unable to attend due to insufficient funds. It was to be another year and a half before I would try again. It was in 2013 that I made my second appointment, and this time I was able to attend. It was on 25th October 2013. My appointment was with Dr. Stuart Lorimer. The assessment was due to last for at least an hour, but instead it only took just over thirty minutes. This was because Dr. Lorimer was so impressed with the other consultant reports and his own interview with me. He was in no doubt that I was ready for surgery and so signed me off for it immediately. He wrote to Dr Hutch confirming that he would be recommending me for surgery. Finally, all the paperwork was complete and sent on to Imperial College Hospital.

It was almost a year to the day when I received my appointment to meet the surgeon Mr Thomas. He talked me through the surgery and mentioned that I would have to wear a catheter afterwards. He said this was necessary after creating a new vagina and relocating the urethra. I was also told by the nurses after the surgery that some patients may have to wear the catheter for weeks afterwards as it may take that long and longer for the urethra to work normally. This was not a pleasant prospect, but I was undeterred. The truth is that I had already decided years earlier that even were I to die on the operating table, I would still be happy knowing that I would leave this life with the body I should have had when I was born. I shared this with my friend in Dublin Sarah Duffy, who said she felt the same. We both meant it. Mt Thomas told me it would be six to nine months before I would be called for surgery. This would be between April and June at the earliest, which to be honest I didn't expect. As with every other step throughout this long drawn out journey, I expected to be waiting for the surgery well after the nine months.

Kathy and I planned to take our holidays in February 2015. I was completely burnt out and decided I needed to take an extended rest. Not that I expected to hear from the hospital while I was away, I phoned to inform them that just in case they were looking for me, I would not be contactable for five weeks. I was not prepared for what happened next. The nurse who took the call told me that as I was on the phone she would book me in for my pre-admission assessment! I was pacing around my apartment in disbelief. I even thought for a moment of asking her if she had the wrong person, but I said nothing. And then it came. Then I heard words I neither expected nor hardly believed, *'while I have you here, I might as well put you in for your surgery.'* It was that matter of fact. I was beside myself in disbelief. But it was true, it was really happening, I was finally looking at the end of my long journey towards being the woman I was always meant to be both inside and out. I can't say for how long I ran around the apartment and jumped up and down with joy and delight, but it was a lot.

The first three weeks in Spain could not have been better. I was getting the rest I needed and was building up my strength for the upcoming trip to London for my pre-admission assessment. But this was to change dramatically during our trip to Ronda. We drove up in the car we hired. As we were about to arrive in Ronda I felt my heart fluttering along with feeling dizzy. I put it down to the usual palpitations I still experienced since I was electrocuted when I was thirteen. We got to a car park and I thought we should go somewhere for a coffee and rest before exploring; a big mistake! Coffee and palpitations do not go well together. The first thing that struck me when we left the car park was the air. It was unlike any other air I ever breathed before. It wasn't just cold, there was something very different that I can't describe. As we walked about I felt myself become weaker and weaker to the point where I felt I was about to become unconscious, or worse still, that I was about to die. I called on every ounce of willpower I had to stay conscious. I asked Kathy if we could go for something to eat. This was in order to sit and try to recover myself, all the while trying not to panic or frighten her with what was happening.

We went to a Moroccan restaurant. While we were having our meal, I kept putting my hands under the table to check my pulse. It was so fast I couldn't feel it, and when I did it was frightening. I genuinely believed my heart was going to burst at any moment. We finished our meal and did some more walking about and visiting the shops. I bought two souvenir block calendars; anything to make things look normal. After a while we decided to head back to the car and back to our hotel. But as we headed towards the car park I became so faint I was certain I was dying. I managed to get to a chair just a few feet from a pharmacy, but it was closed; bloody siesta. I remembered that we'd passed the hospital on the way in, so I thought I would go there on our way back. The problem was that there was simply no way that Kathy would be able to cope if anything more serious happened to me. It was at this time it occurred to me that just maybe I might be suffering from altitude sickness. I am not at all good with heights. It also occurred to me that I may be also suffering from severe dehydration, and that just maybe it was both of these that were causing me to become faint. This along with a determination not to leave Kathy stranded and unable to cope led me to the decision to drive as far as possible before going to the hospital. And sure enough, as we began our descent I began to feel a bit better. We drove for quite a while before I realised that I was on the wrong side of a very wide valley. We were on the road to Cadiz instead of the road to Malaga! That is all I bloody well needed on top of everything else.

We arrived at a small village where we stopped off at a filling station. I went straight to the toilets to freshen up by throwing water in my face. I felt so much better, which confirmed my theory that I had been suffering from altitude sickness and dehydration. The guy behind the counter hadn't a word of English so I had to ask for directions in Spanish. Thankfully we understood each other, and I was finally able to make my way back to the road to Malaga; at least that's what I thought. I was told to take the first turn to the right and follow the road all the way until I reached the other side of the valley. The problem was I couldn't see a right turn, all I saw was what looked like a laneway, so I drove towards a fork in the road and took the right turn, only to end up in the tiniest cul-de-sac I'd ever seen. It was a real test of my driving skills to turn the car around and get the heck out of there. I ended up back out on the main road and having to start all over again. After the second failed attempt to find the right turn, I went back to the filling station. He kept saying primero derecha, derecha then used hand movements to give me direction. The penny dropped, and I figured he must have meant the laneway. As I made my approach towards the lane a jeep turned in to it from the opposite direction, so I decided to follow him; and sure enough, we were on the right road and finally on our way back to the main road to Malaga. To say it was a bumpy ride would be huge understatement; it was bumpy as hell, but I didn't care in the least. I was elated and relieved at the same time, and just glad to know I was going in the right direction. The horrible experience stayed with me for the rest of the holiday, and I believe had a negative impact on my ability to recover from my surgery. The palpitations and anxiety attacks were especially bad, and I've been having issues with them and with dehydration ever since. So much for getting plenty of rest and building up my strength for the trip to London for my pre-admission assessment and surgery!

I was just four days back in Cork when I was heading out on the first of my life changing trips to London. The only thing that occupied me through the entire trip was whether something would happen to prevent my surgery from going ahead. The pre-admission assessment would answer that for me, and it very nearly did. I found it difficult to know what to wear in London in March. It was cold but yet it didn't take long to warm up while walking. As I was fully expecting to get the bus to the hospital I decided to wear heels. I also wore warm pants, a top and woollen jumper and my black hooded coat. It was just enough to keep me warm, but not too warm. The bus arrived and as I got on and tried to pay my fare, I was told I had to have an oyster card, which of course I didn't, so surprise, surprise I ended up walking to the hospital, which took about twenty minutes. By the time I arrived I was sweating like the proverbial you know what. And as for my blood pressure, well try 162/106!!! Suffice it to say, this was not a very reassuring start. The nurse doing the assessment tried to reassure me as she took copious amounts of blood and put me through various health checks like checking my pulse, height, weight etc. etc. She had me wait awhile before taking my blood pressure for the second time to see if there was any improvement, but alas it wasn't, in fact, it worsened slightly to 164/108. This was really worrying and sent my mind into a spin that lasted all the way home and for several weeks afterwards. I was put on an overnight blood pressure monitor after I returned. If my blood pressure did not normalise then there was no way the surgery would go ahead. I can hardly describe how that prospect made me feel and the distress it caused me over the several weeks leading up to the final decision on whether to proceed. To have finally come this close; to be finally able to envision my body, mind, spirit, everything about me finally come together as one, only to have it all taken from be because of my blood pressure. It went well beyond a challenge or something I could be philosophical about, it was something I hope never to experience again. I dread to think of what would happen when having come so far, so close to the finish line, all the sacrificing, and enduring assessment after assessment, and everything that waited beyond this surgery; all being lost because of my bloody blood pressure of all things. The stress was quite simply dreadful.

I wouldn't presume to know about anyone else's reaction to having their blood pressure taken, but so help me no sooner do I put that confounded blood pressure sleeve on than my blood pressure goes up, and it takes a while for it to come back to normal. I think they call it white coat syndrome. Whatever it is, I fully expected the problem to continue when I had to wear the overnight monitor. But it didn't happen, my blood pressure was normal, and I was good to go for my surgery. Hallelujah!

I flew to London on Sunday the 19th April 2015 to be admitted for my surgery which was due to go ahead the following day. I was supposed to have one of my friends follow me over after a few days in order to look after me when I left hospital and to help me get back to Cork. But this didn't happen due to a lack of funds, so I had to do it all on my own. Of course, some might have thought why not postpone it until I had enough funds, but it was never going to be that simple. It needed to happen now, it was that simple, with or without help.

I was taken to theatre around two o'clock in the afternoon, after I was given an injection to help me relax. I was taken to a side room where they went through a number of checks and to make sure I was okay. Even then I found it hard to believe that this was going ahead, and yes, I even remembered what I'd said about passing away on the operating table, but not even that could stop me from smiling and being disbelieving at the same time. Then they placed the mask for the anaesthetic over my face and asked me to count from one to ten, and as I did I had a momentary fear that I would resist the anaesthetic. But I was gone!

I awoke from my anaesthetic around 7.30 in the evening in my own bed. I was of course very groggy as I tried to speak with the nurses who were checking up on me. I had a beautiful sleep and woke early the next morning. I felt entirely different to how I ever felt in my entire life. I felt serene, that my body, though newly operated on was going to make me whole. And sure enough, as I looked down to where that disfigurement once was there was nothing but flat padding to protect the wounds. It was finally gone and never coming back. In the meantime, one of the surgical team came to see me and asked how I was feeling. I told her I felt good. She then pulled back the covering of the wound and held a mirror, so I could see how I looked. All I could do was cry with tears of delight. It may have been a fresh wound, but it was a thing of beauty to me, it was the most natural I ever felt in that part of my body. Of course, I knew I had a long way to go with my recovery, but even now it was already worth the long wait. I barely touched the area for fear of doing some harm, but I did stare at it quite a bit, in wonder and sheer delight. The focus now was to help it heal as soon as possible and to do everything I was instructed to do by the medical team.

I got out of bed after a couple of days and did some walking around the wards and nurses station. I was stooped over trying to keep the pain to a minimum and to avoid stretching, which might have affected the wound. And then there was the catheter and bag stuck to my leg, which had to be emptied very frequently on account of the copious amounts of water I had to drink.

It was on Tuesday evening that a patient was moved in across from me. I didn't get to see her and thought nothing of her being there, until she started talking in her sleep, or so I thought. She repeated the same thing over and over *'don't do that. Please don't do that.'* But then it got louder and louder and more frequent. And if the nurses tried to attend to her or calm her she just screeched louder and louder and continued the screeching after they left her alone. It was becoming increasingly intolerable and made it impossible to get any sleep. This was especially difficult as my pain was worsening, and my medication was not providing the same pain relief. It was a complete nightmare. It transpired that the lady in question had dementia. She was not supposed to have been in a surgical ward, but due to a lack of beds they put her there. Of course, I had nothing against the lady, but her presence in a ward were patients were trying to recover from various forms of surgery caused huge problems for us. Things became much worse as she was also incontinent. The stench was beyond description. The whole situation was utterly intolerable. They finally moved her from the ward and I heard afterwards that she was sent home. She came back again a couple of days later but this time they put her in a room at the opposite end of the ward.

In the meantime, another patient moved into the same bed. She was not a pleasant woman. She was forever on her phone and talking loudly, day and night, which made it difficult to get any rest. She was in the entertainment industry and it was obvious she wanted us to notice her and be impressed. There was a young nurse from India who was as diligent as patients would want a nurse to be, but for some reason the patient just mentioned treated her with utter disrespect and it was obvious she was just looking for an excuse to have a go at her. She got her chance when the nurse, who was rushed off her feet did not do something quite as quickly as the patient wanted her to. She tore into the nurse and clearly sought to humiliate her by questioning her competence. It was intolerable listening to her and watching this lovely committed nurse become embarrassed and humiliated. I'd had enough. I went to the bathroom and while there thought about what I should do; saying nothing was not an option. I returned to the ward and challenged the patient about her conduct. Predictably she told me to mind my own business. I told her that she had made it mine and everyone else's business by behaving as she did, especially given that she obviously intended for us to hear her. She tried to shout me down, but I told her I would not tolerate her obnoxious behaviour, including her constant use of her phone and her utter lack of consideration for the other patients, not to mention her behaviour towards the nursing staff. Word got around very quickly about what I'd done, and the Indian nurse came and thanked me for speaking up for her. In the meantime, the patient received some difficult news and I tried to be supportive. She later spoke with the nurse and apologised to her. She was moved to another ward the next day.

The following days were dominated by the most excruciating pain, which grew worse by the hour. It was in the lead up to when my packing was due to be removed, and my new vagina was to be revealed for the first time. to be followed by the catheter. The pain was so bad that increasing my pain medication made no difference and I was writhing in pain for nearly three days. The nearest I can compare it was to labour pain. The doctors told me they had to leave the packing in until the Friday as to take it out sooner would cause a prolapse of the new vagina, which would of course have been an utter disaster. So I had to bear it as best I could.

And then the moment finally arrived. It was noon on the Friday when the surgical team arrived at my bed. The doctor began removing all the covering, then she removed the packing; the severe pain disappeared immediately, what I was feeling then was a mix of pain and hypersensitivity. But what I felt above everything was relief. The doctor held up the mirror again, and again I cried, and cried, and then went very deep into myself. I spent the following hours looking forward to the kinds of freedom I would have and the potential humiliations I would never have to face. But there was still a little matter of the catheter and whether my new urethra would work the same as other women. I was very apprehensive about it and what would happen. I was to find out in the early hours of Saturday morning. The nurse came to my bed around 3.30 in the morning and read my chart. She told me she was going to remove the catheter. She also told me it could take up to several hours or longer to work, or possibly I may have to leave hospital with the catheter still in place; not a happy prospect.

She removed the catheter and the bag strapped to my leg, another freedom and another new hope in what might be possible. And so it proved to be. It took less than an hour before I had to go to the bathroom and pee for the first time in my life as I should always have been able to, just like any other woman. The piercing I felt while passing urine for the first time was indescribably bad, but it was more than matched by the most extraordinary feelings of elation and joy. It was very much a case of so far so good. When I left the bathroom, I did so with the certainty that my life was never going to be the same again and that I had finally brought an end to this life long battle to have my mind, spirit and *body* become one. I felt exquisite and deeply grateful for being able to do this amazing thing. There were of course very difficult days ahead but for now, in these moments, I allowed myself to feel the utter joy and exhilaration at seeing my disfigurement gone and already feeling like the *lady* I knew myself to be; except, now it was on the outside as well as inside (decorous or otherwise!).

The last couple of days in hospital were spent walking around the ward and trying to build myself up for my discharge. It was at this stage I felt the effects of going through all this on my own and I was dreading facing the trip back to Cork, especially the train journey to Stansted Airport and the flight home. I left hospital on Monday the 27th April. Before I was discharged I was given a dilation kit and a checklist of things to do and what to expect over the following weeks as my wounds healed. I got a taxi to the Star Hotel on Shepherds Bush Road, where I stayed for two days until my flight on the Wednesday.

I felt the effects of being on my own immediately on arriving at the hotel and having to do everything for myself, especially having to shop for food and water and sanitary pads! As the evening wore on I felt myself shivering very badly, no doubt this was one of the effects of the surgery, but even so it was really frightening, as was the blood I was losing from the wound. It was just as well I brought two sets of pyjamas with me. I looked and felt like a ninety-year old crouched over and walking ever so slowly and carefully so as not to cause any tearing of the wound or causing the stitches to open. I confined myself to bed for the whole time I was in the hotel. I had to ask them to bring up my breakfast as I was too unwell to go downstairs.

And so, the most dreaded day of them all arrived. It was time to say goodbye to London and head to Cork, the place I love to call home. Thankfully I managed to make my way to the airport without incident, but when I got there I had my first taste of how difficult it would be to find suitable seating! I kid you not. I tried to find a seat with foam or a cushion, but they were all taken. I needed one like this to ease pressure on the area of the wound. I thought I was in luck when I saw a cushioned stool. I ordered some food and went to sit on the stool, fully expecting it to flatten and spread so as to avoid any pressure on my sensitive area. But bloody hell! Instead of the foam pressing downward it moved in and up like a lift in a carpet to you know where. Jeeesus! I yelped, what the fuck! Sorry but sometimes I had to say it as it was. I lifted myself up and eased myself back down in the hope of the foam doing its job, but not a bloody chance. I had to shift my bum about on the edge of the stool while trying to eat. I'll never eat anything so fast again! Amazingly though this is as bad as it got, apart from the crouching and slow walking and having to lift my case on and off the plane.

Thankfully the flight was uneventful. When I arrived at Cork Airport, I got a taxi home, where I happily stayed for the next few days. I rang a number of my friends to let them know I was home. Thankfully they all wanted to know how they could help me, and I was certainly glad to accept. They brought me food and helped me around the apartment and kept me company. I then had to start the slow road to recovery. This included taking painkillers, taking care of the wound. It also involved having two baths a day and dilating while in the bath, not the best of fun it has to be said, especially given how tall I am for such a small bath. That was a challenge I hadn't anticipated! I had to regularly inspect the wound, which was not at all pleasant, especially as I thought it was getting worse at times. I had to take pictures of the area and send them to the hospital. Thankfully they always gave me reassurance that it was healing properly; and so it was that slowly but surely it healed up. It took longer than I expected, but nowhere near as long as the overall recovery, which lasted well over a year.

The biggest problem I experienced in the first few weeks after surgery was having to use the toilet every few minutes. It became obvious that there was a problem with my urethra. I assumed it might be an infection. It was awful and led to countless sleepless nights on account of constantly running to the toilet. I had an appointment in June for my post-surgery review, so I left doing something about the problem until then. As it happens, when Mr Thomas checked the area he discovered a piece of residual skin had grown over the urethra and it was this that caused all the misery. They booked me in to hospital in July, for a procedure to remove the skin. It was an overnight stay in hospital and thankfully they solved the problem.

The recovery time was not at all pleasant, which I'm sure was partly due to my age; I was just shy of fifty-five when I had the surgery. The biggest problem was palpitations, anxiety attacks and hypertension on a constant basis. They were so severe at times I was certain I was going to die. I was so sure of it at times that I just lay in my bed and resigned myself to it, remembering what I had said many times over about how grateful I truly was to have gotten this far and to be able to experience myself at my most natural, be it for ever so short a time. I experienced great peace from this and I'm quite sure it actually helped in my recovery.

I went back to work not long after returning home, mainly because I desperately needed to get some income. I looked and sounded like death warmed up, which of course didn't go unnoticed by everyone, including my clients. One of the first things I had to do was conduct a number of job interviews. They can be exhausting at the best of times, but bloody hell! And then there was a full day's health and safety training and another day doing customer care training. The training itself was great, but oh my god did they take it out of me. How many times did I think about how nuts I must have been to be doing it, but there was little option? The following year was to be a constant struggle with recovery and money worries, until the recovery reached the point where I could start relaxing, but the money was another matter entirely. I did try to get more work in, but that proved difficult. In the meantime, I was helped by some friends to get by and that made all the difference.

Around the autumn of 2015 some small amounts of work came in and as a result I was finally able to do something I'd wanted to do for a long time, start a life coaching course. I applied to the ILI course and was accepted. I just about had enough money for the deposit, but I trusted the universe to help me, as I had with so many other things, and went ahead in faith. I was not disappointed. As difficult as my financial situation was I managed to get through the course and graduated with two Coaching qualifications in May 2016. I can truthfully say that this course transformed my life as did the books I read and the wonderful people I met along the way. But there were two things above all that made a great difference; the first was giving copies of my book Wrong Body, Wrong Life, to my colleagues on the graduation weekend, and the second was my comments about the course during the feedback session.

The books were meant to be left on the table with a sign saying they were complimentary and inviting everyone to take a copy each, literally nothing more than that. But as it turned out the course Director Adrian held the book up in front of the group and told them there was one for everyone in the audience, courtesy of Sara-Jane. A couple of ladies thanked me for their copies and asked if I would sign them, which of course I was delighted to do. Then came another and another until I ended up signing everyone's copy. During the round up on the following day, Sunday, we were asked to share our thoughts on what the course meant to us. I mentioned that the course proved life changing in helping me to finally resolve a number of major life issues for once and for all, which holds true to this day. One of the issues I resolved was my self-confidence, another was on becoming a motivational speaker, Lifecoach and writer, all of which I had wanted to do and had been encouraged to do for a long time. The course gave me the confidence to do all three. The only question was where would I even start?

One of the other issues I struggled with over the time of the course was my health issues, which necessitated my having to take myself up to CUH to have myself checked out after several very frightening anxiety attacks. Thankfully my heart and blood pressure were given the all clear, but physically, psychologically and emotionally I still struggled and continued to feel very fragile; there are times when I still do and so have to mind myself. But overall everything was moving in the right direction.

It was a Saturday in March when I was out walking in Glounthaune that I found the inspiration for the title of this book. I was feeling very poorly and stressed. While walking, I started coaching and motivating myself by recounting my many achievements and how they pointed to my potential for achieving even greater things in the future. As I got nearer to my apartment, I suddenly blurted out, 'Jesus that is no ordinary life you've lived Sara!' And in that exact moment I exclaimed, 'that is the title of my book,' which I had not yet started.

It was in January 2017 when I was to realise the impact of giving the books and speaking at the course roundup. I received a call from the lovely Alina Amir. Alina is one of my fellow graduates, who received a copy of the book and heard me speak at the roundup. She asked me if I would be interested in speaking at an International Women's Day Event being held in Symantec in Dublin on the 8th March. She told me that they were inspired by my book and what I said at the course roundup. Of course, I agreed, then swallowed hard and asked what on earth I'd done. Just a week before I was due to speak, I was asked if I would do a second talk! I was gobsmacked but agreed to do it. I was asked to give them a theme for the day and for my talks. I came up with the "Power to Change." They were delighted with this and so everything was settled for the eight. The talks were a great success and confirmed me as a motivational speaker for life change and personal growth. It truly was a red-letter day.

A few months after my surgery I was sitting on my sofa having my dinner and watching the evening news when an item came on about the Gender Recognition Certificate application form being published. I nearly choked on my food. I could hardly believe what I was hearing. We were going to be able to apply for our Gender Recognition Certificate and thereafter our Birth Certificates. O my God! I was completely ecstatic. And you can guess what my priority was after hearing that news. I could barely eat my dinner after that. I went to the Department of Social and Family Affairs website to where they announced the new application form. I downloaded it immediately and printed it. I tried filling it in immediately but there were some details I wasn't sure of, so I waited until I spoke to someone in the department the following day, after which I completed the form and posted it in. Talk about an anxious wait. I expected it to take a while, but it only took a few days for the Gender Recognition Certificate to arrive; it was issued on the 15th September. But there was a big surprise included, they enclosed the application form for the new Birth Certificate! No prizes for guessing what I did next and how quickly I did it. The Birth Certificate was issued just one week later on the 22nd September 2015! Just about three weeks in total between the first application and receiving my very own Birth Certificate! Everything I had believed in, everything I spoke about, everything I strived for and sacrificed in order to see this day come had been worth it, and as a result, my journey towards becoming my true self was complete. I could finally go out into the world as a full Irish citizen in my proper gender. The effect was immediate, I didn't care anymore what people thought of me. I was simply Sara-Jane Cromwell, Female, and bloody proud of it! My extraordinary journey was completed, and I could get on with starting a whole new life and a brand-new story. And that is precisely what I'm doing now, and it was all of my own making.

Something truly soulful and spiritual happened to me two days after receiving my Birth Certificate. I was sitting at the kitchen table staring in wonder at the Birth Certificate, and I kid you not when I say that I was met by all my younger selves, from infancy upwards. They came to thank me for having the courage to have done all that I could to make our life become one, past and present, and for always. It was incredibly emotional as I felt my life and my gender reach a state of completeness, knowing that forever more I AM Sara-Jane Cromwell.

Of course, the everyday realities were still there and had to be dealt with, but how I dealt with them changed dramatically. Financially speaking, things remained extremely difficult and it was the kindness of others that really helped me survive and muddle through, until one day I called in to see one of my clients about some outstanding work that needed to be done and to see if he would be willing to go ahead. He said he would and gave me a small deposit to get started. But much more valuable than this was his suggestion that I attend a meeting the following Wednesday, for the launch of a new business website for Carrigtwohill. I went along to the meeting and was impressed by the website, but I was puzzled as to who was behind it. I was told that there had been a defunct business association but that some individuals were looking to start it up again. It was then suggested that those present meet up and discuss reigniting the business association. We met up a week or so later and set up a committee, of which I became secretary. The Business Association is up and running for the past three years and is proving very successful. What has been great for me has been the number of business people I have come into contact with and how many new clients I have managed to acquire. I am very proud of my work with the Business Association, which I stepped down from in May 2018, and thoroughly enjoy working with my colleagues on behalf of the local business community. I am twenty-three years in business in 2019, something I could not have imagined when I started all those years ago in Newcastle West.

I have always believed in being actively involved in any community I live in, and this was the case since moving to Glounthaune in 2012. I was extremely apprehensive after I moved in, especially after an article published in the Evening Echo. It was an update on how I was getting on in my journey. I wasn't sure how people would receive me, and because of this I did not go into the pub next door for nearly a year or more. It would of course be silly to think there wasn't any prejudice towards me, and it was a nerve wrecking experience going to the pub for the first time and a short while after; and there were some awkward moments, But overall my experience in the pub and in the wider community has been simply wonderful. I have become involved with the Tidy Towns and enjoy being part of the community here.

I currently write for the Glounthaune News and the Glanmire Area News. I am also involved with Caring for Carrigtwohill and was involved in the national competition Pride of Place. We won the National Pride of Place Award for our population category in 2017. I can truthfully say that I have never felt more at home in my life than I did living here in Glounthaune and being part of the community of Carrigtwohill. It is also important to say that never in my life have I been made to feel as appreciated as I am within these communities. I am thrilled to be placing this on record. Sadly, I had to move out of Glounthaune in May 2018 and moved into Cobh in June.

I cannot finish this story without mentioning another hugely important full-circle moment in my life, and that is the ending of my spiritual disenfranchisement and being unable to attend church. When I was CEO of GIDI, I attended a Carol Service at the Unitarian Church on Stephen's Green. One of my colleagues had been invited to speak at the service and I travelled from Cork to lend my support. I was very taken by the welcome we received and the fact that there were so many from the gay community. The following year I was invited to attend a memorial service for the LGBT community. The service was to remember those who had died by suicide or who had attempted suicide. It was a very moving service, and once again I was impressed by how warmly we were welcomed by the Unitarians, especially their minister Bridget Spain. I wasn't in the mind or spiritual space to look into the Unitarians in terms of their beliefs and practices etc., but they definitely made a very positive impression on me.

Fast forward to an October Sunday morning in 2015 and you will find me lying in bed, reflecting on the absence of spiritual searching and fellowship and how much this is having a negative effect on my life. So, I decided to find a Unitarian Church in Cork, and if successful I would look up their beliefs and practices. I discovered that there is indeed a Unitarian Church in Cork. It is in Prince's Street, just down from the English Market. I got to read some of what they believe, and it really spoke to my mind and soul. As much as I really wanted to visit the church, I didn't feel well enough. I wanted to be in better health for visiting and not to be preoccupied with health issues, and I had committed to my Life Coaching course, so it was important not to over-stretch myself. I decided to wait until I finished the course before taking on any other commitments; it proved to be a good decision.

In April or May 2016, I finally made the decision to visit the church, and from my very first visit I felt completely at ease. But not only this, I've made new friends. My first three services were enough to convince me that this is where I was meant to be. What made this obvious was announcements given by the minister Michael O'Sullivan. Before going any further, I should point out that my original intention when attending church was to say absolutely nothing about my gender journey. I did not want this defining the rest of my life. I'd been there done that and was moving on. But the Universe had other plans which I was not aware of, until that is, the minister made these announcements. They were to do with the Unitarian Church being the only denomination to attend the launch in City Hall for Cork's LGTB Week. Nothing for me to be concerned about there. The following week he raised the LGBT issue again and on a number of other occasions he mentioned that the church would be marching in the Cork Pride Parade in July, and that we would be the only church to do so. I should also point out that Michael had no idea about my situation, nor did any other member of the congregation, until I told them that is. How could I not tell them when the reason I was attending was because of their support of the LGBT community, and how could I be selfish and cowardly in keeping that to myself. It gave me an even greater purpose for attending and eventually applying to become a Unitarian, which I did in November 2016.

As at the time of writing, the Church has participated in three Pride Parades, with other churches beginning to follow our example. It was on the whole a very positive and uplifting experience. The onlookers were in great spirits, and it was wonderful to see so many families and young children. It speaks really well of us Irish and how we integrate with the LGBT community. There is of course a great deal more that needs to be done, but we should acknowledge the positive change and progress that has and is taking place. I felt very proud being a Unitarian on those occasions and continue to do so.

I met with our minister Michael and shared with him my very extensive experience as an Evangelical Christian, about being a preacher, Sunday School teacher, and how I was preparing for ministry before everything changed so utterly. I mentioned that I never lost my sense of calling and therefore enjoyed the opportunities to participate in our church services. It was more for information purposes originally, but as Michael described how difficult it could be, I could see that it was no more than I would have expected from past experience. I told him I was undeterred; then to my amazement he told me we would treat our conversation as step one. The idea of my preparing for ministry has been very well received, so who knows what the future holds. For me the great thing about being a Unitarian is that we are open, welcoming and inclusive. We live as we speak, and we have the most wonderfully unassuming space in which we enjoy the most open and uplifting fellowship. Being a Unitarian has brought me to the place where I am more open to my own spirituality rather than following any form of religious dogma. This has enabled me to open myself to Buddhism, which I am now practicing, and I can truthfully say I have finally found my spiritual home.

Another huge positive is the number of invitations I receive to speak and participate in panel discussions on a variety of topics. This is yet another goal being fulfilled and very much in line with the vision I have had for my life now and in the future as a speaker, coach, author etc. I mention these things here to demonstrate how possible it is for a person with Gender Dysphoria or transgender to fit into the wider community, be included, and make a positive difference. But it is more than this, it is about how we can live a much more rounded life rather than be limited by our gender journey alone. And that is why this book is as much a story about overcoming the many abuses, obstacles, challenges and setbacks experienced throughout my life, some of which had nothing at all to do with my gender identity; although they certainly did complicate it greatly. However, what is happening in this past year is truly remarkable by any standard. I am referring to my growing relationship with UCC and the opportunities to engage in dialogue with the Church of Ireland here in Cork. But then as I have always consistently said: all the best things in my life happened and continue to happen here in Cork.

Something I could never have imagined and would never have presumed to imagine was any kind of invitation to speak in University College Cork (UCC), in any capacity whatsoever. And yet here I am doing just that, and more. Since November 2017, I have been invited to speak to students on several UCC courses: Diploma in Women's Studies, Masters in Women's Studies and to mental health and social worker students. I have also been invited to speak and participate in panel discussions at several LGBT events. What I am especially proud of is being given the honour of coordinating the first ever Freshers Fest Workshops for new LGBT+ students. And being the opening speaker at the second EAP Annual Conference. The welcome and respect I receive from my UCC colleagues is truly self-actualising, as is the feedback which I receive from the many students I have the privilege to educate on gender diversity.

Regarding the EAP Conference in October, I had a most momentous time speaking with the delegates about my own journey and about the representation of Transgender people in particular, within the classroom environment and course content and materials. I also managed to get closure on the lifelong hurt I experienced after my English teacher told my mother I was mentally retarded. I had noticed in the lead up to the conference that I was becoming increasingly agitated and scared, which was not like me usually; I do get nervous whenever I speak and teach, but this was very different and it took me a while to figure out why. As it turns out, I realised it was because I was facing a room full of English language teachers, the very type that caused me so much pain and distress over my lifetime. I also realised that despite being published and being praised for my English, I felt very inadequate at the prospect of speaking to them, regardless of the subject I was speaking on.

Once I became aware of what was happening and reflected upon its significance, I purposed to do something positive with it. I decided to confront it head on at the beginning of my talk and in doing so highlight the fact that there are other identities to be considered apart from the more obvious and topical ones. So, I prepared a slide at the beginning of my presentation which said: *Not all identities are obvious or visible.* Not only did I mention my being raised mentally retarded, but I also included being left-handed and the stigma and abuse suffered by so many children, which I know still affects many to this day. This was attested to after a talk I gave recently to the Church of Ireland Mother's Union Conference in Cork. Some of the women came to me afterwards to share their experiences of being left-handed and the horrible things done to them. It was obvious to me from the tears in their eyes, that they were still badly affected by their experiences. It was so moving to know that by my mentioning it in my talk it made them feel that bit better hearing someone speaking about it openly.

Speaking at the Mother's Union Conference was not my first engagement with the Church of Ireland, it was my third in a remarkable development with the Church, including speaking to trainee chaplains and at St. Anne's Church, Shandon. At the time of writing I am awaiting a date for the upcoming workshop for Church of Ireland clergy and chaplains. The workshop is on the issue of marginalisation and exclusion from the church of LGBT+ people, which if successful, can be repeated throughout other dioceses around the country. Something I am especially affected by in this regard is how members of the St. Anne's congregation shared with me how as a result of my talk they felt they were really acceptable to God as they are, for the first time in their lives, especially since becoming Christians. This is a truly astonishing thing to hear from seriously committed and conservative Christians. I sincerely hope these opportunities will continue to grow and we can reach many more within the Church to bring about positive change.

The Mother's Union conference came about through my talk to the trainee chaplains earlier in the year at Northridge House. It was there that I had the great good fortune to meet the lovely Hilary Dring. Hilary and I clicked instantly, and we have become good friends since. Hilary has since become President of the Mother's Union and it was, she who proposed me to her colleagues as a speaker at the conference. The significance and importance of these events within the Church should not be underestimated, given the great potential they have for opening a proper dialogue for change within the Church on the issues of marginalisation and exclusion of LGBT people. It will be slow, but I believe it will be worthwhile to continue with these types of events as they will open people up to a greater understanding of the spiritual and pastoral needs of LGBT people, of which I'm proud to be one.

It was at the end of my talk that I received the shock news about my beloved Pastor and father Liam Joyce. A lady approached me saying she was shaking from the top of her head to the soles of her feet and that her body was tingling all over, and not for any good reason. It was because I mentioned Liam in my talk, about the positive force he was in my life and the extraordinary things he did for me. The lady told me the reason for shaking was that Liam's son David was her son-in-law and that Liam had just passed away! I was rooted to the spot from the shock. And though I had been expecting it for some time given his dementia and failing physical health, it was still a shock, especially after only a few weeks earlier his son Kirk told me that apart from Liam going into a home that there was no real change in his condition. What is extraordinary about this news is how and where I received it. It is most unlikely that I would have heard the news for a long time, if ever, had I not been at the conference and speaking about him. Liam has left a huge legacy behind, where my life is concerned, and the many things I have accomplished and the change I've effected over these many years. His passing is greatly significant too in that he was my last remaining connection with my time as an Evangelical Christian and my call to the ministry. His passing marks the end of an era in my life.

Something else I heard from the lady was the squalid conditions in which Liam's wife Sheena was living. This is quite shocking and upsetting for me to hear. I am profoundly saddened at what has happened to these two wonderful people. They deserved so much better after their many years of faithful ministry. Those of us fortunate enough to sit under Liam's ministry should count ourselves blest indeed; I know I certainly do. God grant you eternal peace my beloved father, Pastor and friend. I am eternally grateful to you for all you have done for me and for giving me the great honour and thrill of being your daughter. Words cannot do you justice.

In many respects, these events are like moments in an inspiring film. Some at the beginning and some at the end. One that especially stands out was being the opening speaker at the EAP Conference mentioned earlier. The EAP is English for Academic Purposes, and the reason it is so important for me is that it is the first time since my mother was told by an English teacher that I was mentally retarded, that I got to speak to educators about this part of my life and how it has been affecting me ever since. It was also intimidating speaking to English language lecturers when my English is completely self-taught, but that didn't matter at all. The feedback after my talk was about how they described it as transformational in terms of how *they* will prepare their curriculums to more accurately represent the diversity within their classrooms, including LGBT students. This is indeed hugely transformative and will undoubtedly have a positive impact on the learning experience of students sitting in those classrooms. I am immensely proud to be associated with this kind of progress within third level institutes. Not bad for someone who left school at eleven years of age! My standing in front of these educators brought me real closure and healing from a lifetime of hurt and being held back in many aspects of my life, to standing there on my own terms and treated as a colleague and fellow educator. Even for someone as reluctant as me to say it, this is seriously amazing! This gives me great hope for dealing with the life-long effects of the damage done from the abuse I experienced as a direct result of this terrible falsehood.

Suicide is never that far away for those who have tried to end their own lives. We do not have to suffer with mental health issues to be suicidal. Life events can be so overwhelming that we lose the ability to cope and things can look so dark and hopeless and the pain so unutterably immense it becomes too great to bear, to the point where we may feel we are better off bringing it to an end. This is especially true for those of us living with the life-long effects of childhood abuse trauma. I mention this here because it was in October 2019, I was last feeling suicidal. It came upon me of a sudden and I made arrangements to carry it out; of course, I had no intention of telling anyone about my plans. However, I had arranged a meeting with my support worker, Teresa Ryan, which changed all that. As luck, or should I say, as fate would have it, I had a meeting with Teresa on the Monday afternoon; the day I was going to carry out my plan (we normally met on the Friday but couldn't, so we arranged for the following Monday instead). I was due go to the pharmacy to get the medicine I hoped would do the job for me but was due to meet with Teresa beforehand. When Teresa saw me, she asked me how I was doing, to which I told her I was not feeling great. Whatever it was about how I looked to her and sounded she asked me if I was feeling suicidal, to which I replied "yes," that I was and that I would not hide it from her. She then asked if I had a plan, and again I replied, "yes, I have a plan." Those two honest answers have led me to where I am two years later. I attended Pieta House for counselling and am receiving wonderful support from the team at the Family Resource Centre in Carrigtwohill. Also, the love and support I'm experiencing from so many people is immense, for which I am enormously grateful.

It is a fact that I never for a moment expected to have so much love and support from so many people; it is truly wonderful and overwhelming.

So, what happened to me and how did it come to be like this, especially when I thought I had dealt with all my big stuff? As it turns out I hadn't really dealt with my childhood abuse and its lasting impact on my life. Yes, I had spoken openly about what had happened and I had genuinely forgiven my parents and siblings for the truly terrible things done to me and their devastating effects on my life. There is no escaping the fact that as things stand I have not been dealing with my abuse in the way that matters most, the awful lifelong effects the abuse continues to have on my life, and that actually I've been living in a state of chronic childhood abuse trauma. Trauma is not a word I ever associated with my abuse, nor for that matter was the neurological impact it has had and is still having. This was an astonishing discovery. I came across it in a book by Bessel Van De Kolk, *The Brain Keeps the Score*, in which the author addresses several types of trauma, including childhood abuse trauma and its lifelong impact on those for whom it is neither recognised nor treated. Every single symptom he discusses including financial I have been experiencing. I spoke about this with my therapist and mental health worker and they have both assured me that this is indeed the case. This gives me great hope for the future.

The big downside to this is very great indeed and it is the reason why so many try to avoid it at all costs. The pain and distress of reliving the abuse is unavoidable if we are to have any real chance of healing. I have not stopped crying for months because of constantly hitting this wall and the feeling that my life is just not working as it should. The mental, emotional and physical pain is truly awful, and completely exhausting. But then there is fifty-nine years of abuse stored in my brain and my body and they won't heal until I finally confront it and its effects for once and for all. This seems completely contradictory to all the positive things I've shared here, that is because I am trying to keep functioning and honouring my commitment to making a difference; something I renewed recently in memory of Liam Joyce. I hope I can do this through sharing what is happening and encourage people suffering with this type of trauma to have it looked into, and hopefully experience their own healing.

I am in one of the greatest battles of my life, but I do feel confident and hopeful that I will come through this as I have so many others. What I want to share with people from this experience is the power of saying "yes" when anyone asks if we are feeling suicidal or if we need help. Saying "yes" will not only save our lives, it will change them in ways we can hardly imagine.

So many things have happened since the last time I thought I'd finished writing, and if I don't stop it will never be finished. But finished I am, and if I'm around in twenty years I will include whatever happens next in my memoir. And so it is, in closing this story, of what I know to be a remarkable life thus far, I wish to make it abundantly clear that I am no longer gender dysphoric. I am simply a woman with all that that means and all I ever believed and wanted myself to be. And I am now living the life I envisioned during my teens: tall, elegant, intelligent and pretty (I hope).

I look forward to a new life and creating a brand-new story, and to doing even more amazing things while continuing to make a positive difference. I wrote the following poem in 2018 and shared it with my church. I think it appropriate for bringing this amazing journey to its wonderful conclusion.

Knowing Who I'm Meant to Be

How are you with your heart?
How are you with your soul?
How are you with your mind?
How are you with the things that make you whole,
The person you know yourself to be?
When you think and feel and speak,
Can you be as you know yourself to be?
Can you laugh and cry, be happy and sad?
Can you love and be loved, and have a broken heart;
Being who you know yourself to be?

Can you have your friends and family surround you and love you,
As you know yourself to be?
And when you're no longer around, when you're gone from here,
Will they mourn you, will they grieve, and will they regret that
They never got to know, and love, and accept you as
The girl, the woman, the mother, the daughter, the sister, the aunt,
The best friend, you know yourself to be?

Or will they understand you, accept you, support you and love you,
And encourage you to become the best you, you know you are meant to be?

I know what I was meant to be;
I know what I already am, and what I have always been.
I am the girl you never got to see;
But now you do see me, and know me
As the woman I know myself to be.

About the Author

Sara-Jane Cromwell is an author, speaker, life coach, mentor and workplace relations consultant. She is also a lecturer with the Adult continuing Education Department with University College Cork (UCC). In her 46 years working in the voluntary sector she has founded and co-founded and played a leading role in a number of organisations including Transgender Equality Network Ireland (TENI), Gender Identity Disorder Ireland (GIDI), and more recently Gender Identity Ireland.

Sara-Jane Cromwell is truly one of the world's life-changers and her book will certainly help change many more lives now and in the future.